THE TOWNSMEN

THE TOWNSMEN

By the Editors of

TIME-LIFE BOOKS

with text by

Keith Wheeler

TIME-LIFE BOOKS / ALEXANDRIA, VIRGINIA

Time-Life Books Inc.
is a wholly owned subsidiary of

TIME INCORPORATED

Founder: Henry R. Luce 1898-1967

Editor-in-Chief: Henry Anatole Grunwald
President: J. Richard Munro
Chairman of the Board: Ralph P. Davidson
Executive Vice President: Clifford J. Grum
Chairman, Executive Committee: James R. Shepley
Editorial Director: Ralph Graves
Group Vice President, Books: Joan D. Manley
Vice Chairman: Arthur Temple

TIME-LIFE BOOKS INC.

Managing Editor: Jerry Korn
Executive Editor: David Maness
Assistant Managing Editors: Dale M. Brown
(planning), Martin Mann, John Paul Porter,
Gerry Schremp (acting)
Art Director: Tom Suzuki
Chief of Research: David L. Harrison
Director of Photography: Robert G. Mason
Assistant Art Director: Arnold C. Holeywell
Assistant Chief of Research: Carolyn L. Sackett
Assistant Director of Photography: Dolores A. Littles

Chairman: John D. McSweeney
President: Carl G. Jaeger
Executive Vice Presidents: John Steven Maxwell,
David J. Walsh
Vice Presidents: George Artandi (comptroller);
Stephen L. Bair (legal counsel); Peter G. Barnes;
Nicholas Benton (public relations); John L. Canova;
Beatrice T. Dobie (personnel); Carol Flaumenhaft
(consumer affairs); James L. Mercer (Europe/South
Pacific); Herbert Sorkin (production);
Paul R. Stewart (marketing)

THE OLD WEST

EDITORIAL STAFF FOR "THE TOWNSMEN"
Editor: George Constable
Assistant Editor: Joan Mebane
Picture Editor: Mary Y. Steinbauer
Text Editors: Valerie Moolman, Philip Payne,
Gerald Simons, Rosalind Stubenberg
Designer: Herbert H. Quarmby
Staff Writers: Lee Greene, Sam Halper
Chief Researcher: June O. Goldberg
Researchers: Loretta Britten, Joan Chambers,
Jane Jordan, Donna Lucey, Michael Luftman,
Denise Lynch, Archer Mayor, Nancy Miller,
Mary Kay Moran, Ann Morison, Margaret Quimby
Design Assistant: Faye Eng
Editorial Assistant: Lisa Berger

EDITORIAL PRODUCTION
Production Editor: Douglas B. Graham
Operations Manager: Gennaro C. Esposito,
Gordon E. Buck (assistant)
Assistant Production Editor: Feliciano Madrid
Quality Control: Robert L. Young (director),
James J. Cox (assistant), Daniel J. McSweeney,
Michael G. Wight (associates)
Art Coordinator: Anne B. Landry
Copy Staff: Susan B. Galloway (chief),
Barbara H. Fuller, Gregory Weed, Celia Beattie
Picture Department: Susan Spiller
Traffic: Kimberly K. Lewis

THE AUTHOR: Keith Wheeler grew up in the small town of Carrington, North Dakota, founded in 1882 at the crest of emigration to the Great Plains. He began his career in journalism on the *Daily Huronite* in Huron, South Dakota, became a reporter for the Chicago *Sun Times,* and in 1951 joined LIFE as a writer. A freelancer now, he has written numerous books, including *The Railroaders, The Chroniclers, The Alaskans* and *The Scouts* in The Old West series.

THE COVER: In Nebraska City, little more than a decade after its founding as a sleepy trading post, Main Street bustles with wagon traffic and a throng of shoppers in a lithograph made from an 1865 sketch by Alfred Mathews. A tint in the style of the period has been added. The frontispiece is a photograph, taken some 20 years later, of a Denver lawman's family outside their clapboard house— all proper with plantings, a picket fence and a bevy of youngsters.

CORRESPONDENTS: Elisabeth Kraemer (Bonn); Margot Hapgood, Dorothy Bacon, Lesley Coleman (London); Susan Jonas, Lucy T. Voulgaris (New York); Maria Vincenza Aloisi, Josephine du Brusle (Paris); Ann Natanson (Rome). Valuable assistance was also provided by: Judy Aspinall (London); Bernard Diederich, James Budd (Mexico City); Carolyn T. Chubet, Miriam Hsia, Christina Lieberman (New York); Mimi Murphy (Rome); Traudl Lessing (Vienna).

For information about any Time-Life book, please write:
Reader Information
Time-Life Books
541 North Fairbanks Court
Chicago, Illinois 60611

Time-Life Books.
    The Townsmen/by the editors of Time-Life Books; with text by
Keith Wheeler. — New York: Time-Life Books, [1975]
    240 p.: ill.; 29 cm. — (The Old West)
    Bibliography: p. 236-237.
    Includes index.
    1. Frontier and pioneer life—The West.   2. Denver—History.
    3. The West—History—1848-1950.
I. Wheeler, Keith.   II. Title.   III. Series: The Old West
(Alexandria, Va.)
F593.T55   1975   978'.02   74-21780
ISBN 0-8094-1490-2
ISBN 0-8094-1489-9 lib. bdg.
ISBN 0-8094-1488-0 retail ed.

CONTENTS

A splendidly wide main street—with the town's well in the middle—marks an ambitious beginning for Mullinville, Kansas, in the 1880s.

1 | Making nowhere somewhere

"A new western village is truly indescribable in language. It can only be compared to itself." So wrote a young lawyer to his folks in the East after arriving in Kansas in 1858. His bafflement was understandable, for surely there was nothing back home quite so forlorn-looking yet so brimming with high hopes as the town he was helping to build beyond the Missouri.

The young lawyer was part of an army of men and women—doctors, merchants, millers, barbers, bankers and blacksmiths—who poured westward in the second half of the 19th Century to transform a near-wilderness into a thriving land, and as one frontier editor said, "to get rich if we can."

The new settlers were a sturdy and resourceful breed. A minister who settled in Nebraska in 1856 reported that they were endowed with "the three P's—poverty, providence and pluck." Beyond that they were equipped with boundless energy. They started towns by the thousands, mostly on the prairies and plains, where farming would support a stable population. They laid out broad streets, and achieved a touch of elegance with brave false-fronted structures. Then they battled fire, flood and pestilence, subdued the lawless, engaged in ceaseless boosterism—and sometimes went on to attain the dream of urban greatness that had inspired them as they put up the first building.

Ten days after its founding in 1886, much of Liberal, Kansas, is still in tents, but piles of lumber give notice of its expansive building plans. The town's name honored an early settler who let wayfarers have a free drink at his well and won the locale a reputation as a good stopping place.

Some towns grew, some vanished, and some—like Kelly, New Mexico—just stagnated. Named after a local sawmill operator in 1870, Kelly developed an impressive row of false-fronted buildings, but then the town's growth suddenly stopped, and it just sat there decaying in the hot sun.

Some towns were built on false hopes. In 1868 the 200 citizens of Bear River City, Wyoming, were hastily setting up enterprises on the assumption that the Union Pacific would stop there and make their community important—but the railroad passed them by without even a sidetrack.

Crammed between the vertical walls of a gulch in the San Juan Mountains, Creede, Colorado, scarcely has room to accommodate its boom after the silver strike of 1889. On a street stacked with lumber, stores go up cheek by jowl, while prosperous-looking townsmen cluster to talk silver.

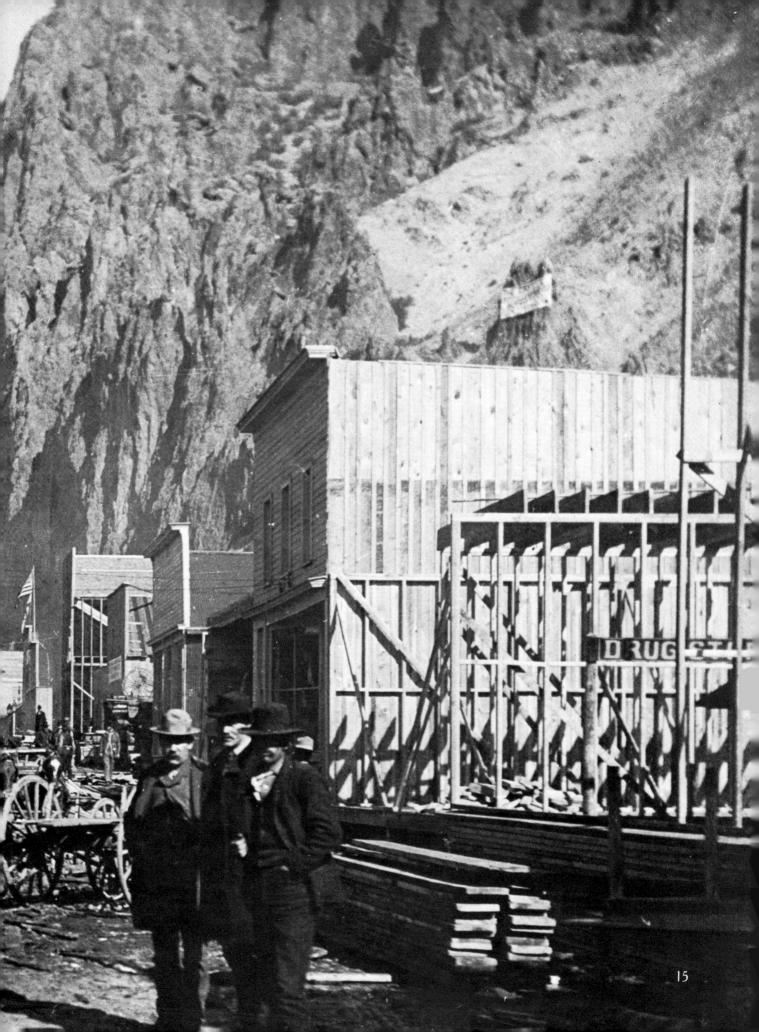

Placing civilization's stamp on the wilderness

At sunset one evening late in 1877 a stage approached Garland City, Colorado, newly designated by the Denver & Rio Grande Railway as a branch-line terminus in the San Luis Valley. Aboard the coach, making a tour of the West, was Helen Hunt Jackson, who would achieve considerable renown a few years later with her novel *Ramona,* an evocation of the passing of the old Spanish culture in California. But on this occasion she was privileged to witness a birth of sorts.

She had no inkling of what she was about to see. "Up to within an eighth of a mile of Garland City there is no trace of human habitation," she later wrote in describing her arrival; "Where is the city?" Then the coach rolled down a steep road into a ravine that "twinkled with lights, and almost seemed to flutter with white tents and wagon-tops." An earsplitting din filled the air and, when the stage pulled to a halt, Mrs. Jackson asked a bystander what was happening.

"The building of the city," he replied matter-of-factly. "Twelve days ago there was not a house here. Today there are one hundred and five, and in a week there will be two hundred." This prediction showed every sign of being attainable. Ox teams were dragging logs about; men wielded hammers, picks and shovels at a frenetic pace; wheelbarrows rumbled in every direction. As darkness settled over the town, the noise gradually trailed off into silence, but the next morning, as Mrs. Jackson recalled, "the chorus began again, dinning, deafening on all sides; the stir, the bustle, every

motion of it began just where it had left off at bed-time. It was like a scene in an opera."

With minor variations, the same operatic scene was being played all over the West in the second half of the 19th Century. During those 50 years literally thousands of new towns arose, sometimes briefly, on the Western prairies, plains and mountainsides. Some observers saw the phenomenon in poetic rather than operatic terms. When Albert Richardson, a roving reporter for the Boston *Journal,* passed through Wyandotte, Kansas, in 1857, he noted for the record that the village was four months old and had 400 citizens; then he rhapsodized: "Its beautiful site on a gentle, symmetric eminence, overlooks low wooded bottom-lands of Missouri on the east, Kansas City on the south, and the Missouri River for miles below. A few pleasant white warehouses and residences, and unpainted plank shanties were erected. Many more were going up; and meanwhile waiting settlers dwelt under heaven's canopy or in snowy tents. Everywhere busy workmen were plying ax, hammer and saw; and the voice of the artisan was heard in the land."

The town-builders themselves tended to be less romantic. When Edwin Bernard, one of the founders of Fremont, Nebraska, first laid eyes on the townsite in the Platte River valley during the autumn of 1856, he found "hardships and privations on every hand." Many times during the ensuing months he wondered about the wisdom of putting down roots in this domain of "Indians and wild beasts." He and his fellow settlers suffered through a hard winter, compelled to bring in all their provisions from Omaha—a round trip of a week, at best. With the coming of spring the town perked up: "All was bustle and stir in the settlement; every man felt well and full of hope." But at least one young inhabitant—a lad who had emigrated from western New York with his family—was unimpressed. At supper one

Two of the busiest craftsmen in Guthrie, Oklahoma, take a break outside their shop in April of 1889. The town, having sprung up on newly opened government lands just a few days earlier, needed signs as fast as Walker & McCoy could turn them out.

Editor James Curren (*center*) works at a hand press under a tree to get out an issue of the first daily paper in Kingston, New Mexico, in 1886. A newspaper was among the top priorities of a new town, and many a journal published its early issues outdoors until a building became available.

evening, when his grandmother reminded him that he had forgotten to say grace, he retorted: "I don't see what we have to give thanks for; we live in beggar houses and eat beggar victuals, and have to sit on old trunks and three-legged stools instead of chairs."

Despite this bleak commentary, Fremont survived and enjoyed a steady rise in its fortunes. The Union Pacific Railroad came through in 1866; a bank was begun in the back of a hardware store shortly afterward; and the town grew into a prosperous agricultural center. Wyandotte, too, succeeded. It became a county seat, a meat-packing center, and in 1886 consolidated itself with Kansas City, whose sprawl had reached out to touch its border.

But survival, much less success, was never a certainty for a new town in the West. Garland City, for all its air of bustle, was destined to have a life span of only a few months—although its demise was not altogether final. In the spring of 1878, when the Denver & Rio Grande had progressed 30 miles westward, the entire town—walls, windows, furnishings and sidewalks —was taken apart and used to create a new rail terminus called Alamosa. No one lost any time in mourning the passing of the old Garland City. Nor did anyone begrudge the investment of energy in such a short-lived community. As long as their present town had a future, the people of Alamosa were content. And as for energy, Western townsmen had enough of that to build a whole new world.

History has never recorded a social phenomenon quite like the mass impulse that filled the American West with cities, towns and hamlets—and sparked countless unfulfilled schemes for more of the same. Many of the millions of settlers who crossed the Mississippi and Missouri rivers during that time were, of course, only indirectly concerned with towns. They came to wrest a living from the region by tilling its soil, grazing cattle upon its almost limitless grasslands or extracting precious metals from its streams and mountains. But along with them—or only half a step behind—came men and women who proposed to win their livelihood by providing goods and services for the rest of the population. These were the townsmen: butcher, baker, bootmaker, banker, merchant, saloonkeeper, doctor, barber, and many others. Inevitably, their ranks also included desperadoes, shysters, prostitutes and scalawags, but mostly they were serious men and women bound upon the honest mission of building a new society in the wilderness.

The drama of the Western towns was slow in getting underway. In the vanguard of all those who came West were the mountain men—nomadic fur trappers whose minimal sense of community produced little more than a few trading posts along the trails they had carved out of the wilderness. Yet the first American town to be incorporated in the West, Oregon City, was the creation of a fur trader, and an English citizen to boot—Dr. John McLoughlin. A white-maned, hawk-nosed giant of a man, McLoughlin directed the activities of the powerful British-owned Hudson's Bay Company in Oregon country. He found himself in something of a dilemma when American pioneers and missionaries began to filter into his fiefdom in the 1830s. The company forbade him to lend any support to the newcomers, and he was well aware that their presence in increasing numbers could only hasten the decline of the virgin wilderness from which the profits of the fur trade were wrested. On the other hand, he felt certain that the future of Oregon country would inevitably belong to the Americans. Eventually, he decided in their favor and hit upon a way to turn his shift of allegiance to profit: he would lay out a town and sell lots to the incoming settlers.

In the autumn of 1842, McLoughlin hired a pioneer named Sidney Moss to plat the town—mark off its streets and lots—at a site beside the falls of the Willamette River. Moss was totally unqualified as a surveyor; he got the job only because he owned a pocket compass. Two years later, McLoughlin seized upon Jesse Applegate, one of the first genuine surveyors to penetrate the region, to enlarge the town. Unfortunately, Applegate had lost his surveying instruments on the way west and had to make do with a practiced eye and a rope four rods (66 feet) long. His rope stretched in wet weather and shrank in dry, which—along with the earlier compass work of Moss—explains why Oregon

City matured with some of the most oddly shaped lots in America.

McLoughlin himself retired from the Hudson's Bay Company under criticism for aiding the Americans, and he became an American citizen himself in 1851. By that time, towns had sprung up by the score along the continent's far edge, amid the gold-bearing foothills of the Sierra Nevada, and across the valley of the Great Salt Lake, chosen as a new Zion by the Mormons in 1847. As the decade wore on, new flurries of town-building were set off by the push of pioneers onto the fertile eastern reaches of the prairies—producing Wyandotte and Fremont, among other towns—and by gold and silver strikes in Nevada and Colorado, spawning Virginia City, Denver, and a multitude of glittering rivals.

The Civil War slowed the westward movement, but after this national storm passed, the real rush began. Homesteaders and townspeople surged onto the prairies and plains by the tens of thousands, filling up the regions of Kansas, Nebraska and Dakota. By 1890 there were villages of at least some pretension every 10 miles or so across the central grasslands. The spacing was no accident. It allowed a pioneer farmer to make a trip to town—to buy nails, have a wagon fixed, get a haircut or consult a county commissioner—and still get home in time to feed his livestock in the evening.

In addition to the towns that proliferated to serve the needs of a permanent farm population, many other towns on the plains and prairies came into being as layover points for people and goods in transit. The first transcontinental routes of passage had been blazed by emigrants' wagons rolling through the grasslands on their way to the Far West. Also, the Missouri River followed its serpentine 2,714-mile course through the region, and it was plied by hundreds of steamboats carrying passengers and goods on the first leg of the cross-continent journey or northwestward toward gold fields discovered in Idaho and Montana in the early 1860s. These land and water routes afforded natural stopping places, and where men stopped for any length

20

Convivial boarders — including the prominent artist George Ottinger, seated in front of a beer dispenser — get together with their landlady in Silver Reef, a Utah town whose nine-year life span ended in 1885.

of time, a town was likely to spring up—if only to provide rest and supplies for those who intended to go on.

Gradually the railroads reached across the grasslands, forging a transcontinental link in 1869 and putting down tens of thousands of miles of track. A strategic location along this steel network guaranteed the good health of a town. Ellsworth and Dodge City, Kansas, enjoyed rip-roaring boom times in the 1870s and 1880s because they represented the meeting points of cattle drives from Texas and railroads that would haul the beef to market. Sioux City, Iowa—founded in 1854 on the banks of the Missouri River—hit its stride in 1868 when a Union Pacific spur line arrived, transforming the town into a major port for steamboat traffic along the Big Muddy. The Mormon community of Ogden, Utah, was twice blessed when the U.P. came through in 1869 and a railroad from Salt Lake City connected there with the transcontinental line in 1870.

Railroads not only invigorated existing settlements by fostering commerce, they actually created towns by the hundreds. By government grant, the roads owned some 181 million acres of land along their rights of way, and they sold off a great part of these holdings to help defray the cost of constructing the trackage. Cheyenne and Laramie, Wyoming, were two of the sturdier communities launched by the Union Pacific as it laid tracks westward in 1868 and 1869.

Conceiving and selling towns in the West was one of the hottest business angles of the time, and railroads held no monopoly on it. Under the terms of the Townsite Act, passed by Congress in 1844, a group of settlers or speculators—or a combination of both—could

Sturdy pillars for a fledgling society

One of the major frustrations of frontier towns was their inability to recruit professional people. The Kansas community that in 1858 advertised in a Boston magazine for "a score" of female schoolteachers was courting sure disappointment, despite the plaintive plea that "We want them immediately and they would do much good." And hundreds of towns were in the same fix as the Wyoming community that in 1884 reported on its supply of doctors thus: "No balm in Rawhide. No physician here."

Ultimately, many towns were to establish their own colleges to train men and women in the learned arts and sciences. But until that time, the West counted itself lucky in attracting such rare individuals as the five at right, whose talent, dedication—and gumption—made their towns feel almost rich in professional know-how.

JURIST—David Josiah Brewer, born in Asia Minor to an American missionary family, attended Yale and Albany Law School, but gave up the chance of a potentially lucrative legal practice in the East to settle in Leavenworth, Kansas, in 1859. He was soon made a judge, serving in the county, state and lower federal courts. After three decades the East lured him back with an appointment to the bench of the U.S. Supreme Court, where he was to serve for 21 years.

SCHOOLTEACHER—Angie Brown, educated in both Massachusetts and Kansas, journeyed to Arizona in 1875 to teach. In one hamlet, she held class in a well to escape the wind that whistled through her regular schoolhouse—a former chicken coop. In another village, invading Apaches terrorized her classroom until cowboys drove them off. She later applied for certification as a U.S. Indian Service teacher and passed her examination with an almost unheard-of score of 100 per cent.

stake out 320 acres and take possession for the nominal sum of $1.25 an acre. The land was then divided into lots of 125 by 25 feet, which were sold to prospective townsmen for whatever the traffic would bear.

Potential profits of anywhere from $50 to upward of $1,000 per lot naturally encouraged feats of all-out salesmanship. Without a blush, speculators would dub the most rudimentary community a city. The practice was so common that *New York Tribune* correspondent Bayard Taylor complained on a visit to Colorado in 1866, "I only wish that the vulgar, snobbish custom of attaching 'City' to every place of more than three houses could be stopped."

Speculators were also capable of prodigies of optimism. In 1857 a group of fast talkers arrived in Davenport, Iowa, and persuaded about 30 settlers, mostly Germans, to hitch their futures to the town of Grand Island, Nebraska, just formed on the banks of the Platte River. According to the promoters, Grand Island was almost certain to become an important railroad junction — but that, they declared, was just the beginning. The extraordinarily auspicious position of the townsite, close to the center of the continent, suggested that the nation's capital would someday be moved there, since it was obviously misplaced in Washington, at the country's eastern edge.

These grandiose dreams faded fast. The financial panic of 1857 cost the Grand Island promoters much of their investment. Two years later, an emigrant heading for the Western gold fields set fire to Grand Island because he hated Germans. Every house except one burned down. The town was quickly rebuilt, but when

DOCTOR—Owing to its carefree way with weapons, no town in the West needed a competent surgeon more urgently than Dodge City, Kansas. In 1872, it acquired Philadelphia-trained Dr. Thomas L. McCarty by chance when he stopped to look up a relative while en route to Denver. McCarty liked what he saw of Dodge—then three months old—and soon set up practice in a drugstore. He went on to become a school superintendent, found a hospital and raise a physician son.

MINISTER—Daniel Tuttle of New York State needed all the spiritual strength he could muster when, in 1866, he was designated Episcopal Bishop of Montana. He had to preach in saloons and cope with Sunday-school teachers who gambled or got "woefully drunk." But there were advantages to bringing the Holy Writ to a gold-rich region. To help raise his church in Virginia City "my own wicked people, whom I loved and prayed for, in their generous kindness gave me $3,000."

EDITOR—Massachusetts-born Daniel Anthony, a brother of suffragette Susan B. Anthony, published the first issue of the Leavenworth *Conservative* on January 28, 1861—and the very next day scooped all other Kansas papers with the first report of the territory's achievement of statehood. An uncompromising champion of abolition and other controversial causes, he frequently tasted the wrath of his readers: he was shot at five times, beaten and—at age 67—horsewhipped.

The people of Merna, Nebraska, assemble before a store constructed of sod and outfitted with a false front. Shortly after this portrait was made in 1886, the townsmen abandoned this spot and relocated the community two miles away to intercept the course of an approaching railroad.

24

Proud false fronts for frontier commerce

False Front

GROCERIES

Awning

CASH

Wooden Sidewalk

Outside Stairway

The first townsmen to raise a semblance of a skyline above the immense void of the West were hardly in a position to muse on architectural subtleties. Sources of brick, plate glass and even sawed lumber were likely to be weeks and hundreds of miles away, and, in any event, the ranks of the early Western townsmen included few craftsmen skilled in the use of such materials. Under these circumstances, building a town was largely a matter of making do with whatever nature provided; the result almost inevitably was an architectural hodgepodge.

In northeast Kansas, a townsman might erect a store or dwelling of the abundant local stone. In Idaho and Colorado he used logs, and squared them off lengthwise with a broadax if he wanted to be highfalutin. Out on the timberless plains he used slabs of sod that were piled on top of one another like bricks and roofed over with more of the same material supported by pole rafters.

Such improvisations were strictly temporary. As soon as sawed lumber became available—produced by a local sawmill or imported by wagon, rail or riverboat—the first makeshift structures were replaced. Moreover, the town's main street almost invariably adopted, as its salient motif, a structural oddity known as the false front. From the Canadian to the Mexican borders, hardly any commercial building—store, saloon or livery stable—was built differently after lumber came to hand.

The false front appears to have been, more than anything else, a product of unabashed braggadocio, a desire to appear substantial and imposing. Since this mendacious façade—which perhaps included a massive cornice overhanging frankly phony windows—hoodwinked nobody, it was a nearly useless conceit. Nevertheless, the façade did frequently serve as a sort of billboard where the proprietor could blazon forth his business title and advertise his wares.

If the false front was a harmless fraud, other characteristic features of the Western main street were genuinely practical and necessary. In the case of two-story buildings, an outside stairway was easier and cheaper to build than one inside; it also saved room and provided a separate entrance to the second-floor quarters. On the front of the building, a roofed portico—sometimes with awnings as well—offered passers-by shelter from the elements and a natural place for gossip; its pillars furnished handy hitching posts. The raised wooden sidewalk kept feet above the street's dust or, in wet weather, its mud.

The street itself was apt to be broad as a field, partly because plenty of land was available, partly to give teams and wagons ample room to turn around. But despite such spaciousness and the imposing effect of the false fronts, main street in the Western town presented a dreary prospect, since most buildings went unpainted, and even the exceptions were graced with only a coating of leaden gray.

the Union Pacific came through the area in 1866, it missed Grand Island by a few miles. Whatever structures could be dismantled and moved were soon relocated so that the luckless community could at last be joined to a railroad.

Such resourcefulness in the face of disaster was the hallmark of the Western townsmen. Sometimes their adaptability came into play even before their town existed. The same year that Grand Island was founded, 300 westering emigrants, mostly strangers to one another, were stranded when their steamboat ran aground on a sand bar in the Big Blue River in Nebraska Territory. By the time their craft was dislodged, the beleaguered passengers had come to know one another so well and had developed such a sense of common purpose that they decided to create the town of Beatrice at the site of their misfortune.

Whatever the circumstances that gave birth to a new community in the West, a predictable cast of characters appeared to nurture it and champion its development.

A newspaper, as the journalist Albert Richardson put it, was "mother's milk to an infant town," and one of the first citizens of any community was the editor, often hired by the promoters of the place. His function, in the beginning at least, was not so much to report on local events as to sing the praises of his community for the benefit of any prospective settlers among the newspaper's out-of-town readership. No effusion was too extreme. The none-too-literate editor of the *Winfield Courier* touted his Kansas community thus: "We would say to all men everywhere, who contemplate coming West to engage in business of any kind, come to Winfield. No better or more desirable place can be found in the state of Kans. Situate on one of the most beautiful and romantic streams imaginable, on as pretty a site as could well be selected, built up with neat substantial, and some even elegant buildings. Composed of a class of people, who, for energy, enterprise, are not excelled."

Frequently, a newspaper preceded the town itself. William H. Adams, editor of the *Kansas Weekly Herald* of Leavenworth, printed his first issue on a riverbank in 1854 and wrote that "All the type in the present number has been set under an elm tree." When the first house in town was built, the paper moved in.

An editor's performance as a publicist was closely monitored by his fellow townsmen, for their future depended largely on the efficacy of his proselytizing. Just how strongly they might feel about lackluster work was discovered in 1878 by the editor of the *Barber County Mail* of Medicine Lodge, Kansas. Printed with worn-out and broken type, the publication was so hard to read that dissatisfied residents invaded the editor's premises and seized him with the intention of tarring and feathering him. No tar was available and no one was willing to contribute the contents of a precious feather bed, but a way was found. The editor's critics coated him with sorghum molasses and feathered him with sand burrs, both of which were in abundant local supply. Then they capped the punishment by riding him around town on a wooden rail. The editor sold the paper shortly thereafter and left for parts unknown.

Any community that hoped to grow beyond infancy needed a hotel—to accommodate prospective townsmen as well as transients—and a hotelkeeper was generally among the first arrivals. His hospitality was often crude. When Sidney Moss opened the first inn west of the Rockies after platting Oregon City in 1842, his establishment did not possess a single bed or chair; guests paid him five dollars a week to sleep in blankets on the floor. At another frontier hotel, a guest who expressed dismay at the condition of the roller towel was told by his host, "There's 26 men used that towel before you and you're the first one that complained."

Along with a newspaper and a hotel, a saloon invariably appeared on the scene early to dispense the fiery potables—and perhaps a variety of entertainment—that made life in a hard land supportable. Saloonkeepers were particularly numerous in towns whose prime customers were cowboys or miners. Abilene, with a year-round population of about 800 in 1871, had 11 saloons to accommodate the 5,000 or more trail-parched cowboys who arrived from Texas in late spring and summer with herds of longhorns to be shipped east. In mining towns, the saloons often stayed wide-open 24 hours a day seven days a week to squeeze the last dollar out of the prospectors.

Predictably, professional gamblers, prostitutes and entertainers swelled the census figures in such communities. However, their numbers were subject to sud-

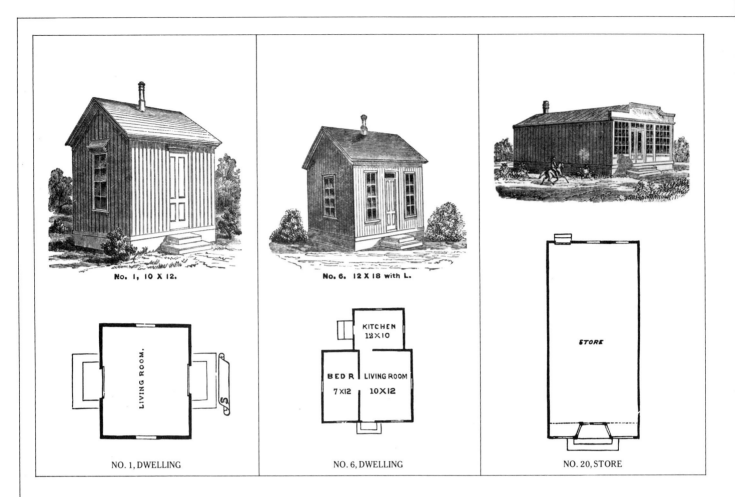

NO. 1, 10 X 12.

NO. 6, 12 X 18 with L.

LIVING ROOM.

KITCHEN 12×10

BED R 7×12

LIVING ROOM 10×12

STORE

NO. 1, DWELLING

NO. 6, DWELLING

NO. 20, STORE

An array of mail-order architecture

Would-be townsmen who were deficient in construction skills could avail themselves of a literally ready-made solution. Prefabricated structures of every description, from one-room dwellings to 400-seat churches, could be ordered from Midwestern lumberyards like Lyman Bridges of Chicago, whose catalogue for 1870 is shown here. The prefabs were shipped west in freight wagons, boxcars or riverboats.

One group of aspiring townsmen had 10 such structures with them when their boat ran aground in Kansas' Kaw River, at a community called Boston. The newcomers had planned to form a town that would be named Manhattan, in accordance with the wishes of their financial backers in New York. But when the mishap occurred, they threw in their lot with Boston, and in return for their prefab dowry, the name of that town was changed to Manhattan.

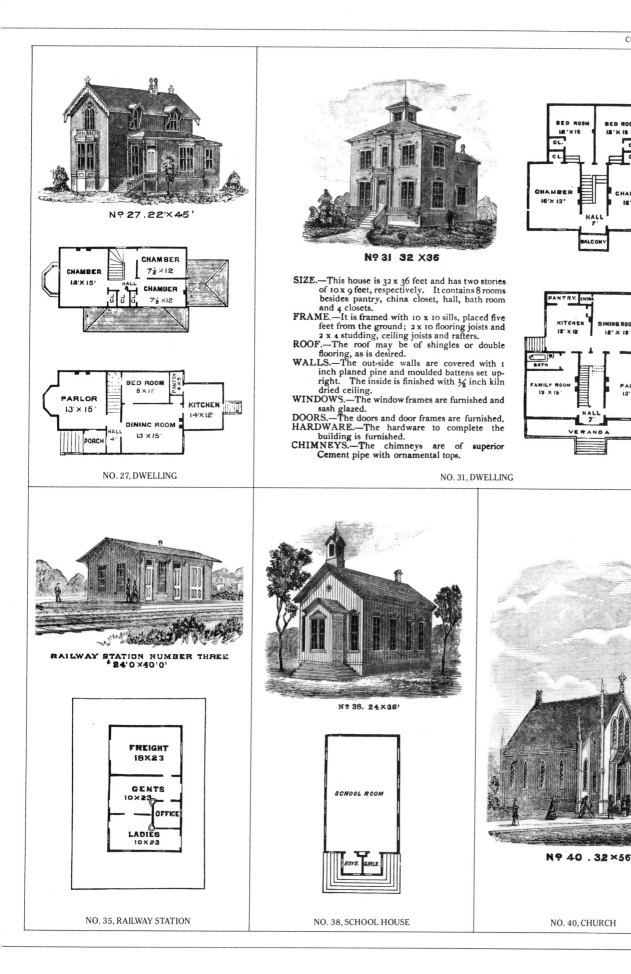

NO 27. 22'X 45'

CHAMBER
13'X 15'

CHAMBER
7½×12

CHAMBER
7½×12

HALL

CL CL CL

PARLOR
13'X 15'

BED ROOM
8'X 11'

PANTRY
4×5

KITCHEN
14×12'

HALL 4'

DINING ROOM
13'X 15'

PORCH

NO. 27, DWELLING

NO 31 32 X 36

BED ROOM
12'X 15

BED ROOM
12'X 15

CL.

CL.

CL.

CL.

CHAMBER
16'X 13'

CHAMBER
16'X 13'

HALL
7'

BALCONY

PANTRY. CHINA

KITCHEN
12' X 15'

DINING ROOM
12' X 15'

BATH

FAMILY ROOM
13 X 15'

PARLOR
13' X 16'

HALL
7'

VERANDA

SIZE.—This house is 32 x 36 feet and has two stories of 10 x 9 feet, respectively. It contains 8 rooms besides pantry, china closet, hall, bath room and 4 closets.

FRAME.—It is framed with 10 x 10 sills, placed five feet from the ground; 2 x 10 flooring joists and 2 x 4 studding, ceiling joists and rafters.

ROOF.—The roof may be of shingles or double flooring, as is desired.

WALLS.—The out-side walls are covered with 1 inch planed pine and moulded battens set upright. The inside is finished with ½ inch kiln dried ceiling.

WINDOWS.—The window frames are furnished and sash glazed.

DOORS.—The doors and door frames are furnished.

HARDWARE.—The hardware to complete the building is furnished.

CHIMNEYS.—The chimneys are of superior Cement pipe with ornamental tops.

NO. 31, DWELLING

RAILWAY STATION NUMBER THREE
24'0'X40'0'

FREIGHT
18X23

GENTS
10X23

OFFICE

LADIES
10X23

NO. 35, RAILWAY STATION

NO 38. 24×36'

SCHOOL ROOM

BOYS. GIRLS.

NO. 38, SCHOOL HOUSE

NO 40 . 32×56

NO. 40, CHURCH

den, violent reductions, for gunfire was more likely to erupt in a saloon—their place of business—than anywhere else in town. An Irish fiddler named Kelley, employed in a saloon in Idaho City, Idaho, grew so apprehensive over the hair-trigger tantrums of the local miners that he insisted on an ingenious safety measure. He had the proprietor build a platform that was rigged to the ceiling by a system of pulleys and halyards. Whenever gunfire broke out he was hoisted aloft, where he played on, presumably above the line of fire.

In farming regions such precautions were not necessary. There a saloon was generally a far more sedate place, where patrons lingered long over a nickel glass of beer, nibbled on pickles and other snacks that were set out by the proprietor, and discussed their affairs in tones of high seriousness.

No town was complete without a blacksmith, whose services were needed to shoe horses and oxen, sharpen plows, repair wagons and perform a multitude of other maintenance tasks for the community and outlying areas. So essential was this craftsman that town founders often offered blacksmiths free building lots as incentives to settle in their communities. The same practice was used to attract an operator of a livery stable—an establishment where visitors could shelter their horses while they attended to business in town. Another service of the livery stable was the rental of a buggy and team to a salesman who wanted to make the rounds of the countryside or to any young swain who wanted to treat his girl to a moonlit ride on the prairie.

But the chief focus of a new town's commercial life was the general store, called a shebang—a term that may have derived from the Gaelic *shebeen,* or speakeasy. Liquor in bottled form was available there, along with almost anything else that a frontiersman might crave: sugar and salt, molasses and meat, gunpowder and ammunition, crockery and coal oil. Everyone within walking or riding distance called at the shebang regularly, hovered over the shelves of goods, loitered amid the deliciously mingled odors and the warmth of the pot-bellied stove, and came away with a heartening sense of well-being. The merchant was usually the most popular townsman—and the most indispensable.

Few new towns were lucky enough to attract the full array of skills and talents that contributed to the convenience of life in the East. "What we want now most,

When the Missouri River went on a rampage in 1881, the only way the townsfolk of East Atchison, Missouri, could stay dry-shod was by poling rafts along the main street. Choosing a townsite on a river was a risky trade-off of ease of transport for peril of flood. This one lasted three days.

is mechanics," the *Kansas Weekly Herald* pleaded in 1854, at a time when the word mechanic was used to describe any skilled artisan. "We have several kinds but not enough of them. We have not got a Sadler, Shoemaker, Tailor, Cabinet Maker, Hatter nor Milliner in the place."

Given the lack of specialists, townsmen often had to settle for second-rate work from untrained, inept or overextended practitioners of all kinds. When newspaperman Thomas A. McNeal arrived in Medicine Lodge, Kansas, by stagecoach in 1879, he debarked dust-laden and unkempt, and went in search of a shave from the town barber. He was directed to a man in the livery stable who was "acting as chambermaid for partially civilized bronchos." Putting aside his horseshoeing implements, the alleged barber stropped a razor on his boot top, seated McNeal in a chair, bent the customer's head back over his knee, lathered him, scraped away the whiskers and grime with a few impatient strokes, and charged him 15 cents.

Of all the shortages of skills, the one that affected Western towns most acutely was the scarcity of qualified doctors. Many of the practitioners who arrived in frontier towns were impelled there by a lack of success back East, sometimes directly traceable to a lack of competence. Even the capable men did not always find greener pastures beyond the Missouri. A Western doctor was expected to minister to the surrounding countryside as well as to his town. Because of the great distances between rural patients and the general shortage of ready money, many doctors found it impossible to make a living and turned to other pursuits.

Yet the need for medical practitioners was undeniably great. The health of the Western townsmen was perpetually threatened by poor sanitation. Many communities got their drinking water from sloughs or polluted streams. Sewage was sometimes piped directly into the streets. The droppings of horses and of wandering pigs and chickens drew clouds of flies.

When the wind was right, a traveler could scent a town before he saw it. The editor of the *Wichita Eagle* was not exaggerating too much when he reported: "A fair sample of what we may expect in the way of variety and kinds of smell, and the different thicknesses of the stratas, was given last Saturday, when it was a little warmer than any previous day this spring, with a stiff breeze flowing from the south. Pedestrians on Main, Market and Water streets, anywhere north of Douglas Avenue, were regaled with quintessence of putrifaction. A tall man who was sitting on the sidewalk said, as he got up and passed through with his nose, that there were two hundred and forty distinct and odd smells prevailing then and there." Turning dead serious, the *Eagle* added, "All agree that some sanitary measures are needed, and heavy fines should be imposed on those who will throw slops, old meats and decaying vegetable matter at their doors or on the street."

In the absence of public health precautions, epidemics were inevitable. Time after time, communities were ravaged by cholera, typhoid, diphtheria, pneumonia, pleurisy and smallpox. An outbreak of cholera in Kansas City in 1855 killed so many people so swiftly that one woman resident complained it was impossible to sleep at night because of the hammering of carpenters building coffins. And since few frontier houses had screens on the windows to keep out mosquitoes and other insects, nearly everybody suffered chronically from malaria—called the ague or mountain ail. In some areas, whole families were wiped out by the disease.

Perhaps in reaction to the sheer enormity of their jobs, many doctors became alcoholics, and the Dakota territorial legislature passed a law making it a misdemeanor for a doctor to poison a patient while drunk; the charge was increased to manslaughter if the victim died. Still, many impressive feats of medicine were accomplished by physicians who were called upon to preside over difficult births, perform operations without proper anesthetics on kitchen tables or remove Indian arrows —a surgical procedure not taught in Eastern medical schools. Even plastic surgery was performed in frontier towns: Dr. Thomas G. Maghee of Rawlins, Wyoming Territory, carried out 39 separate operations in 1886 and 1887 to rebuild a sheepherder's face, which had been partly shot away.

Almost as scarce as competent doctors in the new towns were qualified schoolteachers. In most communities, education was a catch-as-catch-can proposition at first. In 1863, for instance, John Adams—founder and namesake of Adams, Nebraska—persuaded an educated newcomer to undertake the schooling of his four children in return for room and board, plus the gift of a pregnant heifer. The school, begun in Adams' front parlor with a slate, a Bible and a supply of tattered books brought from the East, soon acquired the other eight children in town as pupils.

As soon as townsmen could spare the time, they built a proper schoolhouse, often with everyone in the community contributing labor and materials. Hiring a proper teacher was less easy. The highest pay was only about $35 a month, and there were grievous drawbacks to the usual pay-supplement scheme of having a teacher "board around" from family to family. Fairness to the townsfolk decreed that the teacher should stay longest with families that had the most children in school; but this arrangement worked a hardship on the teacher, since large families usually meant cramped quarters and small portions at mealtime. Not surprisingly, most schoolteachers regarded their job as a way stop to marriage or some more comfortable line of work.

Among the professionals needed by frontier towns, lawyers were most likely to be available in the requisite numbers—and understandably so. They could earn anywhere from a few hundred dollars to more than $1,000 a month at the relatively routine legal work of settling land claims or mining claims, two prime sources of frontier litigation. Another reason for the abundance of lawyers was the ease of gaining admittance to the bar in new territories. The only requirements were that the applicant be at least 21 years old, supply evidence of good moral character and pass an examination before a judge—who usually limited his quiz to a few vague and simple questions, since he probably had little legal training himself. Most young men who aspired to the bar served an apprenticeship in the office of an established lawyer, but even this was not necessary. Before the Civil War earned him fame as a general, William Tecumseh Sherman gained admittance to the Kansas bar merely by showing that he had a rich fund of miscellaneous information.

Yet frontier communities produced a few crack lawyers, sometimes out of unlikely material. James Hawley was a prime example. A native of Iowa, he arrived in Idaho City, Idaho Territory, in 1863 to dig gold, but he soon found that the hard manual labor of prospecting was not to his taste. He took a job selling subscriptions to the *Boise County News*. The paper's editor, sizing up Hawley as a promising and clearheaded young man, got him interested in a legal career by lending him cop-

ies of such classics of the profession as Blackstone's and Kent's *Commentaries*.

Hawley went on to earn his law degree at San Francisco City College, tangled with the police while celebrating the receipt of his diploma and fled to China, where he became involved in the Taiping Rebellion. Later, still hungry for adventure, he returned to Idaho and took up prospecting again, this time enjoying some financial success. But in the course of winning a suit against another miner over ownership of a claim, he realized that he wanted to devote his life to the law after all. He became a trial attorney and participated in 300 murder cases. President Cleveland named him U.S. Attorney for Idaho Territory in 1886, and he went on to become Idaho's 31st governor.

Whatever else Western townsmen lacked, they had an abundance of spiritual guidance. Many church denominations dispatched pastors westward during the era of town-building. On the prairies and plains, the Methodists were often first on the scene; but Presbyterians, Congregationalists, Baptists, Roman Catholics and Episcopalians did not lag far behind. Even so, the influx was insufficient to cope with the number of potential souls to be saved, and many preachers became circuit riders. If sturdy of limb and firm in the saddle, they sometimes managed to squeeze in three sermons and 50 miles on a Sabbath.

On occasion, a minister had cause to question the depth of his flock's piety. A flood delayed one Methodist circuit rider on his way to Hog Thief Bend, Nebraska, where the entire town had assembled to celebrate the wedding of the town belle and her swain. Unwilling to postpone the festivities, the guests decided that the sheriff could perform the ceremony just as well. The bride's mother expressed grave doubts concerning the legality of such a union but was overruled by unanimous vote, and the lawman did his duty. According to the custom of the time, the guests proceeded to serenade the newlyweds by singing rude songs and drumming on kettles late into the night. Two days later the errant preacher finally arrived and insisted on tightening the knot with a proper religious ceremony.

A popular mode of spiritual uplift, particularly among Methodists, was the camp meeting, usually held in a grove just outside of town and sometimes lasting as long as a week. These occasions, attended by both the

The citizens of Creede, Colorado, stand amid still-smoking ashes and rubble after a blaze consumed half their community on June 5, 1892. Preoccupied with the quick riches to be gained from the nearby silver mines, the town had neglected to organize itself against the contingency of fire.

34

townsmen and the rural populace, were considered doubly beneficial since they combined worship with socializing. Now and then the presiding evangelist would achieve a truly astonishing triumph for the Lord. At one such meeting, the renowned Jim Lane—Union general and Kansas Senator—acknowledged his besetting sin and turned his chewing tobacco over to the minister's custody. The man of God, almost overcome, delivered this paean of thanks: "Glory to God! This great man, who has led the hosts of his country in battle, stood upon the forum of the capital and in the serried ranks of war, has given up his last idol!"

It was not always that easy to spread the word, especially in pre-Civil War days, when many churches of an abolitionist persuasion sent preachers west to inveigh against slavery. In 1855 the Reverend Pardee Butler so offended proslavery sentiment in Atchison that a gang of secessionists kidnapped, tarred and feathered him, branded the letter "R" (for "Rogue") on his forehead with black paint and set him adrift on a raft on the Missouri. The parson was rescued but did not repent. As he recalled: "I pledged I would come back. They pledged that if I did, they would hang me." He did return the next year, and once again his foes tarred him. No feathers were handy on this occasion, so they used tufts of cotton. Butler moved on to other Kansas towns more sympathetic to his cause.

Generally, resistance to men of the cloth took a milder form. The first sermon in Bismarck, Dakota Territory, was preached in a saloon where a Sunday poker game was in progress. The players were tempted to throw the sermonizer out, but they concluded that he was inoffensive and not seriously interrupting play, and they even took up a collection of $40 in chips. The proprietor then invited the divine to get into the game and see whether he could increase the Lord's stake, promising to stand by with a gun to make sure that nobody dealt off the bottom of the deck. The minister declined, cashed in the donated chips and took his leave with as much dignity as he could summon.

Spiritual solace of any kind must have been heartening to the townsmen, for life in a frontier community was undeniably hard. Building up a trade from scratch in a remote region was toil enough, but sometimes it seemed that the settlers were locked in mortal combat with nature itself. The weather on the high plains and in the mountains was capricious. Perhaps the only thing that was predictable about it was its excessiveness. In the Nevada silver country, winds that were ruefully known as "Washoe Zephyrs" came swirling off the flanks of the Sierra Nevada from time to time and ripped through Virginia City and Carson City with such ferocity that houses were unroofed; and on the central grasslands the wind hardly ever stopped blowing. Erratic cloudbursts in spring or summer could bring a flash flood roiling down a creekbed. Or a wet spring, combined with the snowmelt from the Rockies, could send a great river spilling over its banks to devastate the works of the townsmen, who too often ignored the counsel of friendly Indians against building a house in a watercourse. In March 1881, when the Missouri River flooded, three quarters of the town of Vermilion, Dakota Territory, simply disappeared.

At the opposite extreme, great droughts periodically afflicted the plains, causing great suffering on the farms and in the towns as well. In late summer and fall the grasslands turned sere, and the land was at the mercy of fire, caused by a haphazard lightning stroke or man's carelessness. "The fires this fall have been unusually terrific and destructive," reported the *Western Home Journal* of Ottawa, Kansas, in 1867. "The long dryness and high winds together have made combustible material and given it wings." Prairie fires did not spare the towns, for fields and weeds usually ran well into the village limits. Both Skyston and Leola, in Dakota Territory, were nearly destroyed by fire during their early days. Three times within an 11-month span from August 1892 to July 1893 flames roared through Alliance, Nebraska.

Some of the worst conflagrations originated in the towns themselves. Creede, Colorado, never truly recovered from a fire that began in a saloon and swept forth to destroy half the town in 1892. Aware of their peril, townsmen everywhere stood ready to fight for their homes and businesses with bucket, shovel and wet gunny sack. Such tools were feeble weapons against rampant flames and, as soon as they could afford it, towns laid in more effective equipment. The first organized fire departments were volunteer bucket brigades furnished with ladders at public expense. Some towns dug cisterns to supply the fire fighters with water at stra-

Riding tandem on a steer decked with patriotic headgear, three farm boys of Heber City, Utah, head for a July Fourth parade in the 1880s. Processions on this holiday were swelled by buggy-mounted floats.

tegic points. Then hand pumps arrived, but they tended to freeze up in cold weather. Topeka ran into another problem: the town bought an efficient man-powered fire pump from a Schenectady, New York, company in 1869 but failed to order enough hose; to reach a fire it was sometimes necessary to bring the water forward in relays, pumping it from cistern to cistern.

Winter's weapon was the blizzard. In towns in the mountains, residents were regularly snowed in for weeks at a time. On the plains, snow was whipped by berserk winds that could rush hundreds of miles without encountering an obstacle. The Easter blizzard of 1873 was one of the worst assaults — all the more disabling because it came late in the year and took people by surprise. When this blizzard struck, the inhabitants of Hastings, Nebraska, had to string guide ropes between buildings to find their way through the white maelstrom, but soon the snow piled so deep that the ropes were no longer practicable. By the time the storm abated, the drifts were at the level of the eaves, and citizens had to tunnel through them to get the town moving again. In Central City, Nebraska, during the same blizzard, a boy sent on an errand to a print shop only a block away was finally dug lifeless out of a drift.

Hard as life on the frontier unquestionably was, it was far from joyless. For the most part townspeople were young — a man of 40 was considered well along in years — and they were robust and possessed of a deep-dyed optimism. Whenever they found the leisure to play, they played with gusto.

Saturday was the high point of the week in any town: the population was swollen by country folk who came in to buy whatever groceries they did not raise themselves, to sell their eggs and cream, to shop for youngsters' graduation suits at the shebang, to shoot snooker at the pool hall, play pinochle or perhaps try their luck at poker or keno in the saloon. Endless gossip was traded in the barber shop, at the livery stable or on the porch of the hotel. Then, in the evening, when most of the country people had returned to their homes, the townsmen might indulge in one of their most cherished diversions — social dancing.

At these affairs, any female from eight to eighty could count on a full dance program. Women were in short supply in practically every frontier town, and in certain areas the disparity between the sexes was positively des-

CONCERT
— AND —
FESTIVAL!
At the STATE HOUSE,
Thursday Evening, June 3, 1869.

Object---to procure an Organ for the Congregational Church.

Singing by a Quartette, composed of
Mr. J. C. STIRE, | Mrs. J. J. JONES,
Dr. W. A. BURR, | Mrs. S. B. POUND.

1. "What delight, what joy rebounds."
2. "When you and I were young, Maggie."
3. "Far away."
4. "The Mountaineer's song."
5. "Engaged."
6. "Sweet and Sour."
7. "Don't you go, Tommie."
8. "Pass under the Rod."
9. "Down by the sea."
10. "Lottie Lee."

Admission Fifty Cents.
Each Ticket entitles the holder to a dish of Ice Cream and Cake. Refreshments will be sold at the tables.

STRAWBERRIES
ARE EXPECTED.

Doors open at 7½ o'clock. Concert will commence at 8¼.
Tickets for sale at the Drug stores and at the door.

Patronage of Strangers and Citizens requested.

"Nebraska Statesman" Print.

perate. According to the 1860 federal census, the white population of Colorado was made up of 32,654 males and 1,577 females. To hold a dance under such circumstances, men had to assume the role of female partners, signaling the switch by tying a handkerchief around one of their arms. This somehow had the effect of making the real women look overwhelmingly lovely; and their feminine allure was further enhanced by the practice of wearing wedding dresses when they had nothing else that was suitable for a festive occasion.

In wintertime, towns organized lyceums — literary societies — for weekly or semimonthly debates, lectures and song fests. The debates — with speakers arguing such volatile issues as slavery, the efficacy of capital punishment or, in one case, "Resolved: that farming does not pay" — were a favorite part of the programs, if only because the debaters tended to present their cases in bombastic style. The townsmen also attended schoolchildren's recitations, and sometimes pitted themselves against the youngsters in spelling bees.

There was an almost infinite variety of pastimes to be savored outdoors — sleigh rides in winter, turkey shoots in summer and, for the youngsters, the constant challenge of snaring rabbits or prairie dogs just outside the town limits. Foot racing was a passion, and men trained themselves for the contests by jogging around with bags of buckshot tied to their ankles. Horse racing was another popular diversion; since the West was chronically short of currency, spectators would sometimes bet their shirts and other prized possessions on the outcome. Usually the races were held just outside of town, but now and then the main street served as the track. Only spoilsports objected to the pounding of hoofs and the whooping of spectators: one such kill-joy was the editor of the *Neosho Valley Register* of Iola, Kansas, who in 1874 sourly editorialized that "an excellent way to fix a street is to plow a deep ditch across it. It prevents horse racing."

The greatest sport of all was baseball, at least in the years after the Civil War. Every town and hamlet had a team, and the fortunes of the local nine were a matter of intense concern to every citizen. It was no game for the frail or fainthearted. Gloves were usually in short supply, and the contests themselves tended to be epic struggles. In 1871 the Blue Belts of Milford, Nebraska, played Seward, 10 miles away, and beat them in a four-hour marathon by the score of 97 to 25.

Nothing galvanized the energies of towns quite like national and regional holidays — Arbor Day, when trees were planted on the timberless plains; George Washington's Birthday, which furnished a welcome winter break; and, most glorious of all, Independence Day. Patriotism was intense west of the Mississippi and Missouri rivers. Because most regions had not achieved statehood, there was still a sense of not belonging, a feeling of being cut off from home. To compensate, Westerners celebrated the Fourth with a fervor they would remember all year long.

A measure of decorum was maintained on the holiday in the form of solemn patriotic speeches by the town's leading citizens. These orations almost always included readings from the Declaration of Independence and the Constitution, and they were followed by toasts to virtually everyone and everything in the nation's history deemed worth honoring.

After the speechifying and the toasts, the festivities on the main street, or in a grove outside town normally reserved for camp meetings, evolved into a kind of delirious melee. Gunpowder was set off under the blacksmith's anvil for a cannon-like salute, and firecrackers battered ceaselessly at the ear. Spectators drifted from foot races to horse races to contests in which men and boys tried to climb greased poles or attempted to capture an oiled pig.

When the celebrants wearied of the games, they settled down to eat — sometimes to gorge. Blue Springs, Nebraska, began its preparations for the 1859 Fourth three weeks in advance. A committee of three men was assigned to provide catfish for a feast; a 250-pound hog was procured to supply lard for cooking; and the womenfolk began grinding quantities of corn into meal. When the great day arrived, the three-man committee had more than a thousand pounds of live catfish penned up in a weir in the town creek, and the women had the ovens roaring hot. The result was described as one of the finest corn pone and catfish fries ever witnessed west of the Missouri River.

In the long run, the morale of any Western town depended less on such festivities than on sober estimates of its prospects for growth. Every community, no matter how small, aspired to cityhood, and for some of them the dream came true almost overnight. In 1854, Omaha consisted of one log house, 16 feet square. By 1856 the town's population had grown to 1,600, and some of its choicest building lots sold for $2,500. And only a year later Omaha boasted 3,000 people, and its lots were valued as high as $4,000 each.

Boulder, Colorado, was more typical in its rate of development. Founded in 1859 as a supply town for the nearby mining camps—and consisting of only a few mud-roofed log cabins—the little settlement barely survived its first few years. But as time went by, more precious metals were discovered and two local Colorado railroads entered the town. By 1880 it had become the seat of Boulder County, the gateway to the mountain mines and a popular summer resort. It could boast of two banks, six churches, two weekly newspapers and a population of 4,000.

Yet for every Omaha or Boulder, there were many towns that stayed small. And there were many others that did well for a time, then withered away when local mineral deposits played out or cattle herds stopped coming. Thus, a townsman needed courage—particularly in the beginning, when his chosen community seemed so vulnerable. He also had to believe in the destiny of his town and in the commitment of his fellow citizens to work toward that destiny.

Believing was not always easy. When Richard Cordley, a Congregational minister, reached Lawrence, Kansas, in 1857, the town was three years old, but it had a dreary, almost moribund look about it: "There were not only no sidewalks, but no streets. The roads ran here and there, as each driver took a fancy. The houses seemed to be straggling around on the prairie as if they had lost their way." Almost entirely bare of trees or other greenery, Lawrence gave the newcomer a "lonesome, desolate impression."

In spite of this prospect, the minister kept an open mind, and before long he was able to report that "this first impression soon wore off as the inner life of the place began to reveal itself." The town had more residents than he had thought, and he was pleasantly surprised to find that they were not all "the traditional roughs of the frontier." He found people reading "the best Eastern papers"—not just in town but across the surrounding prairie as well.

Soon Cordley glimpsed the true spirit of Western townsmen. "These people had not come as adventurers to see how they would like it. They had come to stay and see the thing done." All over the West they stayed and saw it done, and by the close of the century the word frontier had almost lost its meaning.

The congregation of St. John's Episcopal Church—the first house of worship in Wichita, Kansas—lingers after a Sunday service. Constructed with stockade walls and a roof of sod slabs in 1869, the church doubled as Wichita's school on weekdays—until the roof collapsed after two years.

A head start on tomorrow's promise

A school was high on the priority list for almost every new Western town, but only the more prosperous towns could afford such an imposing temple of learning as the structure at right, with rooms enough to divide the student body into grades. A one-room schoolhouse, and one lone teacher, had to serve for most communities—in their early days at least.

Almost every town encountered difficulties in hiring and holding someone to teach there. The standard offer of free room and board at the homes of pupils scarcely compensated for the low wages of $10 to $35 a month. And even that meager income was anything but steady since wages were paid only when school was in session, and children on the frontier attended school for only five months a year on the average. Indeed, this latter frustration cut more ways than one. "Sometimes I wish I could have these children under my care for a year," one young schoolteacher confided wistfully to her diary. "How some of them would advance!"

Built of the abundant local stone in 1870, this two-story school was the pride of Columbus, Kansas.

43.

44

A schoolteacher in Kelly, New Mexico, poses with her charges for a group portrait in the doorway of her one-room schoolhouse during the 1880s. On the frontier, men and women shared the teaching load—and both sexes served as school janitors in addition to their instructional duties.

With an adult guest stationed at the school organ *(left)*, pupils in Leoti, Kansas, prepare to take a musical break from their books. Such interludes were infrequent; most of the time the students were buried in McGuffey's Readers — literary anthologies celebrating hard work, honesty and piety.

cal economy. But the railroads themselves created jerkwaters wholesale as
they laid tracks westward, often bypassing—and intentionally killing—existing
population centers rather than lose an
opportunity for corporate profit.

Yet it scarcely mattered that the legions of town-makers included profiteers and deceivers. Their feverish
rivalry served to provide prospective
citizens with an endless number of
choices for locating their new homes in
the West. The promoters, as one Kansas land official said, were the embodiment of a "day of great beginnings."

Youngsters at the public school of Scofield, Utah, encircle their fife-and-drum corps during a patriotic pageant in the 1890s. Public schools like this were often established with funds from the sale of federal lands, specifically donated for that purpose by Congress when new territories were formed.

2 | Of building lots a

Like so many other opportunities that beckoned in the West, founding a town seemed easy at first. A promoter simply commissioned surveyors to journey out to a spot in the middle of nowhere and mark off the streets and lots. But when the entrepreneur addressed the task of translating these lineaments into buildings, people and perhaps a fortune for himself, he quickly discovered that he would need every ounce of guile and energy he could muster.

The odds were heavily against his creation taking hold. In the second half of the 19th Century, would-be towns

sprang up at a p the supply of se abounding, most promo blatant puffery—or outrig sentations—of their embryoni nity's advantages. Even edite Greeley, who faithfully bo West in the New York Tribu bled that the discrepancy be claims and reality was "enou a cheerful man the horrors."

At times the competiti ruthless. Many a town was the reasonable hope that would pass through and inv

47

Youngsters at the public school of Scofield, Utah, encircle their fife-and-drum corps during a patriotic pageant in the 1890s. Public schools like this were often established with funds from the sale of federal lands, specifically donated for that purpose by Congress when new territories were formed.

48

49

2 | Of building lots and ballyhoo

Like so many other opportunities that beckoned in the West, founding a town seemed easy at first. A promoter simply commissioned surveyors to journey out to a spot in the middle of nowhere and mark off the streets and lots. But when the entrepreneur addressed the task of translating these lineaments into buildings, people and perhaps a fortune for himself, he quickly discovered that he would need every ounce of guile and energy he could muster.

The odds were heavily against his creation taking hold. In the second half of the 19th Century, would-be towns sprang up at a pace that far outstripped the supply of settlers. With rivals abounding, most promoters resorted to blatant puffery—or outright misrepresentations—of their embryonic community's advantages. Even editor Horace Greeley, who faithfully boosted the West in the *New York Tribune,* grumbled that the discrepancy between the claims and reality was "enough to give a cheerful man the horrors."

At times the competition turned ruthless. Many a town was founded in the reasonable hope that a railroad would pass through and invigorate the local economy. But the railroads themselves created jerkwaters wholesale as they laid tracks westward, often bypassing—and intentionally killing—existing population centers rather than lose an opportunity for corporate profit.

Yet it scarcely mattered that the legions of town-makers included profiteers and deceivers. Their feverish rivalry served to provide prospective citizens with an endless number of choices for locating their new homes in the West. The promoters, as one Kansas land official said, were the embodiment of a "day of great beginnings."

Surveyors lay out Progresso, New Mexico, an optimistically named community that would expire within a few years of its birth in 1894.

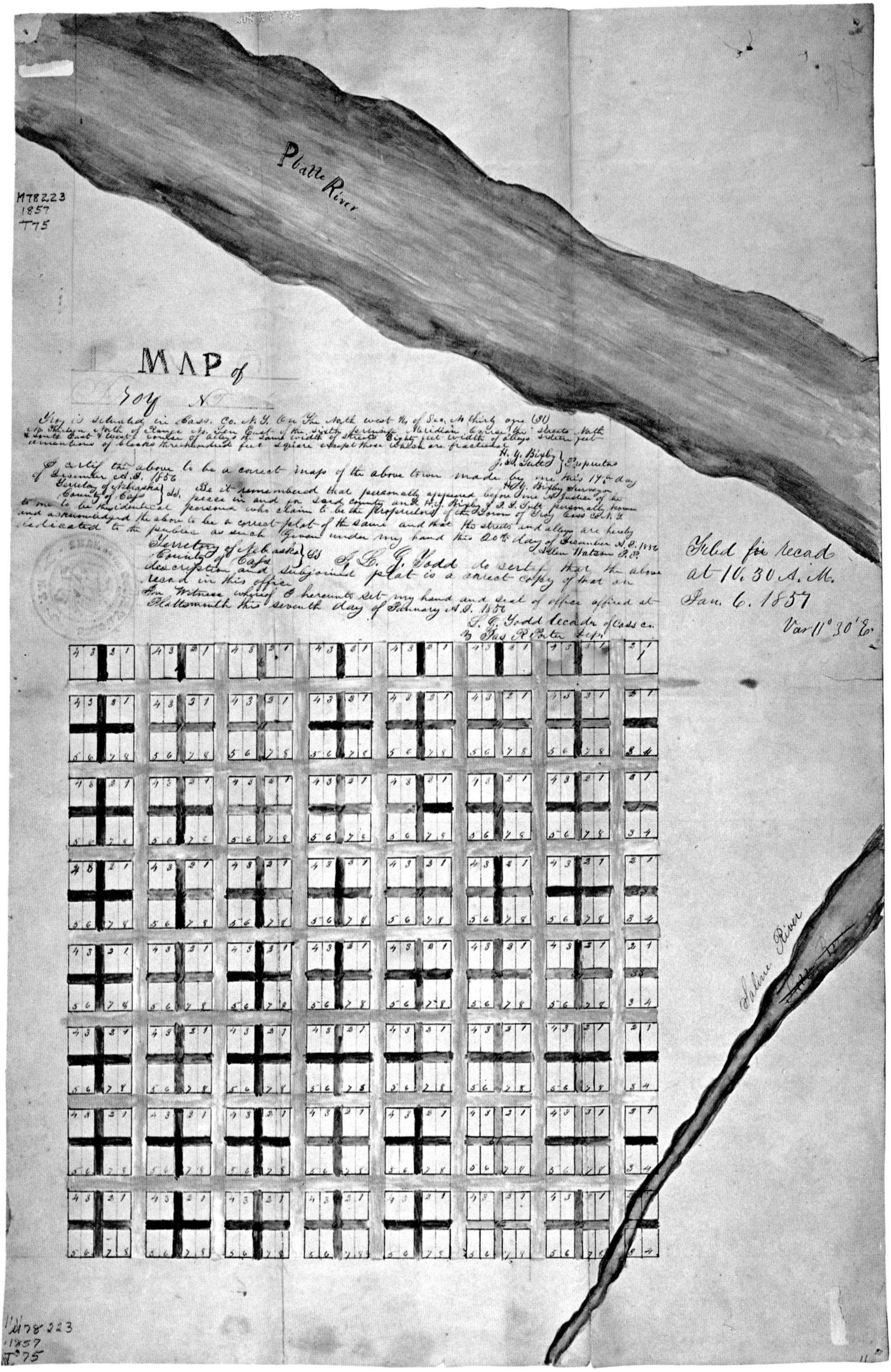
Platte River
M78223
1857
T75
MAP of
Troy N.T.
Filed for record
at 10.30 A.M.
Jan. 6. 1857
Var 11° 30' E
Saline River

"Come!–rush!–hurry!–don't wait for anything!"

For about three decades, from the 1850s to the 1880s, a special breed of men served as Pied Pipers of the lands beyond the Missouri. They were the town promoters, who founded, built and populated thousands of communities all across the virgin wilderness. Many a promoter was simply the leader of an emigrant group whose members were intent on starting life afresh, on terms they themselves would dictate. Others were salaried agents for railroads with huge land holdings. But the typical town promoter of the period was a freelance speculator in real estate. As new territories were opened for settlement, his ilk, generally operating in syndicates of less than a dozen members, acquired acreage that seemed well situated for a future town—or could be made to sound well situated—and sold it off as building lots.

A good example of the kind was J. P. Wheeler, an adoptive son of Kansas who sang of its glories so seductively that it seemed he had lived there all his life. Trained as a surveyor in his native Massachusetts, Wheeler arrived in Kansas Territory in 1855 at the age of 21; the *Atchison Globe* described him as a "blue-eyed, slim, consumptive, freckled enthusiast." Soon thereafter—perhaps while he surveyed the site for the new town of Mount Pleasant in 1857—Wheeler discovered his latent talent for salesmanship. Graduating from a mere enthusiast or "booster" of Western settlement to a promoter or "boomer," he became a land-sales agent for the incorporated group of speculators who had founded Mount Pleasant. A year later

he launched a company of his own to establish the town of Sumner, sited on the Missouri River three miles south of Atchison.

To attract emigrants to Sumner, Wheeler set down his selling spiel in a handsome brochure illustrated in color (*overleaf*), and he sent copies to agents for distribution in the Eastern cities. The pamphlet proved gratifyingly effective, and one reader—another young Massachusetts man named John J. Ingalls—was positively galvanized by its message. Ingalls was a staid, sensible law clerk in a Boston office. Every once in a while, however, a certain restlessness would come over him; "it remains to be proved," he commented in a letter to his father, "whether there is any heroic stuff in my mold." Then a copy of the Wheeler's brochure fell into his hands.

In picture and text Sumner loomed as the coming metropolis of the West. Though Ingalls knew the town could not have been more than four years old (Kansas Territory was legally opened for settlement in 1854), it already boasted steamboat docks, a bustling waterfront business district, a mill, a machine shop, a factory, four churches, many fine residences and several schools, including a noble domed edifice—apparently a college —that overlooked a broad, prosperous panorama.

In no time at all, Ingalls decided that Massachusetts had too many lawyers and that he would do much better to set up his practice in Kansas. He acquired land in Sumner and quit his job. Then, in a fever of anticipation, he journeyed by railroad and steamboat to his future home. Arriving in Sumner on October 4 aboard the *Duncan S. Carter,* he was shocked by what he saw — or, more precisely, by what he didn't see.

The real Sumner had no churches, no fine residences, no schools of any sort and no commerce except for a few listless general stores. In the place where the machine shop was alleged to stand, Ingalls found a crude

A map of Troy, Nebraska, in 1857 placed it at the juncture of the Platte River and a tributary, and gave it 80-foot-wide alleys (*dark lines*). But the town, like countless others, never got beyond a paper plan that eventually moldered in county records.

smithy run by an aging black. Instead of many wide avenues, the town had only one graded street — actually a wandering lane clogged with undug tree stumps. Sumner did have about 200 dwellings, but many of them were made of wagon sideboards or sod slabs, roofed over with hay thatching or canvas.

Swallowing his chagrin and reminding himself that this Western adventure was to be a test of character, Ingalls chose to stay on. It was a decision that worked out brilliantly for both himself and Kansas. By 1860, a year before Kansas won statehood, its rich prairie lands had attracted 107,000 settlers, plenty of whom stood badly in need of the young lawyer's services, Using his practice as a steppingstone into politics, he was elected a state senator in 1862 and moved up to the U.S. Senate in 1873, where he served for 18 years. However, Ingalls never forgot Wheeler's outrageous brochure, which he damned as an "engraved romance" and a "chromatic triumph of lithographed mendacity."

In the strictest sense, its author was a scoundrel. But in those precarious days of frontiering, Wheeler's business ethics were generally tolerable, given the Westerner's belief in self-reliance and in the right — even the duty — to profit by his labors. And, in any case, Wheeler did all he could to make his exaggerated claims come true. Lobbying tirelessly, he convinced the lower house of the territorial legislature to pass a bill in 1858 naming Sumner the seat of Atchison County. If the designation had stuck, an inevitable influx of lawyers and favor seekers would have given town business a shot in the arm. Regrettably, nearby Atchison had artful promoters, too; they got the Kansas senate to kill Wheeler's bill, and in the next election Atchison was voted the county seat.

In spite of that reverse, Wheeler attracted to Sumner about 2,000 citizens and a fair amount of westbound transient trade. But the town suffered other heavy blows in 1858 and 1859 when new stagecoach lines to Salt Lake City and Denver chose Atchison as their eastern terminus. In 1860, much of Sumner was devastated by a tornado. And a few years later, to cap the succession of woes, Atchison was named the starting point of the first railroad through the county — the Atchison, Topeka and Santa Fe.

Slowly, one by one, Sumnerites moved away to towns where business was livelier or promised to

As pictured in an 1857 brochure, Sumner, Kansas, boasts
factories, churches, steamboats landing at a riverfront business district, and even a domed college *(far right)*. Like
most promotional material used to tout new towns to potential settlers, the scene was a product of wishful thinking.

PAWNEE
KANSAS TER.

COME ONE   COME ALL!

PUBLIC SALE OF LOTS!!

In consequence of numerous applications from persons desirous of building immediately, the trustees are induced to announce

A SALE OF LOTS

to take place at an earlier date than that already advertised.

There will therefore be TWO Sales of Lots in PAWNEE, one on the 10th of APRIL and the other on the 15th of MAY next.

The situation of PAWNEE is such as scarcely to admit a doubt of its becoming in a short time a large and important place. Being at the head of navigation of the Kansas it is the most delightful starting point for persons emigrating to our more western territories. A Military road from PAWNEE to Bridgers Pass in the Rocky Mountains affords the most direct route to Utah, California and Oregon, whilst the road to New Mexico is considerably shortened by a new one recently made. The Military post of Fort Riley is scarcely distant a mile from Pawnee and the government business connected with it will mostly be transacted here.

Ample accomodations will be ready for persons attending the SALES. These as above stated will be on the 10th of April and 15th of May next.

TERMS.--Half the purchase money in cash; the ballance on completion of the title.

W. R. MONTGOMERY,
WILLIAM A. HAMMOND,
R. C. MILLER,   } Trustees.
N. LYON,
R. H. HIGGINS.

PAWNEE, K. T., March 12th 1855.   HERALD OF F'D'M PRINT, Lawrence, K. T.

56

An enticing announcement from the promoters of Pawnee, Kansas, invites the purchase of town lots at auction—a common
marketing method. Businessmen, however,
frequently were lured with gifts of land.

be. Late in 1860, Ingalls gave up and departed for the
county seat. By 1866, the population of the ill-starred
community had dwindled to 25. The town's most imposing building, a $16,000 hotel, was torn apart to
supply materials for structures in victorious Atchison.
Wheeler's creation became one of hundreds of early
Kansas towns that perished after a brief life.

If the settlers of a new town in the West were dis-
heartened by a sudden failure of their community or a
long anxious wait for definitive success, very few of
them—and even fewer promoters—were defeated by it.
Like both Ingalls and Wheeler (who went on to found
the town of Hiawatha, Kansas, after his Sumner project), they simply shifted their hopes someplace else,
certain that their luck would turn. The prevailing mood
of the town-building epoch was a strange blend of gritty
determination and grandiose expectations. J. Sterling
Morton—an editor of the *Nebraska City News,* founder of the Morton Salt Company and later Secretary of
Agriculture under President Cleveland—put it this way:
"We felt richer, better, more millionairish than any poor
deluded mortals ever did before, on the same amount of
moonshine and pluck."

Moonshine indeed. The fact was that, after the 19th
Century passed the halfway mark, all of the newly
opened West, and particularly the lands just across the
Missouri River in Kansas, Nebraska and the Dakotas,
had a bad case of galloping euphoria, and the town promoters spread the happy contagion through the whole
country. Opportunity in the West seemed to be knock-
ing at every door, promising immediate and golden re-
turns; Easterners had only to open the door a crack to
be battered by some boomer's hoopla, delivered on paper or in person. Those who had half a notion to go
West anyway were easily swayed by boomers less talented than one whom Mark Twain encountered and
whose ballyhoo he recorded thus: "It's the grandest
country—the loveliest land—the purest atmosphere—I
can't describe it; no pen can do it justice....You'll
see! Come!—rush!—hurry!—don't wait for anything!"

As more and more emigrants answered the call,
towns—and plans for towns—multiplied so fast in Kansas and Nebraska that local newspapers could hardly
keep track of them. The *Kansas Weekly Herald* of
Leavenworth was not only dazed by their wild prolif-

eration but also annoyed to find "each one claiming
some advantages over its predecessors, either in natural
location, timber, adjacent country, proximity to certain
points, mineral resources, the best location for the capital or some other absurd desideratum...when in fact
none, or but a few, of the advantages claimed are possessed." Journalist Albert Richardson, who crisscrossed
Kansas during the 1850s and 1860s, reported: "On
paper, *all* these towns were magnificent. But if the newcomer had the unusual wisdom to visit the prophetic
city before purchasing lots, he learned the difference between fact and fancy. The town might be composed of
twenty buildings; or it might not contain a single human
habitation. Anything was marketable. Wags proposed
an act of Congress reserving some land before the whole
Territory should be divided into city lots. It was not a
swindle, but a mania."

In the rush to seize the best sites, common sense was
thrown to the winds. In 1856, with all of the two-year-
old Nebraska Territory from which to select locations,
two sets of promoters insisted on founding the towns of
Columbus and Pawnee cheek by jowl at a strategic
crossing of the Loup Fork of the Platte River. The
towns were born bitter rivals for the westbound emigrant traffic on the main overland trail, and their an-
tagonism persisted even after they agreed later that year
to merge under the name of Columbus.

Entrepreneurial zeal could account for the birth of
most towns, but the ranks of the promoters were further
swelled by fervent partisans of sundry special causes. In
1856 Henry Stephen Clubb, a wealthy vegetarian from
New York, founded Neosho City, Kansas, as a haven
for anyone who swore to eat nothing that had ever
"walked, swum or flown." In 1871, the Reverend W.
B. Christopher promoted the Kansas town of Cheever
as a stronghold for prohibitionists. ("Settle the Liquor
Question by Pre-occupation" was his punning motto.)
During the 1880s, Ned Turnley, an opportunistic Eng-
lishman who acquired a tract of prairie land in Harper
County, Kansas, built and boomed the town of Runnymede *(pages 66-67)* as a combination training center and sporting resort for feckless young English
noblemen, whose landed fathers paid handsomely to
have them taught the art of large-scale farming.

One idealist intentionally chose a most unpromising
spot for his new town. Nathan Cook Meeker, who

Would-be buyers of town lots and homesteads besiege the back windows of the Garden City, Kansas, land office in 1885—supposedly because its main entrance was already jammed with applicants. The town's drumbeaters, who may have staged this busy scene, soon drew 6,000 settlers.

came to the business of promotion from his post as the agricultural editor of the *New York Tribune,* decided to plant a colony in the arid wastes of Colorado to prove what many considered a crackpot notion: that scientific irrigation could make the desert fruitful. Meeker named his prospective community Greeley, after his famous editor-in-chief Horace Greeley, and advertised in the *Tribune* for emigrants brave enough to join the venture. From the avalanche of 3,000 replies, he selected a 200-man vanguard to lay the foundations of the community in 1870.

Out in the wilderness, Meeker's colonists promptly had dire second thoughts. Said one volunteer, "The first night, I asked myself, who are all these people, gathered together under the leadership of one visionary old man, in the vain hope of building up a paradise in the sands of the desert?" Nevertheless, the townsmen of Greeley persevered, carving out an elaborate network of irrigation canals and wringing rich harvests of wheat, oats, alfalfa, potatoes and corn from thousands of acres of once-barren desert.

Along with the champions of special causes, the leaders of ethnic and religious groups created numerous communities in the West. The town of Amana, Iowa, for instance, was founded by the Ebenezers, a sect originating in Germany. They had first established themselves near Buffalo, New York, but came to feel that the bustling city threatened their pietistic faith and belief in communal ownership of property. Their pastor, a carpenter named Christian Metz, assumed the role of town promoter when he received a mystical commandment: "You shall direct your eyes toward a distant goal in the West to find and obtain there a start and entrance or a settlement." Metz dispatched two delegations to search out the ideal place for a new home. He was a far more patient man than the average town promoter. The final choice of a site was not made for two years, and his flock was not completely settled into Amana for fully seven years.

Many new communities were sponsored by organizations of boosters who had no particular site in mind. The New England Emigrant Aid Society, formed by ardent abolitionists in 1854, recruited thousands of like-minded settlers and sent them in large groups to Kansas in an effort to ensure its admission into the Union as a free state. Some towns, including Topeka, expressed their appreciation—and their desire for continued recruitment—by contributing lots to the society.

Even a single individual could broadcast a veritable army of settlers in the West. In the 1870s and 1880s, a former slave named Benjamin Singleton brought as many as 8,000 Southern blacks to Kansas. A delegation of early comers called on the Governor of Kansas to explain, as he later reported, "that they had borne troubles until they had become so oppressive they could bear them no longer; that they had rather die in the attempt to reach the land where they can be free than to live in the South." Singleton's recruits established many small, all-black towns on the prairies, but only a few of the communities survived their impoverished beginnings.

Various levels of government, too, helped populate the new territories. States and territories set up their own immigration services, which plastered Europe with posters and circulars advertising the West as the land of plenty. Counties appointed commissioners to look after the welfare of the settlers. Many of the newcomers became lone homesteaders; but towns got a goodly share of the arriving throngs.

Yet when it came to settling the vacant spaces beyond the Missouri, not even governmental resources could match the feats of the railroads—although Washington did, of course, make it possible for them to take on the job in the first place. By Congressional action, the lines were awarded immense tracts of public land along their rights of way—as much as 20 square miles for every mile of prospective trackage. The grants were theirs to sell off as they chose, in order to finance the laying of the rails.

The creation of new towns was a particularly lucrative—and frenetic—phase of the railroads' real estate operations. While a line was under construction, surveyors ranged ahead of the tracks and selected townsites every dozen miles or so, and lot buyers swarmed in close behind them. William Bell, a photographer who worked with surveying parties for the Kansas Pacific in the 1860s, described what followed at the scene of each new town:

"As the rails approach, the fun begins, and up goes the price of the lots, higher and higher. At last it becomes the terminal depot—the starting point for the western trade—where the goods are transferred to ox trains, and sent to Denver, to Santa Fe, Fort Union, and other points. The terminal depot quickly rises to the zenith of its glory. Town lots are bought up on all sides to build accommodation for traders, teamsters, camp-followers, and loafers, who seem to drop from the skies. This state of things lasts only for a time. The terminal depot must soon be moved forward, and the little colony will be left to its own resources. If the district has good advantages, it will remain; if not, it will disappear, and the town lots will fall to nothing."

Every 70 miles or so, the transcontinental lines created a major depot, called a division point, where repair shops for the rolling stock would be built. The location of one such town was decided by sheer exhaustion. In 1867, while the Union Pacific was building westward, a surveying party rode out to select a site for a division point at the base of the Rockies, to be called Cheyenne. In the lead was Grenville Dodge, a former Civil War general and the railroad's field boss. The party rode all day without finding a spot that suited all their requirements. Finally, at nightfall, Dodge reined to a weary halt. Sliding painfully from the saddle, he buried a hatchet in the ground and said with a sigh, "By God, Cheyenne will be right *here!*"

Although many a railroad town withered away after the first frenzy of buying was over, this was hardly the fault of the promoters. Agents of the railroads spared no effort in seeking out customers. They escorted them on free trips from points farther east to inspect the new towns and adjacent lands, then lodged them at no charge in the railroads' elaborate hotels, modestly called "reception houses." Railroad colonizers also ranged across Europe, recruiting immigrants and expediting their passage to the American West.

For anyone who decided to buy railroad land—in a town or outside of it—the agents were ready and eager to extend easy credit terms. The Union Pacific asked for only one tenth of the purchase price as a down payment, and the buyer had 11 years to pay off the balance at moderate interest rates. Of course, the railroads' cut-rate friendliness was based on the faultless theory that everyone who settled in the West would repay the investment many times over: the trains would carry more farm produce east, more manufactured goods west, and more passengers both ways.

Most railroads did not care to state this logic out loud, hewing instead to a monotonous siren song of the bountiful Western dominion. But the Burlington & Missouri was perfectly candid about its motive: "Railroad men have every inducement to advance the development of the country which their line traverses," said a company pamphlet addressed to the general public in 1872; "It is to be expected that they will sell low to actual settlers and furnish them with every facility in the way of long credit, cheap rates, etc. It is not to be supposed that railroad corporations surpass all men in disinterested benevolence, but it is beyond question that they know their own interests, and so will take some pains to help you earn a dollar whenever they can thus make two for themselves."

The Burlington & Missouri's reference to its customers as "actual settlers" had some disturbing implications for promoters like J. P. Wheeler. In theory, freelance promoters could buy a choice townsite from a railroad. But in practice, railroads were often reluctant to sell to speculators for fear they would postpone development of the land in anticipation that its value would increase with the passage of time.

Happily, the freelancers could obtain a piece of property from a variety of other sources. For instance, land could be bought from homesteaders who had received full title to their claim; from veterans who had earned a land bounty for service to their country in the Mexican War or Civil War; or from federal land offices, which periodically held large public sales. But perhaps the cheapest and easiest method of getting a tract of property for a new community was to take advantage of the Townsite Act of 1844, which was designed to encourage rapid settlement of new territories as the U.S. government acquired them from Indians and foreign powers. Under its terms, any group of avowed townmakers could obtain 320 acres at $1.25 an acre. The government gradually came to view this law as a bit too generous to speculators, and another Townsite Act was passed by Congress in 1867, stipulating that only groups of at least 100 persons could qualify for the claim. Presumably, such a large body of claimants would be comprised of actual settlers, but speculators easily circumvented the stricture by adding invented names or listing wives and children as claimants.

Once a site was selected, freelance town promotion tended to follow a predictable course. One crucial step

Shares worth several lots apiece were issued by promoters after communities were platted. Some were set aside in the town company's name and

the rest sold — mainly to speculators, who could profit both from rising land values and from dividends paid as the company's lots were marketed.

A plan for Neosho City, Kansas, envisioned an eight-sided village as the home of a group of vegetarians. But the scheme was a literal washout: rains flooded the site soon after the colonists arrived in 1856.

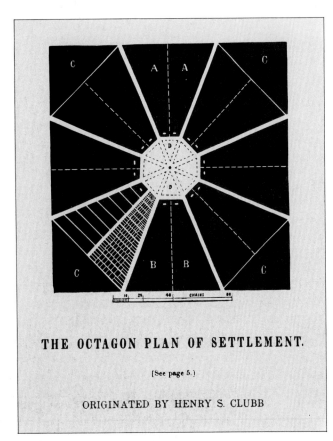

THE OCTAGON PLAN OF SETTLEMENT.

[See page 5.]

ORIGINATED BY HENRY S. CLUBB

was the procurement of a town charter through a special act of the territorial or state legislature. This legal instrument incorporated the group and authorized their company to resell the land either by lots or in the form of shares — the latter being the usual medium of exchange for real-estate speculators. A single share, signified by an impressively engraved note resembling a stock certificate, might represent anywhere from two to 20 town lots. The shares could be converted into actual lots at any time; in addition, they entitled the shareholder to dividends from the sale of lots that were set aside in the name of the corporation.

After attending to the legal preliminaries, the promoters commissioned a surveying team to make the town plat. Streets were laid out, and blocks were divided into numbered lots; many towns were endowed with a rich capital of 5,000 staked-out lots, each one usually measuring about 25 feet by 125 feet. At the height of the town-building mania, so many cities-to-be were platted that a Missouri steamboat captain reportedly declared he could make more money carrying survey stakes than he could by transporting passengers.

The town plat, which was often reproduced in advertising brochures, could take any form the promoter desired. Most boomers settled for a simple, utilitarian grid, but some opted for strange and wonderful conceptions. When Henry Clubb decided to start his vegetarian community in eastern Kansas in 1856, he had Neosho City laid out in the form of an octagon; its eight main streets radiated like spokes from a park in the middle, where he planned to build a reception center for incoming settlers. Unfortunately, Neosho City was sited on swampy lowlands, and its first few buildings were flooded into oblivion by heavy rains only a few months after the colonists arrived. The vegetarians were, in any case, ill-prepared for the wilderness, having brought only a single plow to carve out gardens for the entire community.

A particularly exotic design was prepared in 1873 by the famous town planner, Frederick Law Olmstead, for the site of Tacoma, Washington Territory. His scheme, later modified, was described by a contemporary as "the most fantastic plat of a town that was ever seen. There wasn't a straight line, a right angle or a corner lot. The blocks were shaped like melons, pears and sweet potatoes. One block, shaped like a banana, was 3,000 feet in length and had 250 lots. It was a pretty fair park plan but condemned itself to a town."

Promoters who obtained land under either of the Townsite acts usually showed their true colors as soon as their communities were platted. Thinking in terms of vast cities with endless vistas of real estate to sell, they went to work to expand the 320-acre maximum allowed by law. Journalist Albert Richardson explained how it was done: "They engage settlers each to preempt one of the adjacent quarter sections (one hundred and sixty acres). The settler can only do this by swearing that it is for his homestead, for his own exclusive use and benefit; that he had not contracted to sell any portion of it. The invariable alacrity with which he commits this bit of perjury is a marvel to strangers not yet free from eastern prejudices. When his title is perfected, he deeds his land to the corporation, and receives his money as per agreement. Thus the company secures from five hundred to a thousand acres."

Having laid out the town and accumulated land enough to reap gains from any future expansion, pro-

A poster rallies Kentucky blacks to move to Nicodemus, Kansas. Named in honor of a slave who purchased his freedom, the all-black community had hundreds of residents within a few years of its founding in 1877.

moters plunged headlong into the serious business of selling lots or shares. It took all-out, orchestrated salesmanship for any promoter to make his town stand out from hundreds of others, and if scruples prevented a boomer from uttering exaggerated claims, he was likely to end up a righteous failure.

The promoter's basic selling tool was a printing press. In every town worthy of the name, and in some that were not, the boomer quickly acquired a hand press and kept it busy cranking out a stream of advertising pamphlets and propagandizing newspapers. Some of the newspaper press run was shipped East, and some was distributed to established publications elsewhere in the area, in hopes that they would print a portion of the promoter's good news about his community. (Promoters also donated shares in the town to regional newspapers, on the well-founded theory that self-interest was the best possible bait for a favorable press.) Whenever a new town boasted several newspapers, as many of them did, it was a good bet to be in desperate need of promotion. As James Bryce, an English visitor to the West, shrewdly observed, "Many a place has lived upon its 'boom' until it found something more solid to live on; and to a stranger who asked in a small Far Western town how such a city could keep four newspapers, it was well answered that it took four newspapers to keep up such a city."

In shaky towns, the newspaper editors labored not only to attract more townsmen but also to keep those they had already won. As a matter of course, editors in the Dakotas ran gleeful stories of floods and hard winters in Kansas to discourage faint-hearted townsmen from resettling there. For the same reason, many editors kept close tabs on overboomed towns in their vicinity and warned their local readers against them.

These efforts to expose fraudulent promotions sometimes backfired. For example, the notorious nontown of Fairview, Nebraska, got mentioned often enough to convince a map maker and a circuit-riding minister that it really existed. What followed was comical, sad and predictable. The Reverend Henry T. Davis pointed himself in the right map direction and blithely galloped off to bring the gospel to Fairview. After traveling a good distance, he stopped at a solitary squatter's hut to ask how much farther it was to Fairview. The squatter told him he had passed it two miles back. The Reverend

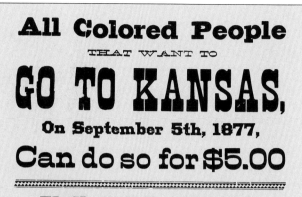

Davis retraced his path with care and finally located the alleged town, which was — and remained — totally houseless. Fairview was nothing but a field full of surveyor's stakes, and the only parishioners that the preacher could scout up were a dozen squatters living in a shanty nearby.

While foiling the opposition as best they could, promoters stayed up late at night inventing schemes to translate their holdings into cash. Brownsville, Nebraska, held a lottery, charging $5 for a ticket and offering prizes that ranged downward from 147 acres on its outskirts to individual building lots in the town itself. Public auctions could be a highly effective marketing method: in 1857 the company that founded White Cloud, Kansas, staged a sale that netted $20,000 at the average lot price of $400 — well above the norm for a town only a few months old. Handing out a few gift lots helped to get an enterprise rolling: in addition to offering lots to desirable tradesmen and professionals, most boomers promised a free building lot to the first couple married in town and to the first child born there. ◉

Living the high life at Runnymede

Surely the most carefree town to spring up west of the Missouri during the 19th Century was Runnymede, Kansas, named for the place where the barons of England forced their king to sign the Magna Carta. The connotations of nobility were indeed apt, for the founder —an English land speculator, Francis Turnly—planned Runnymede as the commercial hub of a colony of lordly estates populated by young aristocrats from his homeland. The bluebloods he had in mind were specifically those whose drinking and gambling habits were a constant trial to their families. Turnly offered to take them off their parents' hands and teach them the arts of farming and stock raising for the paltry sum of £500—or $2,430—per wastrel, payable in advance.

However, most of the 40-odd novices who arrived in Runnymede in 1887 had little use for cows or plows. They were accustomed to a more congenial way of life, and before long the town boasted such un-Kansan amenities as a tennis club, a race track and a polo field. For additional diversion, Runnymede's gentry regularly rode to hounds over the prairie, chasing coyotes when foxes were scarce. After the day's exertions, the bar in the town's splendid hotel reverberated with song and merrymaking until the wee hours.

But even as its residents were living high and importing their wives and sweethearts, Runnymede was dying. Its economy was built on money from home, and when far-off fathers wearied of paying the bills, their playboy sons soon scattered. By 1900, sold to a no-nonsense farmer and stripped of its buildings, the town of Runnymede had disappeared beneath a wheat field.

Runnymede's squires and their womenfolk, including a visiting mother in black, gather at the town tennis club for a midsummer afternoon of some suitably civilized sport.

Founder Francis Turnly *(top left)* and members of Runnymede's elite record their unlikely presence in Kansas for the camera.

The prairie playboys, including some seen on the opposite page, sport another set of costumes—one wag in a woman's dress.

Some of the most adroit maneuvering by freelance promoters was aimed at attracting a railroad, because—rightly or not—they believed that a connection with the growing network of Western trackage would be followed by a torrent of settlers. So universal was the sentiment that in 1869, Governor David Butler of Nebraska declared he could not think of a single town without a railroad that was not seriously attempting to acquire one.

If the town was still in the planning stage or just recently born, a promoter might try to tempt a railroad to build a spur in his direction by offering some outlandish windfall—say, a third of the town company's land plus a decade of immunity from local taxation. Or, if the community had emerged from infancy, he would attempt to wring from the state legislature some special honor that would give the railroad a good reason for coming his way—designation as a county seat or as the site of a university or penitentiary. Another standard tactic of towns already settled was the issuance of bonds to help pay for new railroad construction. Between 1872 and 1890, Kansas towns spent more than $18 million to get these steel rivers of commerce.

Some communities hardly knew when to stop. Hastings, Nebraska, one of nine towns formed in the 24-square-mile area of Adams County, won no less than five major and minor railroads by running up an onerous municipal debt of more than a quarter of a million dollars. By that time, its competitors were either extinct or resigned to lesser stature, but bitter feelings lingered. The editor of a rival town's newspaper wrote that, if the Hastings *Gazette Journal* "should hear of a railroad projected from the Bering Straits to the North Pole it would head the announcement in flaming headlines, 'Another Railroad for Hastings,' and advocate voting bonds to aid in its construction."

Not surprisingly, the rewards for the freelance boomer during this era of no-holds-barred competition were often sadly inconsistent with his industry or business ethics. Innumerable honest, hard-working promoters went broke with their towns after years of struggle, while just as many lazy fast-money artists made off with small fortunes in the wink of an eye. One swindler quickly sold off $20,000 worth of town lots in Burt County, Nebraska—without even bothering to acquire title to the land. Two inspired confidence men conjured up a brochure for the allegedly thriving town of Curlew, Nebraska, and unloaded 10,000 lots at just $15 each by dint of energetic advertising in the East. No house, store or saloon ever raised Curlew above the level of pure hallucination.

To the dismay of moralists, one of the most successful promoters was probably the most unscrupulous rogue in his trade. He was a Baptist minister named Isaac Smith Kalloch, and for all the wrong motives, he crowded into his outrageous career the full range of work performed by the best of the honest town boomers. In his flamboyant heyday in Kansas, Kalloch created the important town of Ottawa, left an indelible mark on the more important town of Lawrence, founded one newspaper and edited several others, started dozens of substantial businesses, built a railroad, invented a college and was elected to the Kansas legislature. Kalloch was a whirlwind of energy, a fountainhead of scandal, a god to thousands and a devil to thousands more.

Isaac Kalloch was born into a family of preachers in Maine in 1832. In his teens he was expelled from Colby College for "pranking"; the college president declared in a letter to Kalloch's father that "his connection with the college is useless to him and injurious to us." Despite the dismissal, Isaac completed his ministerial studies while working as a teacher and reporter. He was ordained at 18, married the same year and, in his early twenties, became pastor of the huge Baptist Tremont Temple in Boston. A spellbinding evangelist, he was thought by many parishioners to be at least the equal of the famous Brooklyn preacher Henry Ward Beecher. One observer said that he was "flowery in his style, highly gifted in the act of pleasing his audiences, whether he instructs them or not."

In 1857, Kalloch's career hit a rough spot. He was brought to trial on a charge of committing adultery with the wife of a friend in a Cambridge hotel; Kalloch claimed he had gone there to review his notes for a lecture. The preacher cut an impressive figure standing in the docks. He was a big man, broad-shouldered and slim-hipped, standing more than six feet tall and weighing 240 pounds. While pleading his own defense, he displayed his habit of tugging thoughtfully at the forelock of his red mane—a mannerism that women found engaging. Employing his deep, melodious voice to full advantage, he was freed by a hung jury. His congregation later passed a resolution that he had "come out of the fire like pure gold, doubly refined."

Though the Temple elders voted Kalloch innocent, the trial somehow left him restless. In 1858, he resigned his pulpit and made a journey west. It was natural enough that he picked Kansas for his destination; for years he had enjoyed singular success in raising donations from his abolitionist flock to supply pioneers in Kansas with shipments of "Beecher Bibles." It turned out that these articles of faith, when uncrated on the other side of the Missouri, were Sharps rifles, the arsenal of the antislavery faction in Kansas.

Kalloch readily accepted an invitation to preach in Leavenworth, Kansas. There, in addition to holding forth against slavery, he made a name for himself as an advocate of temperance. Far from practicing what he preached, Kalloch imbibed freely; he managed to get himself admitted to the Kansas bar by buying drinks for his examiner, Judge John Pendery. He also took a job with the New England Emigrant Aid Society, helping to colonize Kansas with Free State believers.

Through the society, Kalloch formed alliances with three men who would be the nucleus of the syndicate by which he wrought his later wonders. In the trio were Charles Robinson, a forty-niner who had returned from California to become an agent of the Emigrant Society and in 1860, the first governor of the state of Kansas; the Reverend Tecumseh "Tauy" Jones, a half-Indian graduate of Colgate; and the Reverend Clinton Carter Hutchinson, an ex-Vermonter who had somehow wangled appointment as U.S. Indian agent to the Sac, Fox, Chippewa, Munsee and Ottawa tribes.

After Kansas was stricken by the severe drought of 1860, Kalloch retreated to the East again, to raise relief supplies. He stayed four years, preaching with huge success in Boston and New York.

But he once again became the subject of scandal in Boston when the Temple superintendent complained that he was comforting women members of his flock late at night in his study. One of his numerous enemies put the matter less euphemistically and asserted that "the sanctity of the Temple was not proof against his defilement." Kalloch resigned and preached a farewell sermon. While admitting that "it is human to err," he conveniently concluded that "I have done no more than what, after long and serious deliberation, I believe God to approve and require."

In 1864 he returned to Kansas to put into action a scheme he often espoused from the pulpit: the creation of a Baptist institution of higher learning, to be called Roger Williams University. In the fertile valley of the Marais des Cygnes River (Swamp of Swans) Kalloch found what appeared to be an ideal seat for the university and for a new town to surround it. The site happened to lie at the center of the Ottawa Indian reservation, which had been ceded to the tribe in perpetuity. This fact, however, was no impediment to a man who subscribed to the current Baptist notion that "land was a sort of a burden to the Indians."

The first step was to convince the Indians of the truth of this view. The Reverends Clinton Hutchinson and Tauy Jones, having some Indian connections, were sent as emissaries to broach the university project. They assured the tribal elders that the proposed institution would be unique in its commitment to the education of Indians. As soon as the doors opened, the university would establish 50 full Indian scholarships.

The plan was attractive to Chief James Wind of the Ottawas and, when the project promoters generously offered to make him president of the board of trustees, he concluded that everything was on the up-and-up. The tribe thereupon set aside 20,646 acres to establish the school and provide for its maintenance. The Indians agreed to permit the sale of 5,000 acres at once to pay for a school building; and they consented to the subsequent sale of 15,000 more to provide support. Then Chief Wind was persuaded to resign as president of the board in favor of Isaac Kalloch—a move that probably came about through a combination of whiskey persuasions and the chief's imperfect understanding of the legal nature of trusteeship.

With Chief Wind shunted to the sidelines, the schemers promptly went into action. The first 5,000 acres were sold for only $1.25 per acre to one James Young, who, not by chance, was the father-in-law of the Reverend Hutchinson. Then sales of additional land to support the college were completed. Kalloch himself disposed of 2,872 acres for $15,000. This was a reasonable return, but he submitted to the trustees—and collected on—a bill for expenses of $18,255.08. He also set aside for himself 900 acres of choice timber

Guests gather on the veranda of the imposing Grand Pacific Hotel, built by the Kearney and Black Hills Railroad in 1889 to lodge — and impress — potential buyers of lots in Calloway, Nebraska. Railroad surveyors laid out Calloway on the scale of a big city, but their creation sold poorly.

and farmland that adjoined the presumptive campus.

Soon the trustees laid the cornerstone of Roger Williams University. For the next year, the cornerstone remained the university's sole physical manifestation. At that point a three-story building was raised and, predictably, Kalloch was hired as president at $4,100 a year. Equally predictably, few Indians were ever admitted to the student body, although the university was graciously renamed Ottawa College.

Meanwhile, Kalloch and his associates had proposed to the Ottawas that it would be a good idea to establish a town adjacent to the campus, since a flourishing municipality would surely enhance the value of the lands the Indians still had. They agreed and Ottawa, Kansas, was surveyed in March 1864.

As the town father, with the community's interests close to his heart, Kalloch founded a newspaper, the *Western Home Journal,* became a partner in a store and a sawmill, organized a cemetery company, ran a ferry for a year and then replaced it with a toll suspension bridge, the first in the West. (He charged such high tolls that the indignant townspeople finally insisted on buying him out for the cost of the bridge— $10,000.) For good measure, he purchased an abandoned building in a nearby ghost town, moved it to Ottawa, and outfitted it with pews and a pulpit. He named it the Second Baptist Church to suggest that Ottawa had more than one church. In fact, there was no First.

For a while, Kalloch served as pastor of the Second Baptist Church, but finding his other activities too pressing, he brought in a colleague, the Reverend Isaac Sawyer, whose chief recommendation was a handsome daughter. When the daughter became unaccountably pregnant, rival newspaper editors recalled Kalloch's imbroglios in the East and began calling him the "Sorrel Stallion of the Marais des Cygnes." As usual, Kalloch answered with moralizing platitudes—this time from his editorial post rather than the pulpit. "Gossip and slander," his message ran, "are the deadliest and cruelest weapons man has for his brother's heart."

Like any properly motivated town boomer, Kalloch kept in mind the need for a railroad; but, being no ordinary man, he decided to supply his own. In June 1865, when Ottawa was less than a year old, he helped lay the corporate foundations of the Leavenworth, Lawrence and Galveston R.R., which would

be known familiarly as the "Lazy, Lousy and Greasy."

Kalloch put together a board of old friends and associates whose sympathies—or venality—he could trust. U.S. Senator Samuel Pomeroy—nicknamed Beans for his efforts in raising relief supplies during the drought of 1860—was made a director, with the special function of greasing the rails in the Congress. Governor Charles Robinson, who had recently survived an impeachment for assorted high crimes and misdemeanors, became a director. Kalloch took the title of general superintendent.

Senator Pomeroy quickly proved his worth by persuading Congress to grant the L.L. & G. 62,500 acres of public lands. Not to be outdone in generosity, the state of Kansas tossed in another 125,000-acre gift. Kalloch, well aware of the advisability of avoiding realestate taxes, began selling off this largesse at once.

To raise more capital for his railroad, Kalloch hustled about the region convincing local governments to put up bonds as proof of their sincere interest in getting a railroad. In visits to three county commissions, he advised sparsely settled Anderson County to bond itself for $125,000; Ottawa's home county of Franklin was persuaded to raise $200,000; and Douglas County had to come up with $300,000, because it embraced Lawrence, the biggest and richest town in the region. For immediate capital, Kalloch talked the commissioners of Douglas County into handing over $32,000 in cash, ostensibly to pay delinquent L.L. & G. taxes. No such tax payment was ever recorded.

At this point there arose an unexpected hitch in Kalloch's even progress. Any bond issue required the endorsement of a county's voters, but the commonfolk of Kansas were growing increasingly wary of mortgaging their futures for the sake of railroads. The commissioners of Douglas County held a referendum on short notice, before the opposition could get organized. Infuriated by this tactic, a number of citizens won a court-ordered writ of arrest for anyone who attempted to take possession of the bond certificates—which had been hurriedly printed up by the authorities.

Kalloch, ever resourceful, persuaded the commissioners to assemble at midnight and write out a single crude —but legal—bond note for $300,000 at 7 per cent. With the document in hand, and having reason to suspect that vigilantes were looking for him, he took cover in a cornfield overnight. At daylight, he managed to hire

a wagon and team and fled across the border into Missouri to wait for passions to cool. The opposition was, in fact, handcuffed, since he had done nothing illegal. After a prudent interval of a few weeks, he returned to Ottawa. The grateful directors of the L.L. & G. voted him a cash bonus of $25,000 in appreciation of his sagacity and agility.

The L.L. & G. soon ran into a distress common to most railroads in that period. Government land grants were made conditionally and could be revoked if the rails failed to reach specified points by established deadlines. Railroads also had to fulfill performance schedules set by the counties issuing bonds, otherwise the bonds were forfeited. In the case of Franklin County, the rails had to reach Ottawa by January 1, 1868, and time was running out. But Kalloch simply laid rails flat down on the prairie without ties or ballasted roadbed. He got a locomotive into town on time, although observers reported that it wobbled quite a bit.

Later in 1868, Kalloch attempted—and nearly pulled off—his greatest swindle. His cronies in Wash-

ington, using unknown inducements, persuaded the Department of the Interior to set up a special commission to negotiate a new treaty with the Osage Indians, who then owned about one fifth of all Kansas. The precise purpose of the commission, while never spoken aloud, was to relieve the Osages of their excessive land burden and pass it along to the L.L. & G. Kalloch in deference to his proven skills as a confidence man, was elected leader. When he and his cohorts on the commission met the Osage chiefs, they were well prepared for the conference, having brought along four barrels of whiskey. It took the entire liquor supply, but Kalloch finally convinced the chiefs to sell to his railroad, for the price of 20 cents an acre, more than eight million acres of the Osages' 8.8-million-acre domain.

News of the treaty triggered national outrage. Members of the House of Representatives accused the commission of "grossly and fraudulently" misusing the Indians. And the Governor of Kansas protested that the railroad was getting the land—practically as large in area as Massachusetts and Connecticut combined—for a "mere bagatelle in comparison to its real value."

To seal the questionable bargain, Kalloch needed a vote of ratification in the Senate. But with cries of scandal in the wind, normally friendly Senators feared to bring the treaty up for a vote, and the deal fell through. However, Congress suddenly had second thoughts about giving all that land back to the Osages, and a year later it was opened to white settlement.

Balked in this stupendous real estate deal and having done just about everything that he could for—and to —the town of Ottawa, the Reverend Isaac Smith Kalloch decided to move to the larger arena of Lawrence and there go into politics. This proposed change of scene caused other Kansas newspapermen to express serious misgivings. Adopting an ominous tone, they raised Kalloch's rank a degree or so, to the "*Snorting* Sorrel Stallion," and warned virtuous women throughout the region to retreat into seclusion. In Lawrence, at a public meeting held to denounce Kalloch's coming, Editor John Speer of the *Kansas Tribune* said, "He is not looking at all to the public good; he is looking for County bonds . . . he is looking at pretty women and gloating over the frailties of our nature."

Not at all abashed, Kalloch sold his interests in Ottawa, invested in a Lawrence newspaper and bought the elegant Eldridge House hotel, a brick establishment that was described as the finest west of the Ohio River. With his leftover funds, he became a big-scale stock breeder and pioneered a purebred dairy industry by bringing in blooded Jersey cows and Essex hogs; he also bought a vineyard whose assets included 20,000 gallons of wine. To top off these agrarian endeavors, he became president of the Kansas Agricultural Society. And, as planned, he went into politics and was elected to the state legislature in 1873.

At length, all Kansas was too small to contain Kalloch's talents. His departure was hastened by the financial panic of 1873, which left him severely reduced in wealth. To make matters worse, Kalloch's crony, Senator Beans Pomeroy, was defeated in that year's race for reelection; the victor was none other than Lawyer John J. Ingalls, formerly of Sumner.

Kalloch sold out again and prepared to move on to the West Coast. He did not neglect to take a parting shot at his most relentless critic, Editor Speer. In a closing issue of his Lawrence newspaper, Kalloch wrote contemptuously, "The long, lank gelding calls us a stallion....If we are to be called a horse, we would prefer being considered a stallion to a gelding."

So saying, Kalloch went off to San Francisco and to another colorful, tempestuous career. In 1879 he was elected mayor, but only a few months after his victory a bitter political foe, Charles De Young, the editor of the *San Francisco Chronicle,* hid in a hansom cab and shot Kalloch down in the street. He survived, though barely, and was revenged a year later when his son Milton shot De Young dead.

As for the town of Ottawa, it slowly grew in population, amenities and general well-being. In 1866, a townsman set up an icehouse and took on customers at $2 a month. A debating and cultural society was organized the same year. In 1867 came the first strawberry festival and the organization of a 13-piece silver cornet band for the entertainment of the townsmen. Kalloch's railroad steadily improved its service. The city gasworks began operating in 1883. A mule-drawn streetcar system began keeping regular schedules in 1887, and in that same great year the town's electrically powered fire-alarm system was hooked up.

Ottawa—the product of the wiliest and most irrepressible town promoter of all—survived and thrived.

An excursion train to Horton, Kansas, disgorges a load of prospective settlers in 1887. Their inspection trip was provided free by the Rock Island and Pacific Railroad, which founded the town through a subsidiary company and also established repair shops there to get the local economy rolling.

Guthrie, Oklahoma: fastest town in the West

A fever of excitement attended the birth of almost every Western town, but few communities matched the frenetic genesis of Guthrie, Oklahoma, in 1889. It took just 24 hours to transform Guthrie from a somnolent watering stop for Atchison, Topeka and Santa Fe trains into an exuberant city of more than 10,000 inhabitants.

Guthrie's overnight metamorphosis was directly due to its location inside the region known as Indian Territory — later Oklahoma. Deeded to several tribes by treaty with the U.S. government, the territory was off limits to all but a few whites. Among the exceptions were federal lawmen and employees of the Atchison, Topeka and Santa Fe, which ran through the territory and maintained five small stations, Guthrie included, within a 3,000-square-mile chunk of the Indians' domain that was called the District.

In early 1889, responding to pressures by covetous farmers and towns-men, Congress acquired the District from the Indians and declared it open to white settlement. President Benjamin Harrison set the opening time for "twelve o'clock noon" of April 22 — and also hinted that Guthrie would someday become a territorial capital.

When the momentous day arrived, thousands of palpitating adventurers were poised at various starting lines on the boundaries of the District. U.S. cavalrymen held them in check until precisely noon. Then, as bugles sounded, the land rush began. Hordes of mule- or ox-drawn prairie schooners rumbled forward in clouds of dust. Some men wobbled along on high-wheeled bicycles; others sprinted toward the goal on foot or galloped ahead by horse (including four circus midgets on a single mount). Finally, to the toot of whistles, six trains steamed forth, quickly gaining the lead.

Even before the trains had come to a full stop in Guthrie, most of the passengers leaped off and began pounding the stakes they had brought along to claim lots that had been marked off by federal surveyors a few days earlier. Hard on their heels came the horsemen, wagon drivers, cyclists and runners. Before nightfall a tent city was up and brawling, and within a week frame houses and stores had appeared.

Predictably, disagreements over land ownership arose in all the confusion. These were amicably settled by the flip of a coin or by an arbitration board. But there was considerable chagrin over the discovery that about 300 of Guthrie's new citizens had contrived to get to Guthrie ahead of time. Many of them were railroad workers — or had been. "At one second past noon," a federal land official later observed, "the Railway Company was short a large number of employees, as if by magic." Their shrewd coup earned them the label of "sooners" — a nickname that all Oklahomans were eventually to adopt.

Racing to claim desirable lots or trying to figure future sites of commerce, settlers swarm across Guthrie on opening day.

Day-old Guthrie improvises a mayoral election by having voters form lines — one for each of the two candidates — and then wait to be counted.

Using crates for desks, two lawyers launch profitable practices. Clients paid them from 25 cents to two dollars to file land claims.

Because some wily citizens circled back in line to be counted a second time, the mayor eventually had to be selected by a small committee.

A pair of businessmen, their weapons in clear view, establish title to their premises. Most settlers came heavily armed in case of trouble.

A thoroughfare in five-day-old Guthrie — its frame buildings already underway — teems with new residents searching for legal counsel on their claims or for a 25-cent drink of murky river water from a bucket. As one settler recalled: "Just about anything you wanted to do, you waited your turn."

For the families that were arriving to join Guthrie's firstcomers, merchants display pots, pans, buckets—and dolls—at an open-air emporium.

Spectators crowd around to get a view of lawmen ousting a claimant from a contested lot. Evictions were generally accepted by the victims in a

Guthrie's arbitration board convenes a month after the land rush to thrash out the inevitable claim disputes over who was where first.

sportsman-like manner—but occasionally with embarrassment. Some overeager settlers had mistakenly staked their claims in the middle of streets.

Builders and patrons of going concerns mingle at a cross-roads as Guthrie's month-old skyline takes shape. By this time the city had a hotel, three newspapers, three general stores and numerous restaurants. But saloons led the business parade: 50 had been established in the first week.

3 | The merchants on Main Street

Because they purveyed the goods that kept new communities alive, merchants ranked as the elemental townsmen. In many cases, they began their stewardship of the civilizing process under arduous circumstances: Omaha was nourished through its earliest days by a crude emporium that dispensed groceries and whiskey from a dank dugout whose roof was a layer of sod.

But the first merchants in any town quickly expanded to a true general store, cluttered with goods calculated to meet practically any need or whim. Mayer Goldsoll, one of many immigrants who brought Old World merchandising skills to the West, described his establishment in Ellsworth, Kansas, as a source of "anything you may call for, from a $500 diamond to a pint of salt." While the proprietors of most general stores could not claim to have diamonds in stock, they did offer salt, along with foods of all kinds, clothing, toys, blankets, plows, saddles, guns and hundreds of other items.

A general store also functioned as a social center of its community; people gravitated there as much to gossip around the potbellied stove as to pore over the shelves. "Every item of news," wrote one frontier merchant of his own role, "has general dissemination from his establishment, and thither all resort, at least once a week, both for goods and for intelligence."

In time, as a town put down strong roots, the general store found itself flanked by shops catering to specialized needs: meat markets, hardware stores, even ice-cream parlors. The pictures on these and the following pages, though a sequence drawn from different towns, sum up Main Street, Anytown—the milieu of the indispensable merchant.

Aproned butchers take a break from their labors in one of the meat markets of Hays, Kansas — a shipping point for Texas longhorns.

93

Sustenance for the townsman's body and spirit was typically provided by establishments like the modest saloon in La Junta, Colorado — bannering a local brew on its false front — or the restaurant in Casper, Wyoming, where an entire household, dog included, could enjoy a home-style meal.

Storekeepers and their cracker-barrel cornucopias

The pioneer proprietor of a general store west of the great American rivers was an all-purpose practitioner to the human condition. No matter that he started with the modest aim of selling goods at a profit, he soon discovered that his obligations and opportunities were almost beyond inventory.

The parameters of his occupation could be roughly measured by two of the staple items found on his shelves: whiskey to enlarge the spirit and Bibles to assuage the soul. The terrain in between encompassed virtually all of the gradations of human needs and whims. His store was the place of first resort for everything from coal oil to calico to canned oysters, and much more. He was depended upon for wedding clothes, for the baby's croup medicine, for McGuffey's Readers that youngsters would take to school, and for home remedies such as paregoric, epsom salts, castor oil, camphor, opium and snake root. From his shelves the ailing took down Ewall's *Medical Companion* to study symptoms and prescriptions, and it was he who supplied the candles and crepe when all was over. He became, perforce, family confidant and counselor, banker and creditor, and a civic leader whose premises provided the community's public forum.

An establishment that typified general stores everywhere was the Frontier Store in Abilene, Kansas. During the late 1860s, when Abilene was young, this emporium presented an unprepossessing face to the outer world. Across the façade was its name in erratic lettering. On either side of the door were windows

crammed with goods that could barely be discerned through a thick coating of dust.

But to step inside was to enter a wonderfully self-contained world of gentle gloom, muted sounds of leisurely activity, and odd yet familiar aromas. The place smelled of just about everything: the rich fruitiness of plug tobacco, the leather of boots and belts, fresh-ground coffee, cheese, dried and pickled fish and the subtle musty-sweet tang of fresh fabric in bolts. Not an inch of space was wasted. On one side of the interior stood a counter for groceries; on the other, a counter and shelves piled high with dry goods; hardware—along with the proprietor's high desk and stool—took up the rear. From the rafters hung the vague shapes of hams, slabs of bacon, cooking pots and stocking caps. And arranged around the floor was a treasury of kegs and barrels brimming with sugar, vinegar, flour and molasses; canisters of condiments and spices; sacks of whatever produce the season offered; big glass jars of striped candy sticks and peppermint balls.

When eyes became accustomed to the dimness they would be drawn inevitably toward the center of the store and the potbellied stove—unlit in summertime, an island of warmth in winter. Nearby was the open cracker barrel, so situated to keep its contents crisp when the stove was glowing, but left there throughout the year.

Practically every male customer who came into the store spent some time in the rough circle of chairs around the stove and cracker barrel. Some of the patrons were farmers in town with their wives for a day; some were townsmen who dropped by to indulge in lazy talk about politics, the weather and news that was essentially gossip. Those who chewed their tobacco used the pan of ashes in front of the stove for a spittoon—missing almost as often as they scored.

The owner of the Frontier Store enjoyed the casual companionship and kept free refreshment in a whiskey

A paragon of frontier enterprise, Peter Robidoux opened up a tent-saloon in newborn Wallace, Kansas, in 1870 and parlayed the profits into an empire that included a 30,000-acre ranch and the biggest general store between Kansas City and Denver.

barrel in the back room for good friends and steady customers, a tin cup tied conveniently to it. But some of his fellow merchants were less cordial. At least one had been exasperated enough to write a letter of complaint to his local newspaper: "I am a storekeeper, and am excessively annoyed by a set of troublesome animals, called Loungers, who are in the habit of calling at my store and there sitting hour after hour, poking their noses into my business . . . and ever and anon giving me a polite hint that a little grog would be acceptable. Do, Mr. Printer, give this an insertion; some of them may see it and take the hint."

The women who came to the store were in the habit of taking up a bench located near the door when they wanted a respite from their shopping. For the wives from outlying areas, a visit to the Frontier Store was a rare opportunity to be with other women and discuss matters of domestic importance, from weddings and babies to frilly bonnets and sewing patterns. Even more pleasurable was their chance to fondle the calicoes and muslins and ready-to-wears they could ill afford to buy. They neither knew nor cared that the latest fashion in Abilene was already a year old in the East and two years old in Paris. It was new to them.

Western merchants understood how avidly the farm women yearned for a touch of beauty in their lives. One commented: "I have often seen a hard-worked country lady come into a store and inquire for all the handsomest goods in the stock, and admire them, comment on them, take out great strips of pretty patterns, and with her knotted fingers fold them into pleats and drape them over her plain skirt, her face illumined with pleasure at the splendor of such material. Bright, harmonious colors, and fine fabrics, over which she would draw her tired hands caressingly, soothed and gratified her. Who could grudge her such a privilege?"

Certainly not the man who ran Abilene's Frontier Store, William S. "Doc" Moon. He knew about lean times. After emigrating from Ohio to Kansas in 1857, he had tried his hand at farming and found its rigors not to his liking. When a tiny community began to emerge a short distance from his farm, he turned his sights toward it, figuring he had the necessary assets to become a merchant — a little money to lay in a stock of goods and a firsthand knowledge of his potential clientele's needs. But after he established his business in a log

cabin in 1864, he discovered that storekeeping was no instant bonanza either. Abilene, then four years old, had a mere 40 or so residents, and only 443 people lived in the whole county.

Three years after Moon set up shop, ramshackle Abilene fell heir to a measure of prosperity when the Kansas Pacific Railroad reached town. Herds of longhorns from Texas began to rumble in for shipment by rail to Eastern markets. Suddenly Moon found himself with new neighbors. The cowboy trade drew saddlers, bootmakers, blacksmiths, barbers, bartenders and entertainers; new general stores opened up and were soon supplemented by such specialty stores as butcher shops, drugstores, bakeries and hardware stores. But Moon himself was too comfortable in his niche to change his ways. His only concession to the boom was to enlarge his Frontier Store slightly and spruce it up with a false front. While a few cowboys came in from time to time, his main customers were still the farmers around Abilene, along with the small local businessmen and their families. Doc Moon remained an ordinary man ministering to ordinary people. Yet to those who depended on him, his importance could hardly be measured.

The pattern of the Western merchant as the indispensable townsman was set decades before Doc Moon opened his unpretentious general store in Abilene. Perhaps more than anybody, the Missouri merchandising team of James and Robert Aull showed the way — and also showed themselves to be as fiercely enterprising as Moon was placid.

Raised in Delaware, the Aulls journeyed in 1825 to what was then the fringe of the Western wilderness. James was 18 years old and Robert about 20. At that time, civilization's hold on Missouri seemed distinctly tenuous. Local settlers were still vulnerable to Indian raids, and their livestock suffered regular depredations from wolves and wildcats.

Having brought along a little money as a stake, James opened a general store in the little Missouri River town of Lexington, while Robert and a partner went into business in Liberty, about 55 miles away. Both brothers prospered, and two years later they joined forces to introduce the institution of chain stores to the American West. They added branches in Independence and Richmond to their first establishments, hired managers to operate them, and supervised the entire operation —straightforwardly called Aull Brothers—from their headquarters in Lexington.

Each winter, James Aull made a laborious pilgrimage eastward by horseback, stagecoach and steamboat to select and order stock for the stores. In the manufacturing center of Philadelphia he bought coarse wool, cotton cloth and other lightweight goods and sent them by wagon to Pittsburgh, where they were transferred to a boat bound down the Ohio River for St. Louis. The boat was also loaded up with heavy merchandise —stoves, axes and plows—ordered from a hardware dealer right in Pittsburgh, thus saving on the high freighting fees from Philadelphia. On the down river trip, a stop would be made in Cincinnati to add such goods as flour or feathers for featherbeds.

All these items were necessities in pioneer country, but neither the Aulls nor their customers were insensible to the more gracious and intellectual needs of life. On James's shopping list would be such items as cravats, green gauze veils, black silk gloves, bonnets and palm leaf hats, violin strings, music boxes, playing cards, chessmen, Pike's *Arithmetic,* Byerly's *Speller, Robinson Crusoe, Don Quixote* and the collected works of William Shakespeare.

Goods that Aull bought in January might be counted upon—with luck—to reach the Missouri stores in April or May. But not to be counted upon was luck itself. All manner of costly difficulties might be met in transit —from Indian raids to shipwrecks to rough handling and outright theft by steamboat roustabouts. One $10,000 consignment of Aull merchandise was an almost total loss when the steamboat *Talma* burned to the waterline only a few miles outside Pittsburgh. The few goods that were salvaged did not appear on the Aull's shelves until July.

Like their competitors, the Aulls served the communities around them in many ways. They became, by necessity, bankers of sorts: when their customers' funds were low—as they invariably were until the seasonal crops could be sold—they either extended credit, settled bills by accepting farm-produced items in lieu of cash, or bartered goods for goods. By taking payment in kind, the Aulls were not merely doing their clients a favor but expanding their own inventory of merchandise. A customer named Aaron Overton paid off his account in

barrels of home-distilled whiskey, while others brought in beeswax, honey, tallow, meat, skins, eggs, butter or cider in exchange for store goods. A few needy clients, with nothing to trade but muscle-power and skills, paid for their purchases in services such as hog-slaughtering, wood-chopping or cutting brush.

If the hardships and isolation of frontier life were dismaying to the Aulls when they first came to Missouri, they were not entirely unprepared for the challenge, since frontiering was still a living memory back East. In that respect, they had a headstart on certain other tradesmen who came all the way from the Old World to face risks that were utterly unknown.

One of the first and most enterprising of these immigrant merchants was Michel "Big Mike" Goldwater, born into a family of 22 children in Konin, a town west of Warsaw in Poland. In 1847, when local unrest attracted the unpleasant attentions of the Russian Czar's Cossacks, he left home and journeyed first to Paris and then London, where he worked as a tailor, married a dressmaker and anglicized his patronym from the original Goldwasser. While there, he was joined by his younger brother Joseph and others of his kin.

Feverish talk of California gold soon spread through Europe and brought the Goldwaters—with a little money set aside from the tailoring business—across the Atlantic, over the Isthmus of Panama and up the coast to California in 1852. Their intention was not to pan for gold, but to employ their commercial background in catering to the men who did.

Big Mike opened a saloon and billiard parlor in the town of Sonora, selling fruit and candy as a sideline. When the Sonora gold field petered out in 1857 he moved to Los Angeles and joined Joseph in operating a saloon in the Bella Union Hotel. They used their profits to open two general stores in Los Angeles.

Yet this was not enough for Big Mike. Yearning for still-untapped sources of profit, he gave thought to the frontier eastward beyond the San Bernardino Mountains. Out there, he knew, were as yet only a few potential customers—gold hunters, hardscrabble farmers and soldiers manning isolated military garrisons. But these few were enough to challenge him. Leaving his stores under capable supervision, he bought four mules and a wagon, and loaded up with "Yankee notions,"

L. A. Fisher's cozy general store in Oakley, Kansas, accommodates a typical melange of merchandise, customers and loungers. Dry goods are arrayed along the left wall; groceries and kitchenware take up the opposite side; and boxes of men's shoes—advertised for sale "at cost"—fill the rear.

knives, tobacco, belts, shoes, ammunition, and even epaulets for Army officers.

By 1860, Big Mike was making regular runs as far as the western edge of Arizona. The traveling store did well. But two years later a drought in California and the uncertainties of the Civil War visited a business panic on southern California, and the Goldwater stores in Los Angeles went broke. Undaunted, Big Mike went to La Paz, Arizona, and took a job in an adobe general store. His diligence soon earned him a partnership, and in time he was able to buy out his partner and ask brother Joe to join him.

Within the next few years the business prospects shifted several times and so did the Goldwaters. Following the booms, they went wherever the action was —or where they could predict it soon would be. In 1872 they branched into the new and growing town of Phoenix, where Big Mike's oldest son, Morris, managed the business. Carrying the frontier merchant's tradition of versatility a step further than usual, Morris somehow got his store chosen as the first telegraph office in Phoenix—perhaps winning the honor by his promise to serve free of charge as an operator. He sat down with a book and telegraph key and undertook to teach himself the Morse code, but the first message he sent was so incoherent that the operator on the other end tapped back, "Get the hell off the line."

When Phoenix did not rise as rapidly as expected, the Goldwaters closed their emporium there and Morris cheerfully transferred his merchandizing activities to the gold-mining center of Prescott. He was shortly joined by his energetic younger brother, Baron. The Goldwater family began to show signs of becoming a merchant dynasty.

In 1883, Big Mike set up another store in the town of Bisbee when gold was discovered nearby, and then he had a harrowing brush with frontier violence. He was minding the store one Saturday night when five armed bandits strode in and ordered him to open up the safe. A sixth robber stood guard outside, and when a passerby tried to sound the alarm, the lookout man gunned him down. In the ensuing fire fight, three more townsmen were killed.

The gang made it out of town—empty-handed—but several days later a posse caught up with them and brought them back to Bisbee to stand trial. All of the gang members except one were sentenced to hang and were promptly dispatched. The remaining bandit, for no recorded reason, drew a lengthy prison term. But Bisbee's blood was up. A band of vigilantes stormed the jail, yanked the prisoner from his cell, and strung him up with a length of rope which, with prudent forethought and a certain sense of the fitness of things, they had bought and paid for at the Goldwater store.

Big Mike retired to California in 1885. But the Goldwater offspring had one more move to make. When Phoenix became the territorial capital in 1889 and was subsequently linked by rail with Prescott, Morris and Baron—true sons of their father—closed the Prescott store, uprooted themselves and once again followed the business boom to its source. There, in Phoenix, they reopened on a grand scale. Goldwater's became the most prestigious store in the capital, and Baron emerged as fashion pacesetter and arbiter of Phoenix tastes. The itinerant Goldwaters, townsmen of many towns, had finally reached home.

Another immigrant merchant who—for a time —won heady profits through a blend of perseverance and luck was Peter Robidoux. Yet he could hardly have been more different from the Goldwaters. Robidoux was French-Canadian; he had no tradition of merchandising in his background; and he was motivated by nothing so much as an adventurous spirit that vibrated to sheer chance.

Born in Quebec in 1850, Robidoux was smitten by wanderlust while still in his teens. It took him first to Kankakee County, Illinois, where he worked long days as a farm hand and attended night school to master English. Within a matter of months he had, as he later wrote to a friend, "saved enough money to take me out West, where I had long wanted to go."

So he quit his job and "went to Chicago, to the C.B. & Q. [Chicago, Burlington and Quincy] station. I told the agent I wanted a ticket. He asked, 'Where to?' I said, 'Out West.' 'We have no station by that name on our schedule,' replied the agent." The young man—he was just 18 at the time—poured his savings onto the counter and announced that he wanted to go as far west as his money would take him. "The agent counted it—almost $70—and informed me that I would have $3.35 left after paying for a ticket to Ellsworth,

Recording one of their myriad merchandising ventures on the early frontier, the Aull brothers made these copies of an 1834 bid to provision Fort Leavenworth, Kansas, and a letter listing character references.

radic gunplay, "were in full blast. Long after midnight the crowd began to thin out. About 3 o'clock the barkeeper tapped me on the shoulder, saying, 'Kid, wake up. We are going to close up.'"

Peter, tired, broke and very far from home, had no place to go. "I asked the price of a bed. 'One dollar,' he said. I just turned my pockets inside out to show that seventy-five cents was all I had. He accepted and led the way up to 'drunkards' heaven' where there were about fifty single cots containing that many drunk men. I lay there with fear and trembling, until daylight, then got out quickly by the outside stairway."

After leaving Ellsworth, Peter moved across Kansas to Hays, to Ellis, to Ogallah, to Monument, supporting himself by washing dishes and waiting tables and putting in time at any other lowly chore that came to hand. For a while he held a job as a lonely water pumper out on the line of the Union Pacific, but he soon quit in the well-founded fear that the Cheyenne might scalp him —a fate that overtook his unfortunate successor only five days later.

In the course of his wanderings Peter had picked up the beginnings of a trade. Tom Daly, the foremost saloonkeeper of Hays, had briefly employed Peter as a bookkeeper, since the lad knew how to cipher and could write a legible hand. As part payment, Daly taught him the principles of storekeeping. It was not exactly a peaceful apprenticeship; liquored-up cowboys so often ran riot in the saloon that another employee who slept above the barroom kept a slab of sheet iron beneath his bunk as armor plate against stray bullets.

Peter found a place to apply the storekeeping lessons when he moved on to Wallace, Kansas, in 1868. Wallace was then no more than an arbitrary roosting place where the bunk cars and commissary of Union Pacific tracklayers were temporarily stationed on the line's way west. Nevertheless Peter took a special liking to the little settlement, for reasons no doubt having to do with the tracklayers and "brave soldiers" of nearby Fort Wallace, all of whom had spending money but little to spend it on. Acquiring a barrel of whiskey and a box of cigars as stock, he set himself up in business in a tent near the tracks.

Soon he laid in more wares and began to prosper, cleaving firmly to the sound business practices of selling nothing for less than one dollar and charging, for all ar-

Kan., as far west as they were running regular trains."

Peter invested most of his change in a meal of bologna and crackers and arrived in Ellsworth with just 75 cents to his name. After sitting in the railroad depot for about two hours, not knowing where to turn or what to do with himself, he finally "ventured across the street to a big saloon with a big sign over the door, 'U.S. Saloon.'"

This first taste of night life, he wrote, was "some new experience for Peter." Soldiers, gamblers, Indian scouts, buffalo hunters, bullwhackers and other leathery sons of the frontier crossed his fascinated gaze. "The orchestra was playing melodious tunes and the ball was on. Drinking, gambling and dancing," enlivened by spo-

103

Standing before the mug-filled racks of their Littleton, Colorado, barber shop, a pair of slicked-up barbers await the day's customers.

A friendly place to hang a mug

HAIR TONICS

STRAIGHT RAZOR

As much a fixture of a town's main street as the general store or saloon was the barber shop. Here, a man could relax in a cushioned chair, peruse the titillating *Police Gazette* and pick up the latest gossip as he received a 10-cent shave or a two-bit haircut.

While the tools of the barber's trade were standardized, the skill of the men who wielded them was distinctly erratic. Many a practitioner was an untrained jack-of-all-trades who made ends meet by moonlighting at another job or selling hot baths in the back room for 25 cents — soap and towel included. But there were also proud professionals like Dodge City's George Dieter, who billed himself as "the eminent tonsorial artist of the Arkansas Valley." The most reliable gauge of a barber's stature was the number of personalized shaving mugs *(opposite)* on his racks, each one emblazoned with the name and occupational symbol of a valued patron.

ADJUSTABLE CHAIR AND FOOTREST

LIVERYMAN

HORSE BREEDER

PRINTER

DRAYMAN

MORTICIAN

RAILROAD CONDUCTOR

MASON

TELEGRAPHER

ticles from boots to booze, twice what anybody else charged farther down the railroad tracks. His cash register was a beer keg with a slot in its head. Whenever a keg filled up with silver, which was sometimes once a day, he shipped it by stage to a bank in Denver.

Robidoux steadily broadened his line of merchandise until he could answer practically any customer request. "I kept for sale *everything*," he wrote in his memoirs. "That was my sign I had painted over the door. I sold everything from a postage stamp to the 'real old stuff'; from a jew's harp to the big Sharp's rifle which was used to kill the buffalo and a real menace to the Indians. Times were good. The soldiers at the fort spent their money freely while it lasted."

Eventually, Robidoux took himself a wife and built a home, fittingly substantial for Wallace's most successful merchant. Wallace became the trading center for the range country, and as the cattle business boomed, Robidoux's Everything Store could not help but flourish. At length he operated not only a saloon—which for the 12 years of its existence was open 24 hours a day—but was also the biggest general store between Kansas City and Denver. He took up ranching himself and made a success of that, too, at one time having over 30,000 acres behind barbed wire and thousands of head of cattle bearing the Robidoux brand. The French-Canadian kid who had worked his way out west to pitch tent in a place without a real town had brought the town to him —and with it, his own fortune.

But hard times struck the ranching country around Wallace in the bitter winters of 1885 and 1886. Robidoux's customers, losing cattle by the thousands in blizzards that raged across the plains, began going broke and giving up. Robidoux himself started devoting more time and attention to his ranch, and taking less and less interest in the plentifully stocked store he had laboriously built up from nothing. He told his wife that if the store ever had a day without a single customer he would lock it up and forget it.

The depression lingered on and deepened year after year. Finally there came a day, in the midst of the financial panic of 1893, when he did not sell a single item from the $20,000 worth of merchandise that was arrayed on his shelves. Robidoux locked the door and boarded up the windows. In his role as a stockman he was in considerably better shape than most of his former customers, but as a merchant he was through. Perhaps as much out of pride in his accomplishments as pain at their undoing, he never went back into his Everything Store again, not even for a roll of barbed wire or a keg of nails to use on his own ranch.

One Western merchant whose allegiance to his role and his town never waned was Robert M. Wright. As the inventor and perennial overseer of Dodge City, Kansas—the hell-roaringest cowboy mecca on the frontier—he showed just how strong the tie between a tradesman and a town could be.

Wright came to the West from Maryland in his teens. Willing to try his hand at practically anything, he pursued a richly varied early career as bullwhacker, manager of stage stations, supply freighter and hay contractor for army posts. In 1866 he moved to Fort Dodge and settled into a storekeeping job as the post's sutler—a licensed civilian supplier of whiskey, canned foods, soap and other articles for the soldiers.

Fort Dodge was located deep in southwest Kansas, on the Arkansas River; it guarded a strategic river crossing at the boundary of an Osage Indian reservation. But with the approach of the Atchison, Topeka and Santa Fe Railroad in the early summer of 1872, it occurred to Wright and a few close associates that the locale offered commercial possibilities that were at least as compelling as the military advantages.

In July, Wright—together with the post commandant, Colonel Richard Dodge, and Major E. B. Kirk, the quartermaster—decided to create a town at a spot five miles east of the fort. With 16 other men, mostly army personnel and civilian contractors, they formed the Dodge City Company, and installed Bob Wright as president. Wright was then only 32 years old and still boyish-looking despite the rigors of his freighting days out on the open plains.

The promoters suffered a brief setback when they were informed that the Townsite Act of 1867 required a syndicate of at least 100 subscribers in order to acquire a full-scale townsite of 320 acres. Accordingly, they lowered their aim and paid the Wichita Land Office $108.75 for 87 acres of Ford County. The Santa Fe tracks arrived in September 1872, and a station was opened in a sidetracked boxcar. By that time the infant town already had two saloons under

Polish-born "Big Mike" Goldwater, an agile entrepreneur with a predilection for boomtowns, operated better than half a dozen stores in California and Arizona, and established a merchant dynasty to boot.

tent, and a general store owned by Bob Wright in partnership with a man named Charles Rath.

Along with the railroad came an instant upsurge of population: trackworkers by the hundreds, teamsters, whores, pimps and gamblers. Within a month, frame houses and false-fronted stores arose along the presumptive future avenue of commerce, Front Street. Tradespeople flocked to Dodge to reap its profits and, incidentally, help in the building of it. There was Isaac Morris who set up a harness shop; George Cox and F. W. Boyd who operated the Dodge House hotel; blacksmith Tom O'Keefe; Mr. and Mrs. William Olds who ran a restaurant; dry goods merchant Alonzo B. Webster; German immigrant Frederick C. Zimmerman, dealer in arms, ammunition, hardware and lumber; and James "Dog" Kelley, restaurateur and saloonkeeper.

"Business began, and such a business!" Wright recalled in his memoirs. "Almost any time during the day, there were about a hundred wagons on the streets. Dozens of cars a day were loaded with hides and meat, and dozens of carloads of grain, flour and provisions arrived. I never saw any town to equal Dodge."

The "hides and meat" came from buffalo and were being shipped to Eastern tanneries by Wright and Rath. Even before the railroad workers and their camp followers had moved on, buffalo hunting had become the pillar of the town's economy. A buffalo hide could be converted into a robe that sold for $2.75 to $5. Buffalo leather also made superior rawhide thongs, used for all the myriad purposes filled by baling wire in a later time. Even the bones had value as fertilizer, and were, as Wright noted, "legal tender in Dodge."

That first winter, Wright and Rath bought and shipped more than 200,000 buffalo hides. They also bought and sold the pelts of beaver, foxes and wolves, "never paying less than $6" for a prime wolf pelt. The partners plowed much of the profit from their export of animal remains into the retail store, stocking it with camp equipment and other supplies for hunters, along with the usual staples for their fellow townsmen.

The buffalo business was a stopgap. Within a few seasons the prairies were picked clean of uncounted millions of the valuable beasts and the trade was exhausted. But a replacement business was on the way. The great resource that was to make Dodge City's future and Bob Wright's fortune was Texas cattle — cattle driven north by cowboys with money to burn.

Dodge City's destiny as the last, boomingest and most long-lived of the Kansas cattle towns was a gift implicit in its location. Situated in the "southwestern sixteenth" of the state, Dodge was not only a convenient point from which to ship Texas cattle but, by the time the herds began arriving in 1876, was also one of the few remaining railroad towns in Kansas still legally open to Texas herds.

Regulations regarding the movement of longhorns, coupled with the westward extension of the railroads, had already been the cause of boom and bust in many a Kansas town. As soon as the Texas cattle began moving up the Chisholm Trail to meet the railroads immediately after the Civil War, the farmers who had already settled in Kansas discovered, to their dismay, that the longhorns were carriers of a microscopic tick. The Texas animals were immune to the parasite, but

The well-stocked interior of Dr. Thomas McCarty's Dodge City drugstore *(page 91)* presents a vista of neatly shelved patent medicines, pilfer-proof glass showcases for jewelry and perfume, and an assortment of ready-to-frame art prints on the far wall for customers in need of home decoration.

this same tick produced deadly splenic fever in local cattle. In 1867 the Kansas legislature decreed a quarantine line, running roughly north-south, designed to limit longhorn drives to the western parts of Kansas, which were largely unsettled. Year after year, with the continuing influx of farmers, the quarantine line was moved inexorably westward and southward as successive counties in the state filled up with domestic herds that had to be protected from the deadly tick.

Thus, one by one, the other cattle towns—first Abilene, then Ellsworth, Wichita and Ellis—were closed off behind the quarantine line, and the Texas cattle drovers were obliged to seek new shipping centers. Finally, only Dodge and a few lesser towns along the Santa Fe railroad were left.

When 200,000 head of cattle descended on Dodge in 1876, Ford County farmers raised cries of protest against the threat to their livelihood. They already had trouble enough wresting a living from the often-parched soil without having their grain fields ravaged by the hungry trail herds and their stock decimated by the imported fever. But Wright, reasoning that what was good for Dodge was good for him, and vice versa, exerted all of his growing business acumen and political influence to insure that the rising tide of longhorns did not abate. Although the trade was seasonal—the cowboys and their herds began arriving in May each year and kept coming until November—it was more than sufficient to keep Dodge in the pink of economic health.

In 1877, Charles Rath decided to sell out to his partner, and Wright began looking for another associate. Well aware that his new cowboy customers were more at ease with fellow Texans than with Kansans, Wright cannily picked a jovial Texan as his new partner. Henry M. Beverley was known to the trail hands and popular with them. He had been a cowpoke himself before going to work in an Ellsworth general store, where he had learned the ins and outs of cattle-town merchandising. Beverley proved to be a tremendous asset to Wright's enterprise. "The Texas drovers seem to think a heap of the 'Old Jedge,'" said the *Dodge City Times* of Beverley, who had somehow managed to acquire a quasi-judicial rank during his cowboy days.

Every season Wright, Beverley & Company dispatched trail agents deep into Texas to entice the herds toward Dodge City by trumpeting its advantages as a

Drugstore remedies

AMPUTATION KIT

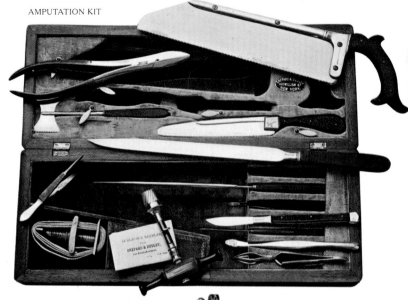

In many towns, the drugstore—that bastion of Western medicine—was run by a doctor, who kept busy filling his own prescriptions and selling soap out front when he was not in the back room taking care of the sick and infirm, and repairing gunshot wounds or sawing shattered limbs.

The hottest-selling items on his shelves were patent medicines, which—if labels were to be believed—could handle just about any and every complaint. One concoction grandly promised to cure 30 different disorders, including "nervous debility caused by the indiscretions of youth." Mostly they relied on a heavy lacing of alcohol to work their proclaimed wonders. Hostetter's Stomach Bitters, for instance, soothed indigestion with a formula packing a 50-proof wallop.

CORK PRESS

STONE MORTAR AND PESTLE

BALANCE SCALE

PRESSED SOAPS

APOTHECARY CONTAINERS

DIET ENRICHER

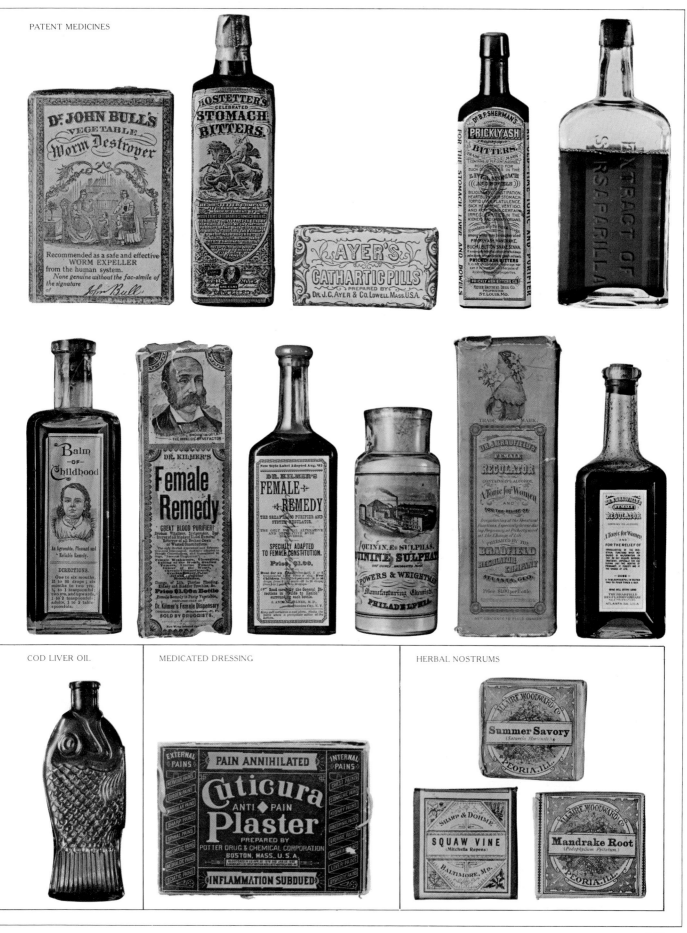

COD LIVER OIL

MEDICATED DRESSING

HERBAL NOSTRUMS

In his mid-30s, Bob Wright had already founded Dodge City and prospered in the buffalo-hide trade. But his merchandising glory days lay just ahead, when Texas cowboys began pouring into Dodge in 1876.

railhead and emphasizing its policy of unrestrained hospitality to those engaged in the cattle trade. Longhorn-hating Ford County farmers denounced the practice as disreputable, but Wright was unmoved. "The interests of Dodge City are with the Texas drive," proclaimed the literature he distributed in Texas, "and public sentiment will not allow the cattlemen to be hampered and harassed by the few farmers so inclined."

The "few farmers" had a pretty thin time of it in Dodge. Like Wright, the Front Street merchants let the local farmer know that they held him—with his near-empty pockets and his resentment of the Texas cattlemen—in minimum esteem. They much preferred to do business with the free-spending cowboys who were making Dodge one of the rowdiest of frontier towns while helping to enrich it. In turn, the Kansas farmers,

whose crops and cattle were under constant threat, became even more bitter toward the tradesmen.

The impasse worsened as the years passed. Farmers kept settling in Ford County, except when drought deterred them; and the longhorn herds kept growing—from 300,000 head in 1877 to nearly 500,000 by 1882. Meantime, Wright took steps toward solidifying the merchants' position. He was elected to the state legislature in 1879 and soon wangled himself a key job as chairman of the committee that determined the location of the quarantine line.

All the while, he kept a close eye on his store, continuing to hire men who were already skilled in catering to the needs and preferences of Texas cattlemen. After taking on Henry Beverley as partner, he employed a man named S. E. Isaacson, who had learned the business in Ellsworth and Wichita. Isaacson became Wright and Beverley's specialist in firearms and clothing. Next, Wright hired a European immigrant who, in his travels, had picked up a working knowledge of Spanish along with the German, Russian and Hebrew of his Old World background. "Sam" Samuels became Wright's ambassador to any Mexican drovers who came with the Texas herds. "Wright, Beverley & Co.'s store was a perfect bee hive," noted a Front Street observer. "About thirty Mexican customers dropped in at the same time and purchased goods to the amount of seven or eight hundred dollars. The Mexicans look upon Sam Samuels as their Moses in this strange land." Wright, coining money, regarded him with a similar fondness.

When the trail-hand business commenced each year, it came in a freshet. Upon reaching Dodge, a cowhand was paid wages of $60 to $90, and he made haste to spend it. First, an observer noted, "the barber shop is visited. Next a clothing store is gone through, and the cowboy emerges a new man, everything being new, not excepting the hat, and boots with star decorations about the tops . . . well, in short, everything new."

Wright was more than ready to make him over or take care of just about any other material need that might arise. The Wright and Beverley newspaper ads proudly offered *the largest and fullest line of Groceries and Tobacco west of Kansas City...anything or everything from a paper of pins to a portable house . . . clothing, hats, caps, boots and shoes, underclothing, overalls...Studebaker wagons, a genuine Cal-*

ifornia or Texas saddle, a nobby side saddle, a set of harness, a rifle, carbine, pistol or festive bowie knife, camp equippage, building hardware." Or you name it, he might have added.

Wright, Beverley & Company, like the other merchants up and down Front Street and elsewhere in the West, pursued an informal sideline as bankers. When a trail boss or herd owner reached town, he would "leave his whole pile" on deposit with the partners; or, if he needed money until the longhorns were sold—which was usually the case—Wright would advance cash on terms as favorable as 4 per cent. This was another source of grievance to the local farmers, who sometimes had to put up 25 per cent or more to borrow from a bank—and who, by now, were vociferously agitating for the westward extension of the quarantine line to

rid Ford County of both trail hands and trail herds.

Leaving cash in Bob Wright's care was a matter of simple prudence for, once a cowhand was off the trail and spruced up for town, his most likely next stops were successively the saloon, the dance hall and the brothel. Front Street publicans christened their bars with home-sounding names like Lone Star or Alamo or Long Branch; the latter establishment was just two doors down from Wright, Beverley & Company, and a brother of Ford County Sheriff Bat Masterson tended bar there. By 1880 the town, with about 700 full-time residents, supported 14 saloons and 47 whores.

In the rich early years of the drives, Front Street's slogan for trail hand exuberance, enunciated for all by Bob Wright, was "live and let live." But, from the first, this tolerant attitude stimulated disquiet among the

113

Newspaper ads trumpet Dodge City's mercantile prowess, capable of supplying anything from watch repairs to new boots for Texas drovers. When the seasonal cowboy trade waned, stores sought the patronage of local farmers, although one merchant so resented their pinchpenny ways that he said he would "rather see the devil coming than a granger."

town's more conservative citizens, primarily people who had no commercial dealings with the cowhands. One objected that both the visitors and their hosts were "walking howitzers." By the early 1880s, when public outcry for peace and quiet had reached full voice, local lawmen required all visitors to relinquish their shooting irons for the duration of their stay in town. As the town's foremost merchant and elder statesman, Wright accepted responsibility for holding the weapons, which were tagged and deposited in his store. "And my! what piles there were" Wright said. "At times they were piled up by the hundred."

The editor of the *Sentinel,* the media voice of the rival cattle town of Hays City, said of Dodge, "Her incorporate limits are the rendezvous of all the unemployed scallawagism in seven states. Her principal business is polygamy without the sanction of religion; her code of morals is the honor of thieves and decency she knows not."

Wright, the most eloquent defender of his town's good name, was deeply offended by such libels and greatly preferred the findings of the editor of the Kokomo, Indiana, *Dispatch,* who visited Dodge in 1878. "My experience in Dodge was a surprise all around," the editor told his readers at home. "I had expected to find it a perfect bedlam, a sort of Hogarthian Gin Alley, where rum ran down the street gutters and loud profanity and vile stenches contended. On the contrary, I was happily surprised to find the place in daytime as quiet and orderly as a country village in Indiana, and at night the traffic in the wares of the fickle Goddess and human souls was conducted with a system so orderly and quiet as to actually be painful to behold. It is not true that the stranger in the place runs a risk of being shot down in cold blood for no offense whatever."

He must have visited on a good day. Strangers ran just that risk. Not often, it is true; but often enough.

As a merchant, Wright's primary concern was for his store, and one of his worries was the possibility of fire. To provide a measure of protection, he worked with other civic leaders in establishing a system of rain barrels located in strategic places. He was not displeased when this municipal innovation paid off in a peripheral dividend of safety in the streets. Gunmen, peace-loving citizens and startled strangers discovered that the barrels made splendid foxholes when gunplay broke out.

Never far from the center of things, Bob Wright sometimes found himself drawn into affairs of the gun

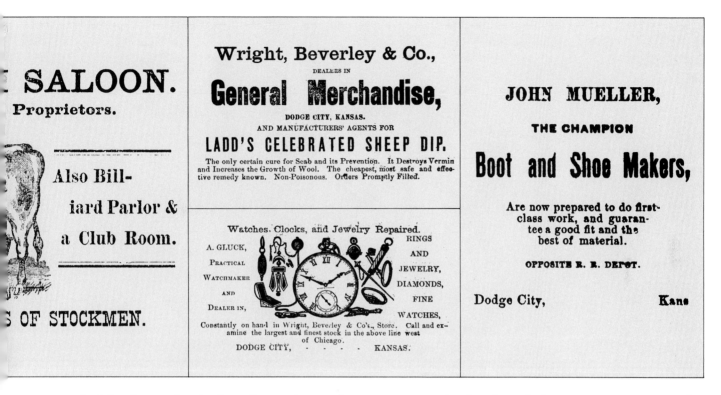
—luckily, always after the fact. One such episode was the matter of Deputy Marshal Jack Bridges versus the Texans. In July 1883, Bridges, aroused from his afternoon siesta by cowboys on a rampage shooting up Front Street, took his buffalo gun and blasted one of them out of the saddle. A difficult economic dilemma confronted Wright when he was appointed foreman of the coroner's jury. The Texans warned him that unless Bridges was punished, Wright, Beverley & Company would face a drovers' boycott. Pondering the issue and deciding reluctantly that some sort of order had to be upheld, he persuaded the jury to bring in a verdict of justifiable homicide. To Wright's relief the threatened boycott did not materialize, for "as soon as the stockmen got over their anger they came to me and said they could see it now in the light I presented it."

Wright did admit tolerantly that Dodge after dark and south of the tracks tended to be somewhat on the hair-raising side, but, as he pointed out, prudent citizens knew how to avoid trouble and strangers would do well to follow their example. "While such things as shooting up plug hats and making strangers dance is all bosh and moonshine," he explained, "none of Dodge's well-known residents would have been so rash as to dare to wear a plug hat through the streets or put on any dog such as wearing a swallowtail or evening dress."

As might be expected, the more rambunctious denizens of Dodge did not take kindly to anyone who rated their way of life as less than salubrious. They once had occasion to demonstrate their resistance to reform when an Eastern medical lecturer, describing himself as a specialist in venereal disorders, wrote to inquire whether Dodge might stand in need of his healing arts. A well-meaning junta of the town's leading citizens wrote back to advise the physician that he would be welcome, since the town—sad to say—was rife with disease and even ministers of the gospel were sufferers.

Advertised in advance, the lecture pulled a capacity audience to the Lady Gay Theater, an establishment which was then controlled—like a number of other things in Dodge—by Bob Wright. The doctor was escorted to the stage by Bat Masterson, Deputy Marshal Wyatt Earp, and the quick-on-the-trigger deputy, Jack Bridges, who had shot the rampaging cowboy.

The lecturer, foolishly adopting a censorious tone, got only a few sentences into his advice on hygienic practices when an outraged voice from the audience cried, "You're a liar!" Masterson stood up, hitched his

In a Durango, Colorado, meat market, sides of beef keep company with a stuffed elk, symbol of the wild game also available on the premises.

Shopping at the "most complete store on earth"

Whatever his business, the Western merchant often found his most formidable competitor to be Montgomery Ward & Co., a Chicago-based mail-order house that touted itself as the "most complete store on earth" and bragged that it could provide—at a 5 per cent markup—"almost any article required by the civilized world."

The company's catalogues, prized throughout the West, were crammed with tempting bargains: 864 shirt buttons ("72 dozen") for 35 cents, a spring bed for $2.75, a farm wagon for $50. Most orders were filled by railroad express, and the company thoughtfully advised its customers to pool their orders to qualify for a lower freight rate on shipments weighing 100 pounds or more. On request, Montgomery Ward & Co. shipped small orders by mail—but from the customer's viewpoint, this was not always the wisest course. The clerks were so scrupulous in observing the four-pound parcel-post limit that they once mailed an overcoat in two packages, throwing in a free needle and thread for reassembly.

This eminently resourceful merchandising operation was the brainchild of Aaron Montgomery Ward, a shrewd dry goods salesman who had traveled extensively throughout the West. Hearing frequent complaints about high prices charged by general stores, Ward decided in 1872 to form what he described as a "house to sell directly to the consumer and save them [sic] the profit of the middle man." The 28-year-old entrepreneur invested $1,600 in goods and set up shop in a 12-by-14-foot room.

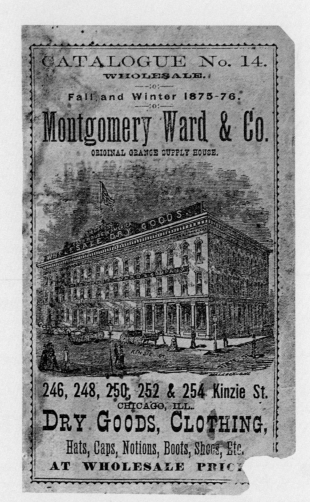

An 1875 catalogue, shown full-sized, handily fitted in a pocket.

His first catalogue was a single sheet of paper listing 167 items. By 1875 the company occupied an entire floor over a livery stable and published a 72-page catalogue (*above*) containing almost 2,000 items. Two decades later, the catalogue had swollen to 624 lavishly illustrated pages offering 75,000 different items.

Embattled storekeepers derisively dubbed their rival "Monkey Ward," and another mail-order house, Sears, Roebuck and Company, was nicknamed "Shears and Sawbuck." Going beyond mere taunts, merchants periodically offered free goods to people who brought in large numbers of catalogues. This effort to cut circulation was no more effective than the name-calling, but at least the merchants could put the booklets to a consoling use—as fuel for spectacular bonfires.

gun around to the front, and said, "I will kill the first man who interrupts this gentleman again." The next heckler's voice brought Earp to his feet to announce that, "This gentleman is a friend of ours. The next time we will begin shooting and we will shoot to kill." A sentence or so later an unidentified voice cried out, "You lie, you sonofabitch!" All three lawmen drew. Guns began going off, the lights went out, the hall filled with powder smoke, windows shattered and the doors were blocked by a stampede. The lecturer, a man of some courage, offered to try again the next night; but Wright, having learned that the plotters now proposed to set off 10 pounds of gunpowder under the lectern, smuggled the doctor aboard an eastbound freight.

Bob Wright may have regretted the day he became affiliated with the theater, but his retail business was making him very rich by the standards of the time. By 1884 he was Ford County's biggest taxpayer and twice as wealthy as Dodge City's next most affluent citizen, George Hoover, who had come to Dodge in its infancy and worked his way up from tent saloonkeeper to wholesale liquor dealer.

In a fitting climax to his career as custodian of the town he had been pivotal in creating, Wright was elected mayor in the spring of 1885. As always, the central interests of Wright the Mayor were those of Wright the merchant: to keep the longhorns coming into Dodge and preserve a wide-open town for its cowboy trade. Under his tolerant governance, Dodge continued to be as lively as ever. "The town is beginning to fill up with cowboys and stockmen," reported a local newspaper in late May. "The saloons, gambling halls and dance halls are in full blast." However, there were ominous portents for the future. Not only did the threat of quarantine loom larger than ever because of increasing pressure on the state legislature by Ford County farmers, but the outcry of the town's conservative element against the drinking, gambling and whoring of the cowboys had finally reached the ears of John Martin, governor of the state. Bob Wright was sorely aggrieved on behalf of his town when he received a curt letter from Governor Martin complaining of Dodge's continuing "depravity" and warning him that the town had to "reform or perish."

"You," he wrote back, "have been imposed upon by a lot of soreheads. We have always been a frontier Town, where the wild and reckless sons of the Plains have congregated, their influences are still felt here, but we are rapidly overcoming them, let us alone and we will work out our own salvation in due season."

Even as Wright penned this message, Dodge City's moral salvation—and its economic near-ruin—were being wrought by an alliance of nature and the forces Wright had long sought to forestall. The year of his mayoralty, 1885, was one of unusually abundant rainfall, as had been the two previous seasons, and a fresh influx of farmers—responding to the promise of fertile fields—poured into Ford County. Thus even providence was now smiling upon a class of citizens whom the cattlemen and their suppliers had so hated and feared for years. A Front Street businessman once revealed the depth of the merchants' feeling about them when he said, "Damn the grangers; I wish it wouldn't rain this summer so that they would starve out."

But it did rain, and the grangers at last had their say. The legislature, no longer able to withstand the farmers' call for protection, that year extended the quarantine line all the way to the western border of the state. After 10 riotous, abundant years, the cattle drives from Texas to Dodge were finally at an end. "Dodge City, once famous for its extraordinary prosperity, its lavishness in prodigality and possession of wealth, at one fell swoop was reduced to extreme poverty," Wright noted long afterward. "For ten long years, Dodge City was suspended in reverses."

Many Front Street businesses failed within the decade from 1885 to 1895. Wright himself managed to escape bankruptcy; he sold his Ford County grazing land and other property at panic prices but kept his store and stuck it out through the hard times. When Dodge City at last recovered, it was a very different place. The longhorns and cowboys were gone forever. In their stead came irrigated fields, orchards, neat farmhouses and vast acreages of golden wheat and green alfalfa. Bob Wright was still there when the hitching rail in front of his store was uprooted to make room for automobiles, and he was as proud as ever. Writing his reminiscences in the twilight of his life, this tradesman who had built, boosted, guided, coddled and protected his town like a loving parent distilled his feelings in a few simple words: "Hurrah for little Dodge! She has a bigger heart, for her size, than any town in Kansas."

A Dodge City institution, Wright, Beverley & Co. boasted in its newspaper ads *(below)* of an "endless variety" of merchandise.

A stock of you-name-it under one roof

"There was no article you could mention that we did not handle," Bob Wright once said of the general store he and his partner Henry Beverley operated in Dodge City. While the merchants stuck to tradition in the way of furnishings (three standard accouterments are shown below), their inventory was special in both size and range.

Wright, Beverley & Co. not only purveyed the usual diversity of items to be found in any general store (*following pages*) but also served as wholesale suppliers to other general stores in the area. In addition the partners were regional agents for the Studebaker Brothers Company of South Bend, Indiana — an arrangement that made available

to them the world's largest product-line of vehicles. And the emporium specialized in eye-catching items favored by cowboys — including, as a Dodge newspaper noted, "the jingling spur, the carved ivory-handled Colt, or the suit of velveteen." On a good day the receipts from these varied merchandising activities might put $1,000 in the till.

POTBELLIED STOVE   COFFEE GRINDER   CRACKER BARREL

TILTING WATER BASIN

KEROSENE LAMPS

CANNING JARS

FLATIRON

PLUM PRESERVES

CAST-IRON BOOTJACKS

APPLE BUTTER

122

WOMAN'S LONG JOHNS

BOY'S BUTTON SHOES

STETSON

STRAIGHT BOOTS

FIRE-EXTINGUISHING BOMB

CHASED GOLD WATCH

BABY CARRIAGE

ROLL-YOUR-OWN TOBACCO

PIPE AND CHEWING TOBACCO

KEROSENE JUG

COPPER DOUBLE BOILER

GROUND COFFEE

BUSHEL BASKET

INK RESERVOIR

SCHOOLBOOK

STONEWARE WATER DISPENSER

LIGHTWEIGHT SLEIGH

With a band, bunting and a big crowd, Wyoming Territory dedicates a new $150,000 capitol building in Cheyenne on May 18, 1887.

4 | Government by guess and by gall

Among the most urgent needs of settlers on the frontier — only slightly less pressing than food and shelter — was the establishment of town, county and territorial governments to keep their affairs from lapsing into chaos. The men who came forward to create and serve in these layers of government were, for the most part, grievously lacking in political experience. According to the forth-right testimony of Bucky O'Neill, an Arizona newspaperman who became mayor of Prescott in the 1890s, they were mainly distinguished by a "liberal endowment of the valuable article known as 'gall.'"

All too often, their brashness led to unfortunate excesses. Many counties, especially in Kansas, were wracked by mini-wars in which rival towns fought —with rigged elections and loaded rifles — to become the county seat. And early town governments often countenanced vigilante action to deal with crime.

Yet the blend of political innocence and aggressiveness freed Westerners to try bold experiments. In 1869 women's suffrage was enacted by Wyoming Territory, the first political body in the United States to take the step *(page 154)*.

Boisterous amateurs at the game of politics

Early in August of 1867, a group of settlers in Cheyenne faced up to a problem that, in one form or another, beset practically every new community in the West. Their town, just one month old at the time, had been growing like a weed, uncontrolled by rules or by organization of any sort; and it had become painfully obvious that these helter-skelter conditions could not be tolerated any longer. If the settlers' property and their very lives were to have any value, they had to create a local government and also establish working relations with higher political levels, setting to the task without a moment's delay.

Cheyenne's need for a municipal government was especially urgent because of the town's sudden and overwhelming success. Already several hundred residents had arrived, lured by rumors that Cheyenne was to be a major depot on the Union Pacific Railroad. And the heaviest influx was yet to come: hordes of brawling railhands and their camp followers were sure to pour into town as the track-laying crews worked their way across the desolate landscape from Julesburg, Colorado Territory, some 140 miles to the southeast. Cheyenne was utterly unprepared to cope with the transients, or even with the rowdies who had already showed up. The

town had no lawmen, and whenever serious disorders broke out, troops had to be rushed in from nearby Fort Russell. For that matter, the soldiers could do no more than serve as a calming influence, since Cheyenne had no court in which to try wrong-doers, much less a jail in which to lodge them.

To make things still more difficult, Cheyenne itself had no legal status in the eyes of any duly constituted authority. Although it was nominally part of Dakota Territory (which included all of present-day North and South Dakota and most of Wyoming) its settlers had yet to file in Yankton —the Dakota capital, 500 miles away—for a charter that would incorporate their town and legalize its existence. Thus Cheyenne was a political orphan in the wilderness, forced to fend for itself.

In Cheyenne, as elsewhere, the work of organizing a grass-roots government was complicated by the limitations of the men available for the task. They were ordinary settlers—primarily merchants and craftsmen with little experience in practical politics. Mostly they were young men, and their youthful blunders were hardly mitigated by their frontiersmen's traits: brash self-assurance and none-too-scrupulous ambition. Even though the new politicians of Cheyenne were, on the whole, more able than the average run of beginners, the community was subjected to an exasperating array of problems during the early years. An examination of Cheyenne's tribulations as it groped for self-government illuminates a dilemma that was virtually inevitable in town-making.

Cheyenne's first politician—and probably its very first citizen—was attracted by the railroad's rumored

Saloonkeeper William Collamer (*left*), first mayor of Yankton, Dakota Territory, was casual about his image, drinking heavily during his term. But Adolph Gluck, a Dodge City jeweler, was so proud of his office he wore a special badge (*above*).

Wooden containers made fine ballot boxes, and Nebraskans used this crate in an 1871 election. However, knotholes were to be avoided: in one election an official was caught stuffing fake ballots through them.

plans; he arrived on July 8, 1867, and pitched camp on what was then an empty expanse of buffalo grass beside Crow Creek. This pioneer was James R. Whitehead, an enterprising 40-year-old wagon freighter who had come to sell a load of house logs to the settlers who were certain to follow him. Whitehead was a restless man and had lived for a time in Kansas as well as Colorado. Like many of the West's self-made politicians, he had practiced law occasionally, probably without any formal legal training. On this and other points in Whitehead's background, Cheyenne's tireless early chroniclers were silent. Perhaps they never asked him; a man's past didn't matter much on the frontier.

In any case, Whitehead quickly became influential among the incoming settlers. By August 1, soon after surveyors laid out the town for its railroad owners, he had acquired a lot on Eddy Street and was erecting a two-story building that would be grandly named the Whitehead Block. With property to protect, Whitehead grew alarmed as unruly transients began to arrive. He alerted other substantial citizens to the danger. These men, encouraged by the railroad managers, called a town meeting to head off trouble, and thus commenced their adventures in do-it-yourself government.

At the meeting, held in a grocery store on August 7, Whitehead and a certain Mr. Spicer made what one chronicler described as "brilliant speeches in which they pointed out the necessity for a city government being organized with the least possible delay." The next day, Whitehead started practicing what he preached. He labored with a shopkeeper and a railroad land-sales agent to draft a provisional town charter; since this legal in-

strument was of doubtful worth, an application for an official charter was hastily sent to the Dakota legislature. Whitehead spent much of August 9 politicking, and it paid off that night when the townsmen met again to nominate officials for the town government.

Whitehead was nominated for city attorney on a ticket headed by mayoral candidate H. M. Hook, a livery stable owner originally from Pennsylvania. The election was called for the next day, so Whitehead didn't have long to wait for the outcome. But it must have been a tense 24 hours for him; he had seen enough of Western elections to know how chancy they might be.

Everywhere in the early West, elections offered irresistible opportunities for vote fraud. At the time, the printing of ballots was unmonitored; parties supplied their own, often on extra-thin paper which permitted a voter to stuff the ballot box with several votes—a practice that was not difficult, since polling places were poorly policed. Such vote-tampering did not always have the desired effect, however, since officials frequently counted up ballots any way they pleased. When two rival candidates practiced fraud, the better cheater usually won, but not always. In a scandalous Nebraska election in 1859, vote fraud was so flagrant on both sides that the U.S. Congress, called upon to decide the contested results, awarded the office to the loser on the supposition that he must have cheated a little less.

All of these horrors were apparently spared Cheyenne on its first election day, perhaps because time was too short to permit rigging. When August 10 drew to a tranquil close, 350 ballots had been cast to elect 11 officials—among them, Mayor Hook and City Attorney James Whitehead. The officials were sworn in on August 15 in a highly informal ceremony: their oaths were administered by an Army officer because no one else in the area had the vaguest link to any legal authority.

As city attorney, Whitehead went to work to draw up a set of laws and ordinances for Cheyenne. It could have been a big job, but Whitehead disposed of it handily by settling for a popular Western expedient: appropriating an established code in its entirety. He persuaded the city council to adopt the statutes he knew best: the criminal and civil codes of Colorado Territory, where he had once practiced law.

As August passed into September, Cheyenne's business community grew steadily, acquiring banks, hotels

PEOPLE'S ANTI-MONOPOLY LABOR TICKET.

1886

State Ticket.

For Governor—
J. BURROWS.

For Lieut. Governor—
M. K. LEWIS.

For Secretary of State—
E. J. O'NEILL.

For Treasurer—
W. H. DECH.

For Attorney General—
M. I. BROWER.

For Auditor Public Accounts—
A. STEDWELL.

For Com. Pub. Lands and Buildings—
L. B. PALMER.

For Supt. Pub. Instruction—
I. D. CHAMBERLAIN.

Congressional Ticket.

For Congress 2nd Neb. District—
W. A. McKEIGHAN.

50th Senatorial District—
GEO. W. PRICE.

Representative 51st District—
JAMES T. KELLIE.

County Ticket.

County Attorney—
ROBERT ST CLAIR.

Our Choice for U. S. Senator—
CHARLES H. VAN WYCK.

Township Ticket.

For Supervisor—

For Township Clerk—

For Treasurer—

For Justice of the Peace—

For Constable—

For Judges of Election—

For Clerk of Election—

For Assessor—

For Road Overseer Dist. No.—

Against the Proposed Amendment to the Constitution Relating to Legislative Department.

Until standardized ballots came into use in 1888, each party printed its own, like this Nebraska ticket. Since the slips were frequently distinctive in shape and color, observers could tell how a man was voting.

and more stores. A postmaster was named to handle the mails that were now moving through on Wells, Fargo stages. And everyone welcomed Nathan Baker, a printer from Colorado, who, on September 19, began publishing Cheyenne's first newspaper, the *Leader*.

Meanwhile other new towns were beginning to appear in what had been an unsettled wilderness only a short time before. Potentially the most important was Laramie, located 50 miles farther west; it would be the next major base of the Union Pacific. Still farther west, gold strikes earlier that year had brought prospectors streaming into the Wind River range of the Rockies; at least 15 mining camps had already sprung up.

Obviously a county government was needed—to build roads connecting the new communities, to provide peace officers and judges whose jurisdiction extended beyond municipal limits, and to attend to a variety of other matters affecting the region as a whole. Theoretically, it was the responsibility of the Dakota territorial legislators in Yankton to foresee these needs and send out commissioners to supervise the election of a county government. But the legislature was not in session, so Cheyenne's politicians decided to take the initiative. They called yet another town meeting for September 27. This session took place on the second floor of the Whitehead Block—space that had been rented as a temporary town hall—and its grandiose achievement was the establishment of the county of Laramie, which embraced almost the entire region that would someday become the territory and state of Wyoming, 97,914 square miles in all.

The officials for the informal county government were elected on October 8; no less than 1,900 ballots were cast. The post of representative to the Dakota legislature was won by James Whitehead and it gave him a chance to kill two birds with one stone. When he went to Yankton to represent the county and get its government legalized, he could also press the legislators to act on Cheyenne's petition for a town charter.

As Whitehead prepared to leave on his mission, the citizens of Cheyenne waited with mounting impatience to celebrate the completion of the railroad tracks from Julesburg. The great day finally came on November 13, but the real climax occurred shortly afterward when an immense freight train steamed into town, filled to overflowing with material from the dismantled Julesburg

Bannered campaign wagons roll through Prescott, Arizona Territory, in 1876, boosting John Behan for county sheriff (he lost) and Hiram Stevens for delegate to Congress (he won). A territory's sole delegate wielded considerable control over federal patronage but could not vote on legislation.

Four times elected Republican mayor of Dodge City, James Kelley was given this gold-headed cane by a clique of gamblers and madams. They also financed Kelley's campaigns in exchange for his protection.

base: food and liquor, equipment, furniture, piles of lumber and even some whole houses. Strangers who had never seen a "hell-on-wheels" town were dumfounded by the spectacle, and for their enlightenment a cheerful railroadman explained, "Gentlemen, here's Julesburg!" The *Wyoming Tribune,* the community's second newspaper, later put it more vividly: "When Julesburg died, its stinking carcass was thrown into Cheyenne to add to the pestilential atmosphere."

Whitehead may have left town before the first train arrived. In any event, he made the serious mistake of detouring to Denver, where he apparently attended to personal business. Thus he reached Yankton well after the legislative session had begun — and discovered that the Dakota legislature, working without his guidance, had already acted on Cheyenne's petition for a charter.

Unfortunately, however, the document passed by the legislators had some grievous shortcomings. In spelling out the legal powers vested in the municipal government, it neglected to list all the licensing fees the town had previously imposed on merchants and professional men in order to raise operating revenues. This vagueness would cost Cheyenne dearly. In March 1868, a territorial judge from Yankton outlawed all fees not specifically mentioned in the charter. Since few of the townsmen were of a mind to pay municipal taxes voluntarily, Cheyenne soon found itself cash-starved and running up heavy debts to pay officials' salaries and build a school and jail. (The town didn't solve the problem until the next year, and then only by getting a new charter properly tailored to fit its needs.)

Actually beginner's luck had run out for Cheyenne even before the townspeople learned of the charter problem. Through the autumn of 1867, crime had increased with the influx of railhands and their hangers-on. In November, a drifter named Shorty Burns allegedly killed two companions. The new city council posted a $300 reward for the accused murderer's capture, but Shorty escaped — at least temporarily. From that time on, conditions in Cheyenne went from bad to worse.

Editor Baker of the *Cheyenne Leader,* well aware that potential settlers might be reading his paper, tried to minimize his accounts of crimes to protect the town's reputation. But he complained editorially about the rising tide of violence, and on December 10 he grimly advised all good citizens to carry and use firearms at night in view of the "frequent occurrences of garroting." By Christmas, respectable townspeople decided something had to be done, and since the town's fledgling police force and municipal court had proved unequal to the job, they took matters into their own hands. By early January, 1868, they had banded together to form a secret vigilance committee.

Apparently the vigilantes organized with the full knowledge of the town officials. In fact, one contemporary reported that the group was made up "largely of the same people who had organized the provisional government." The vigilantes made a tentative debut under cover of night on January 10. Three men had just been arrested for theft, but, as provided by law, they were released on bail, with the trial to be held four days hence. They celebrated their freedom by getting drunk, and were found the next morning staggering down Eddy Street, roped together and decorated with a canvas sign noting that justice, of sorts, had been done. The sign's crude lettering said: "$90 stole...500 recovered. City authorities please not interfere. Next case goes up a tree. Beware of the Vigilance Committee."

Then, five days later, fist fights and shooting broke out at the New Idea Saloon, and when brawling occurred again the next night, the vigilantes came into the open to discourage the offenders. No less than 200 men marched silently up and down the main street, armed to the teeth and wearing gunnysack masks with eyeholes. The troublemakers, thoroughly impressed by this show of force, left town in a hurry.

So far, the vigilantes had done no real harm and some good. But, emboldened by the town's tacit approval of their terror tactics, they committed murder on January 18. The fugitive Shorty Burns had been captured near Fort Laramie and had been returned to Cheyenne to stand trial. The charge was dismissed — lawfully and also justly — for lack of evidence. Nevertheless, the vigilantes seized Burns, spirited him out of town and

hanged him from a telegraph pole. For the first time, substantial numbers of townsmen began to wonder whether the vigilantes might not be a worse burden than the criminals they were ostensibly fighting.

These dissenters soon had an opportunity to express their views. That month Whitehead returned from Yankton, bearing the charter as approved by the Dakota legislature. It required Cheyenne to hold an election to replace officials of the provisional government. The antivigilante faction hoped the new officeholders would be strong enough to restore true law and order.

One candidate for mayor seemed to be capable of doing just that. He was Luke Murrin, a respected saloonkeeper whom the *Leader* characterized as "a stoutly built gentleman, a reliable and energetic businessman — very popular." The townsmen elected Murrin on January 23, along with a completely new slate of officials. Finally Cheyenne had a legal government.

To everyone's relief, Mayor Murrin promptly issued a "call to account" for all members of the Vigilance Committee, "if now existing." The vigilantes declined to identify themselves — or to cease operations. But Murrin's bold opposition had stripped them of their semiofficial sanction, and their membership apparently changed, with misguided do-gooders contritely dropping out and unmitigated criminals hopefully joining up.

For some weeks afterward the vigilantes continued their activities. But at last they went too far. In April of 1868 they killed a brewer whom they were harassing for payment of a small debt he owed a saloonkeeper. The murder caused such public outrage that the vigilantes never risked operating again for fear of being lynched themselves. In 100 or so days of activity they had filled seven graves, only two with victims who might have been executed after due process of law.

Cheyenne's troubles were not over. Its residents were about to discover that controlling lawlessness was only one of the problems facing a new community. Controlling economic growth was another, and in some ways it was even more important. In the spring of

Like many new towns that were trying to impress potential settlers, the tiny Dakota Territory rail stop of Green River in 1868 issued a set of ordinances far more detailed than its uncomplicated affairs warranted.

GREEN RIVER
CITY ORDINANCES.

CHAPTER I.

Be it ordained by the President and Board of Trustees of Green River City, Dakota Territory.

1st. That it shall be unlawful for any person to carry concealed weapons of any kind within the corporate limits of said city.

2d. That it shall be unlawful for any person to shoot or discharge any fire-arm, air gun or other deadly weapons within said corporate limits.

3d. That it shall be unlawful for any person to be on the streets or in any public place in said city under the influence of intoxicating liquors.

4th. That it shall be unlawful for any persons to make loud and unusual noises, or to boisterously or uncivilly conduct himself or herself, or in any way disturb the peace of the citizens of said city as to fight or threaten to fight in said corporate limits.

5th. That it shall be unlawful for any person to be guilty of indecent public exposure.

6th. That any person found guilty of any of the above offences shall forfeit and pay a fine of not less than five nor more than ten dollars.

7th. That it shall be the duty of the City Marshal to arrest any person committing any of the above named offences, and take him, her or them before the proper officers to be dealt with according to law.

Be it ordained, that there shall be a chief and other policemen in numbers sufficient to maintain the good order and peace of the city.

In accordance with the provisions of the law in such cases made and provided, (this being a case of emergency,) it is ordered that the above ordinance be in full force and effect from the date of the passage thereof.

CHAPTER II.
Obstruction of Streets and Alleys.

Be it ordained by the Board of Trustees of Green River City:

1. That all persons are hereby forbidden to keep or maintain any building, tent or other obstruction in any street or alley of said city, and any person who shall leave or fail to remove any such obstruction within three days from the time of receiving notice to remove the same from the City Marshal, except by permission of the Board of Trustees, shall be liable to pay a fine of not less than five nor more than ten dollars for each day such obstruction may remain unmoved.

2. That it shall be unlawful for any person or persons to slaughter any beef, calf, hog or other animal of food within the corporate limits of said city.

3. That any person convicted of any

offense under any of the city ordinances on failing to pay the fine and costs that may be assessed against him or her shall be committed to the city jail of said city until said fine and costs are paid; and that under the direction of the Board of Trustees said prisoners may be put to work on the streets until said fine and cost be paid at one dollar per day for such work.

CHAPTER III.
Licenses.

Be it ordained by the Board of Trustees of Green River City:

1. That no person or persons shall carry on the business of an auctioneer in the city without first obtaining from the Board of Trustees a monthly license for the same, which license shall not be less than ten dollars nor more than one hundred dollars.

2. That no person shall give a public exhibition of any kind without first obtaining a license from the Board of Trustees, which shall not be less than five nor more than ten dollars for each exhibition.

3. That no person shall peddle or retail merchandise or produce of any kind within the city, without first obtaining a license from the Board of Trustees, said license not to be less than five nor more than fifty dollars. Provided, that any person may get a permit from one of the Board of Trustees, in which case he shall not be prosecuted, otherwise he shall pay a fine of not less than five nor more than fifty dollars.

4. That no person shall keep a whisky saloon within said city without first obtaining a license from the Board of Trustees, which license shall be ten dollars per month.

5. That no person shall carry on the business of retailing merchandise of any kind without first obtaining a license from the Board of Trustees, which license shall be ten dollars a month, and that wholesale dealers in merchandise shall obtain a license which shall be twenty dollars a month, and that keepers of feed stables and butchers shall also obtain a license from said Board which shall be ten dollars monthly, and that every keeper of a restaurant, hotel, public boarding house or lodging house shall obtain a license which shall be not less than five nor more than twenty dollars monthly.

CHAPTER IV.
Gambling.

Be it ordained by the Board of Trustees of Green River City:

1. That it shall be unlawful to be guilty of gambling by betting money on any game of chance, whether at cards, dice, faro, monte, keno, or any other game of chance whatever, or for any person to

keep or maintain any house or table for the purpose of any such gaming; that persons guilty of any of the above offences shall pay a fine of not less than five nor more than ten dollars.

CHAPTER V.
Houses of Prostitution.

Be it ordained by the Board of Trustees of Green River:

1. That it shall be unlawful to keep a house of prostitution, every person keeping such house, and every inmate thereof, shall upon conviction be fined in the sum of ten dollars, and each individual case shall pay the cost of arrest and conviction.

CHAPTER VI.
Creating the Office of City Attorney.

Be it ordained by the Board of Trustees of Green River City:

1. That there shall be and hereby is created the office of City Attorney, to be filled by said Board of Trustees.

2. It shall be the duty of the City Attorney to prosecute all actions on behalf of the city and to defend all actions against the city, and to advise the Board of Trustees on such legal questions as may arise in relation to the business of the city.

3. It shall be the duty of the Chief of Police to act as a conservator of the peace and in conjunction with the Marshal to arrest or cause to be arrested and taken before the Police Magistrate any person or persons who shall be guilty of a breach of any city ordinance, and the city police shall be under his control, all, however, being subject to the order of the City Marshal.

CHAPTER VII.
Fast Driving.

1. That it shall be unlawful to drive or ride a horse or mule or horses or mules, at a faster gait than six miles per hour within the city limits.

CHAPTER VIII.
Nuisances.

1. That it shall be unlawful for any person or persons to suffer any filth or filthy substances from their premises to remain in any street or alley, or on other premises where the same shall be offensive to the public or to any persons residing or doing business in the vicinity, and any person permitting the same shall forfeit and pay a fine of not less than five nor more than ten dollars.

CHAPTER IX.

That in all misdemeanors or violations of city ordinances, or ordinance, that the convicted parties shall pay a fine of $5 to $10 and cost of arrest and prosecution.

Approved this 12th of August, 1868.

JOSEPH BINNS,
President of the board of Trustees.

Attest: HARRY OWENSON, Clerk.

1868, the Union Pacific railhands, thousands of whom had wintered in town, went back to work laying tracks westward, and the railroad agents began touting Laramie as the next new important railhead. Cheyenne had expected the Union Pacific to build machine shops and roundhouses; these would help make up for the sudden loss of the railroad workers' business. But as of May, there was still no sign of the anticipated installations.

The anxious editor of the *Leader* wrote: "It is useless to disguise the peculiarities of our situation any longer. Cheyenne is a creation of the Union Pacific Railroad, and by the acts of that corporation does she stand or fall." The example of Julesburg—once a busy settlement less than a day's train ride away, now an abandoned site—was on everyone's mind. Finally the Cheyenne Board of Trade sent an agent to the New York office of the railroad; he reported back that the company did have plans for Cheyenne. That summer, work was begun on the machine shops and roundhouses; moreover, Cheyenne was selected as the junction for a branch line to Denver—a development that assured the community's economic future.

Although some of the boom went out of the boom town with the departure of the construction workers, the economic downturn proved to be a blessing in disguise. For the first time, life in Cheyenne became normal and even orderly. Local government was stabilized on the sound foundations laid down by self-made politicians. In the meantime these political amateurs, desirous of a greater measure of self-rule than their county setup afforded, had already launched a new and more ambitious campaign: they had petitioned Washington for a territorial government of their own.

The mechanics of this step were simple enough. If and when Congress granted the petition, the federal government would send the nascent territory five top administrators: a governor, a secretary (comparable to a lieutenant governor) and three judges. These appointees, aided by a locally elected legislature, were supposed to serve as good shepherds until the new ward of the federal government had a population of about 60,000, qualifying it for statehood. But as Cheyenne and neighboring towns knew all too well, Congress usually played politics in granting territorial status—and it often sent appointees who were venal or incompetent. Moreover, there was one phase of acquiring territorial status that could lead to serious local dissension and turmoil: the competition among towns to be chosen by the governor as the territorial capital. This was a prize greatly to be coveted. Designation as the capital ensured that a town would get a land office, a major post office and a variety of jobs for other federal functions; and because it was the seat of power, the capital would have the inside track on contracts to supply Army posts and Indian reservations in the territory.

Dakota Territory, the governmental parent that Cheyenne now sought to dismiss, had already been the arena of bitter battles over this honor. In fact, the territory had been the product of a long and sometimes ludicrous struggle between town-making syndicates that had invaded the region with no less an objective than to capture the territorial government whenever it was born. One of them actually had manufactured a government and tried to ram it down Congress' throat.

It had all begun back in 1857, four years before Congress granted Dakota territorial status. At the time, the federal government was negotiating with the Sioux tribes for cession of 14 million acres of Indian land west of Minnesota, between the Missouri and Big Sioux rivers. When the government negotiators failed to make headway with the chiefs, their job was turned over to a freelance with excellent credentials, among them the fact that he had a cousin who was married to a rising politician named Abraham Lincoln.

The freelance was John Blair Smith Todd, and he was many things to many men. Starting out as the scion of a prominent Kentucky family, he became a spit-and-polish West Point graduate and an elegant man-about-Washington, adept in the ways of party politics. His 20-year Army career took him to various frontiers, and he was quick to realize that the unsettled Dakota wilderness presented unlimited opportunities for personal gain. So in 1856 he resigned his commission as a captain, got in on the ground floor as an Indian trader and proceeded to turn a neat profit at every phase of developing events, including the business of government.

The cornerstone of Todd's success had already been laid by the time he was called to Washington to dicker officially with the Sioux chiefs. His trading firm had established several posts in Dakota and was properly licensed by the federal government. In getting his

To establish a look of civic maturity—and in the hope of making their town county seat—the 700 citizens of two-year-old Marfa, Texas, saddled themselves with a $71,000 bond issue in 1886 and erected an imposing courthouse and a capacious jail *(at right)* on the outskirts of town.

operation underway, Todd personally had dealt with the Sioux chiefs and this experience helped make quick work of the treaty arrangements. The 14 million acres of Sioux land were purchased at 12 cents an acre. And one of the treaty provisions granted Todd the right to buy, at the minimal price of $1.25 an acre, 160 acres of land surrounding each of his trading posts.

Todd had made extensive plans to capitalize on this real-estate bonanza even before the treaty was signed. He fully expected towns to grow up around his posts. Along with his partner, a wealthy St. Louis merchant named Daniel Frost, he had rounded up several ambitious speculators and formed the Upper Missouri Land Company. At the same time Todd sent orders to his agents in Dakota to extend his string of trading posts. They chose several prime new sites between the Missouri and Big Sioux rivers. What is more, he had already chosen his main post — Yankton — as a likely spot for a future capital.

Todd remained in Washington through the winter of 1858-59, lobbying for the creation of Dakota Territory. His campaign was at a critical stage when disquieting news reached him from his agents on the frontier. They reported that a dangerous competitor had been conspiring to wangle the capital for a town of its own, Sioux Falls City, located 60 miles northeast of Yankton on the Big Sioux River. This rival outfit was the Dakota Land Company, a firm based in Minnesota; what made it so dangerous was that its operators were influential Democrats (one of them was the governor of Minnesota) at a time when Congress was dominated by the Democratic Party. Todd himself was a Democrat, but he had been maintaining a scrupulously non-partisan stance lest the political pendulum start to swing the other way.

In its efforts to outflank Yankton, the Dakota Land Company contrived—in the autumn of 1858—to set up its own homemade territorial government, complete with governor and legislature. To enlarge its handful of Sioux Falls votes and lend credibility to its cause, the syndicate dispatched several small parties of pioneers into the wilderness to form an instant electorate. Each party paused every few miles, declared the spot an election precinct, took a communal pull at a whiskey jug and cast votes in the names of all their relatives and friends. By this means, more than 1,000 votes were re-

Colorado Springs policemen shape up for a station-house portrait in 1887, while their chief sits behind a picket fence on his personal rug. Two years earlier, the town's forward-looking government had ordered the force to switch from civilian clothes to natty serge uniforms and white gloves.

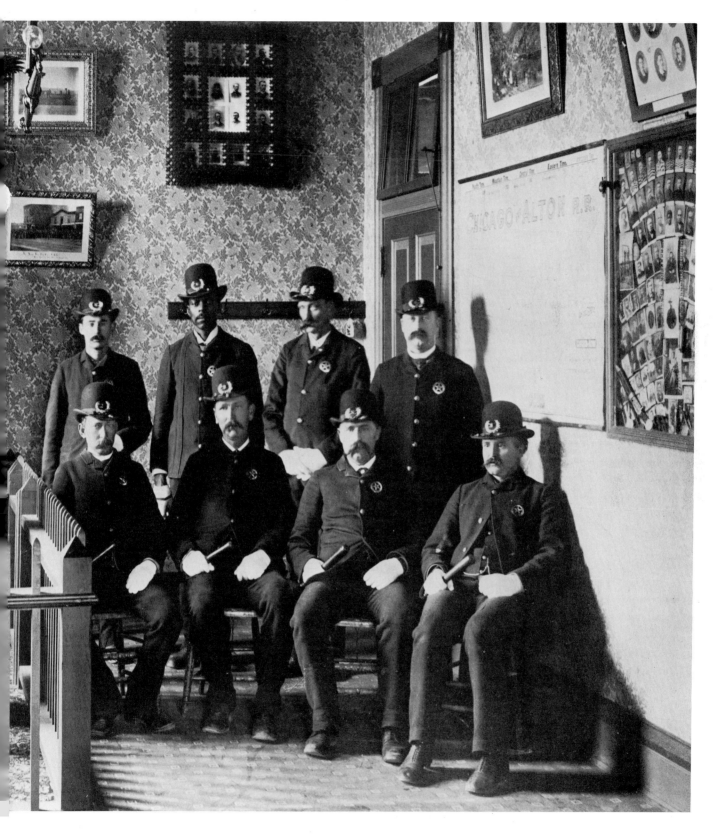

corded in one area that was utterly devoid of settlers.

The officials thus elected actually convened in Sioux Falls City and sent a delegate to Washington to lobby for them. In turn, Todd's Yankton supporters, fearing that Congress would recognize their competitors' political concoction as legitimate, joined with another new town, Vermillion, and passed a resolution denouncing the Sioux Falls government as a farce.

Congress, it turned out, was far from impressed by either of the rival parties. According to one political pundit, the legislators "looked with more surprise than compassion on these early political freaks of Dakotians." In 1860 a bill was introduced to organize the territory, but Congress defeated it. "These people of Dakota," said Representative Eli Thayer of Massachusetts, "are as well off today as they would be if they had our territorial officials over them."

But then, as so often happened in territorial affairs, the battle between the two land companies was decided by events far beyond the control of the participants. First, in 1860, the Republicans gained a majority in Congress, and because Sioux Falls City was the creature of stridently partisan Democrats, its chance of being chosen for the territorial capital was sharply diminished. Then, within a few months, even more momentous developments impinged upon the Dakota scene. The imminence of civil war in the East made it imperative for Washington to solidify the North, and Congress eked out the compromises between parties necessary to confer territorial status on Colorado, Dakota and Nevada, and to admit Kansas to the Union as a state.

The bills organizing the three new territories were passed in February and March, 1861. Then Congress and the new president, Abraham Lincoln, hastily scouted around for some top executives to send West. John Todd was the logical choice for Dakota governor; he knew the needs of the settlers and had a vested interest in their success. But Todd was a Democrat and Lincoln was a loyal Republican and a veteran spoilsman. The President bypassed his relative and instead chose 36-year-old William Jayne, his doctor from Springfield, Illinois, who was not only a reliable Republican but was also the brother-in-law of the powerful Republican senator from Illinois, Lyman Trumbull.

Jayne was typical of the party hacks who all too often were sent to administer the Western territories.

Showing minimal allegiance to the settlers who were his responsibility, he wintered in the East to escape Dakota's ice and snow. And he made himself the object of ridicule by fleeing the territory—along with his fellow appointees—when he feared that an 1862 uprising of Sioux in Minnesota might spread. Their disgraceful flight was reported with malicious glee by Moses Armstrong, a surveyor and sometime journalist who was later elected to the legislature. Armstrong wrote: "With such rapidity do they fly, pale and breathless, that a boy could play marbles on their horizontal coattails."

Governor Jayne did manage to call a government into being shortly after he reached Dakota in May 1861. According to formula, he ordered a general election to choose members for the Dakota legislature, whose two houses were then supposed to work up a body of law for the territory. Like all territorial election campaigns, Dakota's turned out to be a hot race—although for positions a good deal less powerful than the appointive posts filled by Washington. The governor had veto power over just about all the legislature's acts, the territorial secretary controlled the federal pursestrings, and the three federal judges ran the territorial judiciary to suit themselves, so there wasn't much left for elected officials. The most sought-after post chosen by the local electorate was that of the single territorial delegate to the U.S. Congress, who had no vote in Congressional decisions. The delegate simply served as lobbyist for the needs of the territory—or for the interests that controlled him.

Dakota's first legal election took place on September 16, 1861, and the post of delegate to Washington was won by none other than John Todd. He had already scored a bigger coup. Probably at the behest of his cousin, Mrs. Lincoln, Todd's town of Yankton had been chosen by Governor Jayne to be the territorial capital in spite of the aspirations of other communities, particularly Vermillion and Bon Homme. However, one of the few gubernatorial decisions that the legislature could overturn was the selection of the capital; and Todd, well aware of the danger, immediately set to work to consolidate Yankton's position.

His Yankton cohorts in the legislature began swapping votes. In return for pledges to let them keep the capital, the Yanktonites agreed to back J. H. Shober of Bon Homme for president of the territorial council (the upper chamber of the bicameral legislature) and George Pinney, an ambitious lawyer from Bon Homme, for speaker of the house (lower chamber).

When the legislature convened in Yankton in March 1862, the rowdy lawmakers were in a state of high excitement. According to Moses Armstrong, "A little blood was shed, much whiskey drunk, a few eyes blackened, and revolvers drawn." Until the vote was actually taken, Todd and his cronies were fairly certain that the capital would be theirs to keep. But some more swapping had been going on behind their backs. To their astonishment and indignation, Speaker Pinney turned traitor and backed Vermillion for the capital. Immediately Todd's men mounted a drive to unseat Pinney as speaker, but they failed to persuade the necessary two thirds of the legislature to see things their way. Since parliamentary maneuvers were unavailing, the Yanktonites concocted a plan to throw Pinney out a window, with the idea of disabling him just enough to necessitate the selection of a new speaker.

Pinney got wind of the plot against his person and sensibly resigned. His treachery was not forgiven, however. A little later, James Somers, the house sergeant-at-arms and a trusted Todd man, encountered the ex-speaker in Robeart's Saloon, and he *did* throw him through a window—a closed window at that. A few days later, Todd himself attacked Pinney, who this time, showing quick reflexes honed by danger, jumped unaided through still another window. Pinney then picked himself up, and, as an eyewitness later testified, "ran as few lawmakers could run."

Pinney's come-uppance convinced most of the legislature that the Yankton politicians would stop at nothing to hold on to their prize. Opposition from other towns was further reduced when the Todd men raised their political swapping a notch and promised Bon Homme the territorial prison and Vermillion the territorial university—just as soon as those institutions could be cut from whole cloth. In the end, Yankton got to keep the capital by a comfortable margin.

The territory of Dakota was in business, but for years the main commodity it had to purvey was an immense surplus of less-than-irresistible terrain. Its political heartland—the 14 million acres that John Todd had wangled from the Sioux chiefs—could boast no more than a few thousand settlers. Gradually the arable wilderness did attract homesteaders, many of them Scandinavian farmers who felt perfectly at home in—and even sentimental about—the frigid Dakota winters. But Democratic Dakota drifted aimlessly under a succession of ineffectual Republican appointees.

Dakotans were not especially dismayed when their distant outposts of Cheyenne and Laramie began to clamor for a territorial government of their own in 1867. They could easily spare their southwestern county. Moreover they feared that its population, which was growing faster than theirs, would take control of their own legislature if honest, per capita representation prevailed. Dakota politicians generally hoped that Congress would satisfy the demands of their noisy rebels, and the sooner the better.

As for Cheyenne and Laramie, their politicians felt, quite rightly, that the Dakota legislators, who thought in terms of their farm economy, didn't understand the needs of a region whose mainstays were mining and the Union Pacific Railroad. This popular view was neatly expressed by Editor Baker in the *Cheyenne Leader:* "Dakota is a slow coach—we travel by steam."

By the summer of 1868, Congress could no longer ignore the vociferous lobbyists from out Cheyenne way. Since Dakota was agreeable, Congress passed, and President Johnson signed on July 25, the legislation that created the Territory of Wyoming.

The very name of the territory boded well, for it was chosen in the earnest, cooperative spirit that had marked the launching of Cheyenne's municipal government. Wyoming, originally a Delaware Indian place name, was first proposed for the Western region by an Ohio member of the House of Representatives back in 1865; it had since come into common use. The word had several virtues: it was euphonious and easy to spell, and its Indian meaning was something like "on the big plain," which suited much of the territory's geography pretty well. Both the House and the Senate preferred the name over other suggestions that the territory be dubbed "Lincoln" or called after one of the area's Indian tribes or rivers. When the bill reached the West with Wyoming blazoned on it, no one there had much objection. Since Congress had spoken, Wyoming it was.

The same high level of good will attended the formation of the Wyoming government. The first gov-

Hose Company No. 1 of Prescott, Arizona, turns out on July 4, 1888 for speed competitions against the three other volunteer fire companies that safeguarded the community of 1,900 citizens. Prescott's municipal treasury paid for the hose reel, but the firemen had to provide their own outfits.

Unprepossessing but serviceable, the Dakota Territory capitol building — here doing extra duty as a polling place — was erected in Yankton in 1862. Before that, the territorial legislature met in settlers' houses.

ernor appointed to the territory was 33-year-old John A. Campbell, an Ohioan who had risen to the rank of brigadier general in the late war. Although he was a Republican outlander sent by a Republican administration to govern a largely Democratic populace, Campbell quickly demonstrated an unusual dedication to his duties and a sincere desire to get along with Wyoming's Democrat-dominated legislature. Campbell was not merely talking for effect when he declared in his inaugural address, "I trust that this initial point in our history will be marked by no personal dissensions, no mere partisan schemes and no local jealousies."

Of local jealousies there were few. When Campbell selected Cheyenne as his capital, the only possible rival, Laramie, was mollified by being picked as the site of the future territorial penitentiary. And almost at once, the mismatched team of the Republican governor and

the Democratic legislature showed signs of greatness. The very first session of the legislature put on the books two bold acts, one "to protect Married Women in their separate property," and the other to prohibit sexual discrimination in the payment of teachers. These laws were merely a warm-up for an act of radical statesmanship that placed Wyoming far ahead of the rest of the country. In December 1869, Wyoming enacted women's suffrage.

At that time, voting rights for women was a full-fledged crusade that kept ardent feminists campaigning from coast to coast. One of them, the good-looking Anna Dickinson, even stopped over to evangelize Cheyenne in 1869. Nonetheless, Wyoming's enlightened law astonished the nation, and it probably startled most of the territory as well. News traveled slowly to Wyoming's isolated towns, and women's suffrage was an accomplished fact before many people realized what their government had done.

According to Wyoming legend, the instigator was Mrs. Esther Hobart McQuigg Morris, a sturdy 55-year-old woman whose physique and determination served to dwarf her husband John. In September 1869, just before the first territorial election, she held a tea party in the mining town of South Pass City; it was attended by Colonel William H. Bright, formerly with the Army Quartermaster Corps and now a candidate for the legislature. Before Bright bade his adieus, the forceful Mrs. Morris extracted from him a promise to introduce a women's suffrage bill if he was elected. At least that was what Wyoming legend said. But Bright happened to be a 46-year-old man married to a lovely 25-year-old woman who happened to be a suffragist, and he undoubtedly had made his decision beforehand.

In any case, Bright won and was selected president of the territorial council; not only did he introduce the bill, but the nine-man council actually passed it — and by a vote of six to two, with one absentee. Then the bill went to the house, where it also passed. When Governor Campbell signed it into law, Wyoming became the first American political unit in which women had full rights to vote and hold public office. The first woman to exercise the franchise was Louisa Ann Swain, aged 70, of Laramie. On September 6, 1870, she fastened a clean apron over her house dress, headed for the polls, and cast her vote in a territorial election. She made the trip doubly worthwhile by stopping at a bakeshop on the way home to buy some yeast.

Once the deed was done, well-founded allegations were heard that the gentlemen of the legislature had not been motivated solely by a sense of chivalry or justice. The act, said the *Cheyenne Leader,* had been a "shrewd advertising dodge. We now expect at once quite an immigration of ladies to Wyoming." Such a wave of female immigrants was undoubtedly something the legislators had thought of and hoped for; women were dismayingly scarce in Wyoming. Unhappily, an inundation of potential wives failed to materialize.

Wyoming's political progress was nearly as remarkable in another field: the formation of county governments to meet the needs of increasing population. As each new county was authorized by the territorial legislature, the normal procedure was for its settlers to choose their county seat and county officials by popular election. In Wyoming, the original, enormous Laramie County had been divided into five smaller ones by 1869, and each set up its own housekeeping in orderly fashion. This was in sharp contrast to the record of several Western territories and states where large areas were virtually paralyzed by long, bitter battles between towns for designation as the county seat.

As in the case of territorial capitals, there were several good economic reasons why county-seat elections were hotly contested. With selection as the county seat, a town won government jobs, considerable influence over bond issues, and lucrative contracts for public works such as road cutting and bridge building. These plums, and an attendant increase in local commerce if the county had any sort of prospects, were a sore temptation for townsmen in remote, newly opened frontier areas where the business of government was the easiest route to wealth. Driven by need and greed, many townsmen became shotgun politicians and fought small wars to capture the honor.

Perhaps the most bizarre of these conflicts was staged in Gray County, Kansas. The struggle embroiled three small towns — Ingalls, Montezuma and Cimarron; it started in 1887, reached a violent climax in 1889 and dragged on for seven years more before it was settled. The instigator was a Rochester, New York, millionaire named A. T. Soule, who gave the world a patent medicine cure-all known as Hop Bitters. Soule, annoyed by stiffening competition in the East, had decided to go west and invent a county seat as a financial plaything.

His creation was Ingalls, which he named for Senator John Ingalls of Kansas as a favor-currying tactic. Soule proceeded to spend a fortune in an effort to endow Ingalls with the Gray County government. To make the town a prosperous agricultural center, Soule built the 96-mile-long Eureka Irrigation Canal connecting with the Arkansas River. The canal would have been a glittering success — except that it was poorly maintained and often ran dry. To bribe Montezuma to withdraw from the county-seat contest, Soule then linked that town to Dodge City with a gift railroad, which was eventually demolished because no passengers or freight ever went to Montezuma. Soule's agents also spent thousands of dollars buying settlers' votes

Papering the plains with homemade currency

The venturesome spirit of Western politicians never showed itself more clearly — or to worse effect — than in the late 1850s when legislators in Kansas and Nebraska tried to bolster the region's economy by tampering with the money supply. At the time, tight-money policies set by Eastern banks made cash so scarce that merchants sometimes had to do business by barter.

The solution seemed simple: the territorial legislators chartered banks and authorized them to print money. Unfortunately, the lawmakers neglected to set up regulatory agencies that would make sure the institutions were always sufficiently capitalized to redeem their scrip on demand.

A number of towns immediately opened banks and issued bills to finance pet municipal projects. Private bankers dashed off homespun currency for loans and also used it to speculate in real estate. And scores of fast-buck operators added to the money-flood without bothering to acquire a charter.

All but a few of the institutions, including those operated by towns, collapsed in the financial panic of 1857. Omaha's bank, beset with demands for redemption of its bills *(right),* tried to float a bond issue to get the necessary cash, but voters refused to go along and the bank notes were thereby rendered worthless. Some privately owned operations were finally exposed as out-and-out frauds. In late 1857, auditors poring over the books of the defunct Bank of Tekama discovered that the $90,000 in picturesque notes *(below, bottom)* were backed by total bank assets of a shanty, a table and a stove.

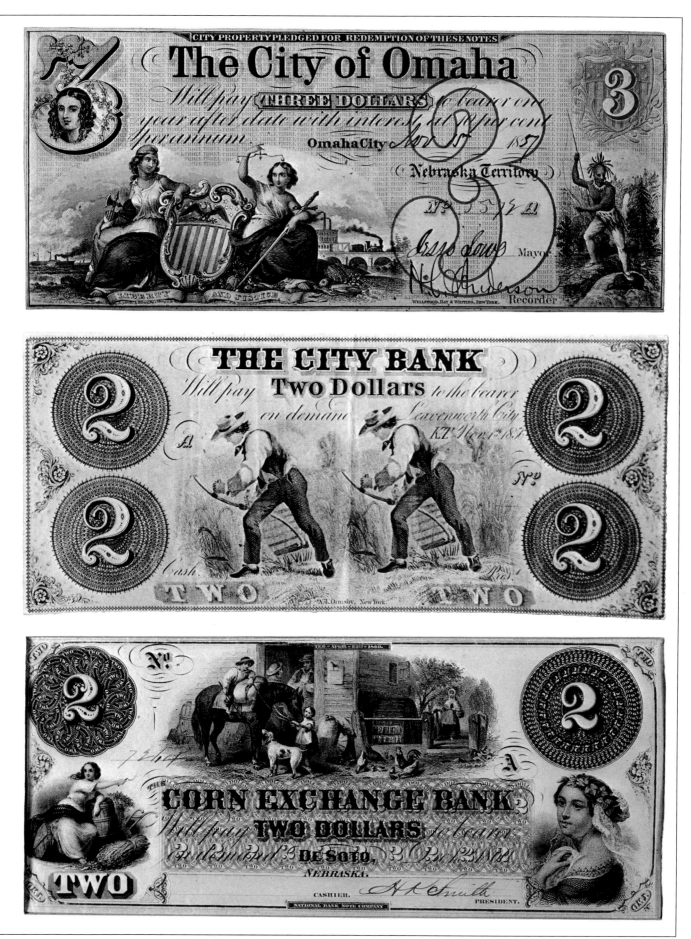

State militiamen bivouac outside Hugoton, Kansas, in an attempt to stop the town's war with nearby Woodsdale over irregularities in an 1888 election to choose the county seat. Before Hugoton finally emerged as the victor, six men were killed and the militia was called out three times.

for the election that would presumably decide the issue.

To counter Soule's machinations, the leading citizens of Cimarron made a $10,000 deal with the Equalization Society, a secret organization formed by 72 rapscallions for the sole purpose of selling their votes in a bloc to the highest bidder. The society members swore to vote for Cimarron on penalty of death. They delivered as promised when the election was held in 1887, and Cimarron won.

But nothing was settled. Ingalls protested the election on grounds of fraud and commenced a long series of court maneuvers. During this impasse, another election was held; an Ingalls man won the post of county clerk and naturally demanded that the county records, which then reposed in the Cimarron courthouse, be transferred to Ingalls. Just as naturally, Cimarron refused to surrender the records.

Ingalls then prepared a maneuver known as a courthouse coup. The town's citizens hired a gang of ruffians, swore them in as deputy sheriffs and sent them to Cimarron to kidnap the records. Some of the invaders did accomplish their mission. But Cimarron woke up to

the raid in time to trap a few deputies still in the courthouse. A lively gunfight ensued. The mercenaries held out for a day before they were forced to surrender.

After the raid, it was all downhill for Ingalls. Soule died in 1893, and when his irrigation ditch proved to be an irreversible failure, settlers moved away in droves. After several years of inconclusive litigation over the election, the choice of a county seat was again put to a vote in 1896, and Cimarron won hands down.

The most discouraging thing about the Gray County war was that it occurred nearly three decades after Kansas was admitted to the Union as a state. Apparently, Westerners were wrong in their widespread belief that statehood would solve all of their political problems. ("A State signifies law and order," the Colorado Springs *Gazette* once pontificated, "a Territory violence and disorder.") However, at the time of the Gray County war, many Westerners had not had a chance to find out for themselves just what statehood could do for them. Between 1867 and 1889, Congress made a state of only one territory—Colorado, in 1876. A

whole generation had to grow up under territorial governments in regions that became the states of Arizona, Idaho, Montana, New Mexico, North Dakota, South Dakota, Utah, Washington and Wyoming.

To excuse the long delay, Congress often pointed to county wars and other persistent forms of Western violence as evidence that the territories were unready for statehood. But national politics was the real culprit. Through most of the 1880s, Congress' reluctance to confer statehood was a result of its internal split, which made concerted action impossible. The Senate was Republican and its majority was naturally disinclined to help a Democratic territory become a state, which would add Democratic senators and representatives to Congress; the same applied in reverse to the Democratic House. But the deadlock was broken in 1888 when the Republicans won control of both houses of Congress. In the next two years, Congress admitted six Western states to the Union: North Dakota, South Dakota, Montana, Idaho, Washington and Wyoming.

Citizens in the territories resented this long political probation. Statehood had been an implicit promise when

territorial status was awarded, and the knowledge that it had to come eventually didn't reconcile men to waiting nearly a lifetime for the second shoe to drop.

The benefits of statehood were never far from the Westerners' minds. On becoming citizens of a state, they would at last be fully enfranchised—entitled to vote for the President, for their own top officials, for two senators and at least one representative who actually had a vote in the U.S. Congress. For these very reasons, moreover, statehood figured to attract more settlers and to curb Washington's infernal meddling in local affairs. To a fair number of thoughtful Westerners, the territories were no less oppressed by the federal government than the 13 original colonies had been under British rule. In Dakota, the Vermillion *Republican* demanded deliverance with a rhetorical question that would have gladdened the heart of Patrick Henry: "When shall we slough off this chrysalis or bondage and be free, independent and self governing?"

Wyoming came to grips with this question in 1888. There was some opposition to immediate statehood; the Democrats, who had lost their former dominance in

As part of its campaign to become the state capital, Anaconda issued a satirical booklet with "statistics" that skewered rival Helena. Montanans chuckled, then chose Helena, because it was more centrally located.

	Helena.	Anaconda.
Men who wear silk hats	2,625	3
Men who wear No. 7 shoes	2,110	5
Men who wear No. 9 shoes	2	3,618
Men who wear silk night shirts	2,910	4
Men who wear cotton night shirts	186	3,016
Men who wear kid gloves	4,552	4
Men who wear overalls	0	3,220
Patches on seats of trousers	1	7
Patches on knees of trousers	0	253
Patches on conscience	1,691	8
Dinner buckets in daily use	2	4,028
Manhattan cocktails, daily consumption	17,699	127
Gin fizzes, daily consumption	18,123	180
Whiskey straights, daily consumption	13,303	1,977
Champagne (qts.), " "	1,245	2
Beers " "	4,088	8,854
Ladies who nurse their own babies	124	2,876
Ladies who do their own washing	8	980
Ladies who dance the minuet	3,773	82
Ladies who do the skirt dance	861	1
Ladies who can kick the chandelier	140	0
Ladies with poodle dogs	774	0
Ladies with pug dogs	2,285	3
Ladies with no dogs at all	1,863	3,555
Ladies who give high fives	2,731	9
Ladies who rip other ladies up the back	1,296	147
Babies born with silver spoons in mouth	435	0
Children with Shetland ponies	590	0
Children who make mud pies	0	2,773
Average number children per family	⅓	5¾
Horses with docked tails	1,182	0
Four-in-hand turnouts	112	0
Yellow donkey carts	215	1
Skeletons in closets	1,343	16
People who eat dinner at 6 o'clock	8,658	456
People who eat dinner at 12 o'clock	370	6,954

Wyoming, called for a delay on the grounds that Wyoming had suffered a long business slump and that a state government would cost $95,000 a year more than the territorial government did. The added expense, warned the Democratic *Cheyenne Leader,* would have to be paid by increased taxation.

In January of 1889, however, the city council of Cheyenne closed a business-boosting deal with the Union Pacific Railroad, which pledged to build new installations in town. This happy turn of events brightened Wyoming's economic picture and persuaded the *Cheyenne Leader* to withdraw its objection to immediate statehood, which all but settled the issue as far as Wyoming was concerned. The main problem now was the fact that older territories, with larger populations, were ahead of Wyoming, waiting in line for Congress to pronounce them states.

As usual, Wyoming seized the political initiative. In 1888, while the Democrats were still demurring, the legislature had sent Congress a formal petition for statehood. And in the spring of 1889, boards of county commissioners in seven of Wyoming's 10 counties

adopted resolutions calling for a constitutional convention—even though Congress hadn't yet authorized one. In July, the citizens of Wyoming elected 55 delegates to draft a state constitution.

The convention was called to order in Cheyenne in September. Many of the delegates were lawyers and they soon began arguing over technical points, such as the composition and jurisdiction of various courts. "The lawyers in this convention," said Cheyenne delegate A. C. Campbell, "have been talking too much." He thereupon started a harangue of his own, prompted by his fear that conservative members of Congress would vote against statehood because of their distaste for the women's suffrage that would go along with it. To solve the problem, Campbell proposed that, when the constitution was voted on by the electorate, women's suffrage should appear on the ballot as a separate article, unattached to statehood. The proposal was patently designed to permit the electorate to cancel women's voting rights and clear the road to statehood. But most delegates wanted no part of the dodge. One declared gallantly, "I am unwilling to stand here and by word or gesture disfranchise one half the people of our territory, and that the better half."

Others took up the protest. "If they will not let us in with this plank in our constitution," a delegate named Burritt exclaimed, "we will stay out forever." Burritt's language gave rise to the legend that the Wyoming legislature sent Washington a defiant telegram declaring, "We may stay out of the Union a hundred years, but we will come in with our women." No such telegram was ever sent, but the sentiment was widely held. Campbell's proposition never appeared on the ballot.

Finally, after 25 days of hard work and gentle persuasion, the convention completed the document and approved it unanimously. In a special election held in November, the people of Wyoming voted for the constitution—and for statehood—by a three-to-one margin.

For a few months longer, Congress withheld the invisible, invaluable prize. A last stumbling block was Wyoming's population; estimates ranged as high as 125,000 and as low as 55,000. Probably the actual figure fell a little short of 60,000—the population level that, by law, territories were supposed to achieve before they could qualify for statehood. But exceptions had been made before, and the House Democrats who

played the numbers game were now fighting a Republican majority they could not defeat.

Congress approved of statehood for Wyoming in the three usual stages, each one setting off frenzied celebrations all over the Territory. The statehood bill passed the House on March 26, 1890, passed the Senate on June 27, and was signed by President Harrison on July 10. By July 23, when Wyoming's fourth and final celebration was scheduled to be staged in Cheyenne, it might have been expected that the citizens of the new state would have exhausted their enthusiasm. Far from it. More than 5,000 people jammed Cheyenne on statehood day. The great crowd watched a two-mile-long parade of soldiers, floats and decorated carriages. Marching music was supplied by two bands, an Army outfit from Fort Russell and some talented railhands contributed by the Union Pacific. The theme of the parade was attractively presented and magnificently fitting. On the main float rode 42 young women, each one representing an earlier state. The float was followed by a little carriage that bore three girls, pink-cheeked symbols of the Goddess of Liberty and the two newly created states of Wyoming and Idaho.

Statehood day was practically ladies' day. The first speech was delivered by a woman, Mrs. Theresa Jenkins, who briskly reviewed her sex's crusade for the vote. It was said that Mrs. Jenkins' voice carried so well because she practiced on the prairie, elocuting for her husband, who kept moving farther and farther away.

Then the famous Mrs. Esther Morris presented Governor Warren with a 44-star flag contributed by the women of the state. Finally came the highlight of the day-long program. Heralded by a 44-gun salute, an original poem was read with feeling by its author, Mrs. I. S. Bartlett. Its last lines made a spine-tingling climax:

*Let the bells ring out more loudly and the
    deep-toned cannon roar,
Giving voice to our thanksgiving, such as never
    rose before.
For we tread enchanted ground today, we're
    glorious, proud and great,
Our independence day has come — Wyoming
    is a state!*

153

A surprise breakthrough for the better half

The passage of the nation's first women's suffrage law *(opposite)* by the Wyoming territorial government in 1869 was intended as a public relations gesture. It was expected to add no more than 1,000 active voters to the electorate, and although it gave women the right to hold office, most men assumed that the ladies would choose to stay home where they belonged. But the newly enfranchised voters were following a separate scenario. They promptly demanded more active roles for women in government, a prospect so unnerving to the all-male legislature that in 1871 it tried—and failed by one vote—to repeal the suffrage bill.

Wyoming's first woman officeholder was 57-year-old Esther Morris, one of the territory's most renowned suffragists. Despite a lack of legal training, she was appointed justice of the peace for the mining town of South Pass City.

Esther Morris

She ran her court with an iron hand for nearly a year and never had a decision reversed by a higher court.

Even as Judge Morris was gaveling rowdies into the calaboose, other women were pioneering as members of juries in Laramie and Cheyenne. Although cartoonists were quick to lampoon them *(below)*, the women jurors took their new duties seriously. In one notable Laramie murder case, a jury of six men and six women was locked up for two and a half days trying to reach a verdict. The men, three of whom favored acquittal, played cards, smoked and drank beer in one room, while the women, unanimously for conviction, sang hymns and prayed next door. Finally the impasse was broken with a compromise verdict: guilty on a lesser charge of manslaughter.

Wyoming's widely publicized example emboldened women throughout the region to seek the same rights. By 1896, women had won the vote in Utah, Colorado and Idaho, and had begun to play a major role in politics and professional life all across the West.

This all-female Wyoming jury was the fanciful creation of a New York magazine artist; actually, women jurors always served with men.

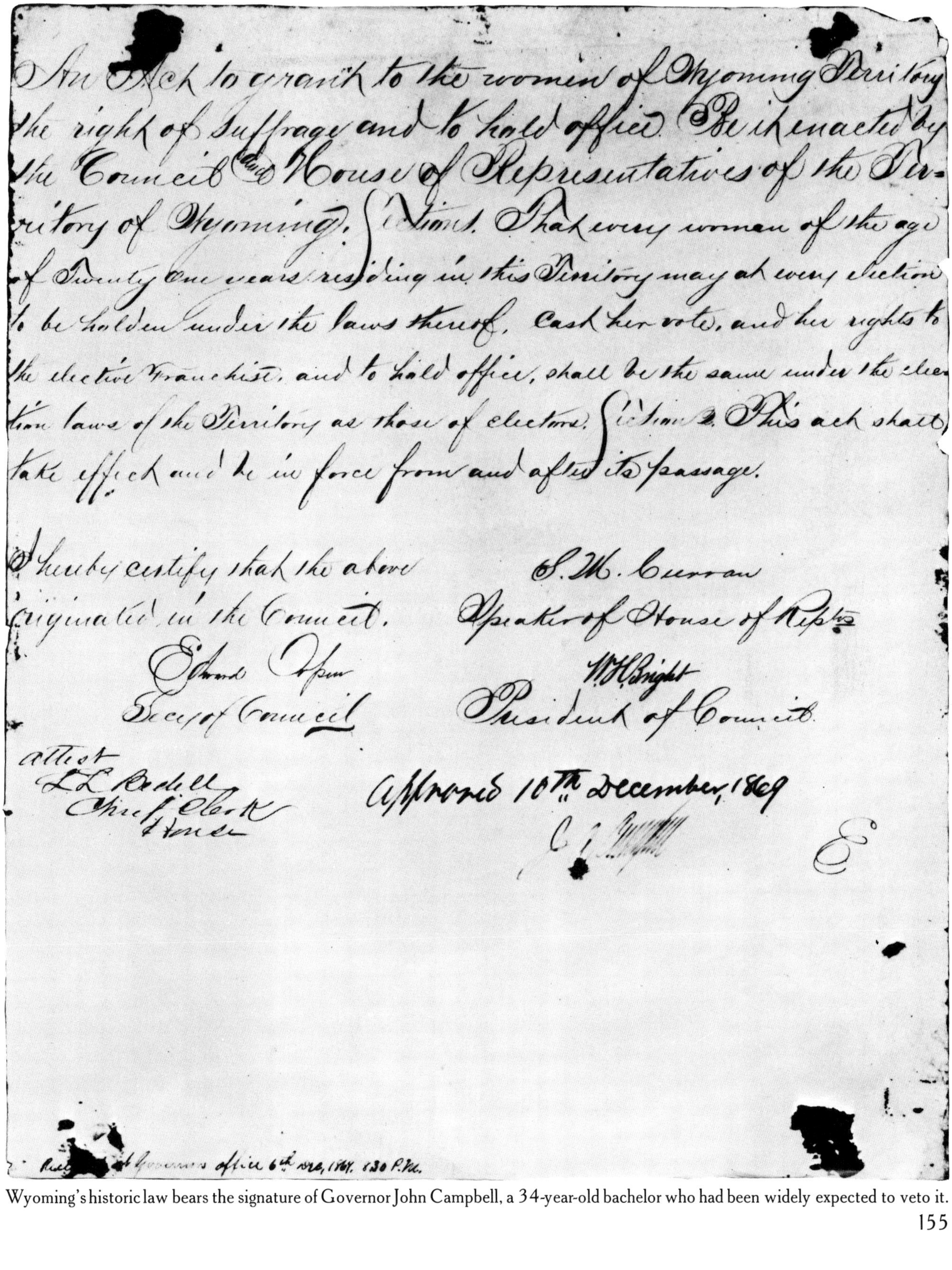

An Act to grant to the women of Wyoming Territory the right of Suffrage and to hold office. Be it enacted by the Council and House of Representatives of the Territory of Wyoming. Section 1. That every woman of the age of Twenty One years residing in this Territory may at every election to be holden under the laws thereof, Cast her vote, and her rights to the elective Franchise, and to hold office, shall be the same under the election laws of the Territory as those of electors. Section 2. This act shall take effect and be in force from and after its passage.

I hereby certify that the above originated in the Council.

Edward Lee
Secy of Council

Attest
S. L. Rockwell
Chief Clerk
House

S. W. Curran
Speaker of House of Repts

W. H. Bright
President of Council

Approved 10th December, 1869
J. A. Campbell

Recd at Governors office 6th Dec. 1869, 130 P.M.

Wyoming's historic law bears the signature of Governor John Campbell, a 34-year-old bachelor who had been widely expected to veto it.

Lillian Heath dressed like a man and toted pistols while studying under the only doctor in Rawlins, Wyoming. In 1893 she began work as the town's first obstetrician.

Grace Hebard was a civil engineer, the first woman admitted to the Wyoming bar, a university professor, a golf champion and the author of numerous Western histories.

Mary Lathrop showed herself a pace-setter as Denver's first woman lawyer and went on to achieve another first when she was admitted to the American Bar Association.

Susanna Salter, a housewife in Argonia, Kansas, became America's first woman mayor in 1887 after she was nominated as a joke and—irked—would not withdraw.

Estelle Reel, a Laramie, Wyoming, schoolteacher, was the first woman elected to a state office, winning the post of superintendent of schools in 1894 by a landslide.

Hired for three months in 1884 in an experiment by the Denver police department, Sadie Likens spent nearly a decade as the first full-time policewoman in the West.

A DEDICATED FEMALE VANGUARD

As the wave of emancipation rippled outward from Wyoming across the West, almost every town proved to have a share of women who aspired to positions that had been traditionally barred to their sex: doctor, lawyer, police officer, politician. Inevitably, most had to work long and hard to achieve the goal. Others, like Susanna Salter, mayor of Argonia, Kansas *(above)*, became pathbreakers almost accidentally and later retreated to a homemaker's role. But everywhere they acquitted themselves so admirably that things would never be quite the same again.

Oskaloosa, Kansas, in 1888 chose Mayor Mary Lowman *(left, seated at center)* and five councilwomen to form the first all-female municipal government in the U.S.

Mary Lease *(right)*, a teacher and self-taught lawyer, rallied Kansas farmers to the Populist cause in the 1890s with exhortations to "raise less corn and more hell."

Company H of the newly formed Wyoming State Guard prepares to join a July 23, 1890, parade celebrating the attainment of statehood.

Several such all-female companies were mustered into service for the occasion and received honorable discharges after the ceremony was over.

"We are always gratified to see a respectable and legitimate amusement come here and carry off our surplus dollars and dimes," wrote the editor of the Omaha *Weekly Herald* in 1866, expressing the desire for wholesome entertainment felt by townsmen everywhere west of the Missouri. And come they did—the entire gamut of show business, from song-and-dance men to Shakespearean actors—journeying from town to town to perform before foot-stamping, coin-tossing crowds.

Few hazards were too great to keep performers from their audience. In 1869, Dan Castello's Circus, the first to cross the country by rail, left the railroad at Cheyenne to make the rugged 85-mile overland trek to Denver. The trip took four days of slogging through bone-chilling rain, and cost the life of the troupe's baby elephant, but the big top played Denver.

The show-must-go-on tradition was put to a different test when popular actor Jack Langrishe and his actress wife were waylaid by desperadoes while traveling to Denver in 1862. The Langrishes escaped with their money and their lives when the bandits recognized them and sent them on their way—after a round of drinks.

Even hometown productions were subject to peril. In 1888, a glee club in Topeka, Kansas, staged a memorable performance of *H.M.S. Pinafore* on a boat anchored in a local creek *(left)*. The drama ended on a note befitting a Gilbert and Sullivan plot: during the last act the floating stage sprang a leak and sank, while all of the players were hauled to safety amidst wild cheering.

Members of a Topeka glee club take their stations on a boat-stage for a routine performance of the operetta *H.M.S. Pinafore.* The boat sank during a July Fourth show, but was raised and returned to service.

Entertainments–some gamy, some grand

The good life for a hardworking Western towns-man meant money in his pocket, a place to hang his hat, a square meal at day's end—and something more. Every man on the frontier knew by instinct that, while his body could be maintained in a condition of rawhide toughness on a diet of beans and bacon, his whole being needed nourishment of another kind: fodder for the spirit, and relaxation for the mind.

Happily, his need was filled by pleasurable diversion in myriad forms. Across the wide Missouri and over the mountains and plains came a kaleidoscopic variety of entertainers, braving rough travel conditions and sometimes even rougher audiences to offer the priceless commodity of amusement. The spectrum of offerings was colorful and vast, ranging from such lowly spectacles as animal fights to lofty lectures on temperance and aesthetics, from prostitution to Gilbert and Sullivan operettas, from crude boxing bouts to the sonorous rhetoric of Shakespeare presented by the most notable actors of the American stage. Spanning the gulf between lowly and lofty were marching bands, song-and-dance acts in saloons, tear-jerking melodramas, and just about every other escape from the workaday world ever imagined.

Local tastes and resources differed—sometimes drastically—but certain types of entertainment were popular and available virtually everywhere. Frontier towns early grew accustomed to itinerant organ-grinders, magicians, jugglers, and troupes of "Ethiopian" (i.e., blackface) minstrels who offered sentimental songs, dancing and rapid-fire badinage. But nothing in the world beyond the

Missouri was more eagerly welcomed than the circus.

Circuses were an old tradition in the West, dating back to Mexican times when shows based on European models came up from the south into California and the Southwest. Around the middle of the 19th Century circus troupes from the East began to reach settlements in the more accessible regions of Kansas and Nebraska. Except that they traveled in horse-drawn wagons over atrocious roads, these pioneering shows were not vastly different from their modern counterparts. They had wild animal menageries, clowns, acrobats, trapeze artists, tightrope walkers, brass bands, performing elephants and equestrians who could stand on horseback as they galloped around a center ring.

By the 1880s, when the railroads had eased the difficulties of transportation, the circus came into its own as the greatest show in the West. When John Robinson's Great World's Exposition—trumpeted as "Ten Big Shows in One"—rolled into Western communities, every childlike heart thrilled to its triumphant parade of "31 Chariots, 4 Steam Organs, 60 Cages, 8 Bands and 2 Calliopes." And the show itself offered one breathtaking sight after another, until the mind reeled: "2,500 Rare and Costly Animals," blared the program, "Lulu, the tattooed lady," "Zola, riding a velocipede over a single wire sixty feet above the heads of the audience," "Zenobia, hurled 200 feet by the ancient Roman war engine, the catapult," and "28 female Siberian roller skaters!"

Wondrous though these tent-roofed spectacles were, they received some stiff competition from another source of marvels: the patent-medicine man, a nearly ubiquitous presence in the West from the 1860s on. No hamlet or even farmhouse beyond the Missouri was too remote to be ignored by this breed of nomadic hustler with his miraculous nostrums—said to cure everything from rheumatism to falling hair—and his special brand

A music hall and opera house—bracketing a coyly marked keno parlor—enlivened Glendive, Montana, in the 1880s. Such grandly named premises often were no more than saloons that offered a few nightly acts.

Boxers square off for an impromptu bout in 1886 at the Bale of Hay saloon in Virginia City, Montana, before an audience of cardplayers and bar flies. There was every incentive to fight all out; at the end of the match a hat might be passed, and a rousing battle usually meant a good purse.

The Highland, Kansas, brass band, tooting away in the 1860s, had a counterpart in just about every Western town. These groups turned out for fairs, played concerts and sometimes serenaded honeymooners.

of entertainment to bring the suckers under his spell.

Sometimes his technique was sublimely uncomplicated. "Doc" Ray Black roamed the entire West with no impedimenta more cumbersome than a Bible, a human skull, a suitcase full of medicines and a set of imperishable vocal cords. After his ballyhoo had collected a crowd, Doc Black would launch into an interminable speech about salvation and the variety of ills that hastened mortals toward it. According to one observer, his listeners' backs would eventually "get to aching so bad they're certain they got lumbago or kidney troubles" —at which point he would sell them the contents of his suitcase to heal the condition. Tonics such as his did indeed induce a temporary feeling of well-being: their alcohol content ranged from 5 to 55 per cent.

Other patent-medicine men, operating on a somewhat grander level, employed sword swallowers, fire-eaters, tumblers, fortunetellers and minstrels to rally the crowd. The Big Sensation Medicine Company ranged across Nebraska with a tent show of imposing proportions. It carried a staff of 31, including a 12-piece band, and provided room under canvas for 1,500 potential pigeons. Its most persuasive come-on was free and supposedly painless dentistry, done on the spot. When a sufferer proffered his aching jaw for relief, a gargantuan husband-and-wife team would go to work on him while the band oompahed its most resounding march to drown out his howls of anguish.

A few of the medicine show companies were more conservative and actually provided entertainment that might be called pure. Every year, Hamlin's Wizard Oil Company of Chicago sent 20 to 30 sales teams West, each equipped not only with such wonder-working medicines as Hamlin's Wizard Oil, Blood Pills and Cough Balsam, but also with a dapper male quartet called the Lyceum Four. Each of the quartets sang in the nightly

show and, as a matter of company policy, voluntarily performed at church services and charity bazaars.

When no medicine shows were in town, many communities were able to turn to their own band for entertainment. Town bands existed all over the West; one such group—Dodge City's Cowboy Band—became nationally famous, as much for its unique appearance as for the quality of its music. Its 18 members were colorfully decked out in cowboy uniforms, including chaps, boots and spurs, sombreros, bandannas, cartridge belts and guns. The band's director used a six-shooter as a baton, explaining to a St. Louis reporter that he kept it loaded "to kill the first man who strikes a false note."

Rough humor appears to have been typical of Dodge City. Another brass band once visited Dodge and staged a parade down Bridge Street as a prelude to a concert in a local hall. Dodge City had a pair of tame buffalo, and they grew restless under the incessant bar-rage of brass and the thunder of the bass drum. A local jokester led the animals down the street and turned them loose behind the unsuspecting musicians—"with a big send off," reported merchant Bob Wright, "driving them right into the thickets of the band." The hapless musicians "not only threw away their instruments, but took to their heels, shouting and holloing, almost paralyzed with fear."

Among the entertainments that appealed to townsmen over a wide area and throughout the life span of the Old West were such bloody spectacles as dog fights, bear fights and badger fights—in fact, almost every conceivable sort of animal combat. In April 1861 a chamber of gore calling itself Sportman's Hall opened up in Leavenworth, Kansas, and offered "Rat killings, coon baiting, cock matches, and similar sports." It was an instant success. "The 'rat pit' establishment," noted the Leavenworth *Daily Times,* "attracts large crowds." ◉

A big-city gift to a Montana boomtown

A ballad sung in the gold fields of Montana during the 1860s described the origins of certain local entertainments with disarming simplicity: "First came the miners to work in the mine/Then came the ladies who lived on the line." Although every Montana town had a "line"—a row of saloons that frequently offered dancing, gambling and female favors along with the liquor—few of them could claim ladies so enterprising as Josephine Hensley, who arrived in Helena in 1867.

Josephine had already served a long apprenticeship in the rawer forms of nightlife in Chicago by the time she took her talents to Helena at age 23. In this overwhelmingly male center of the gold-mining area, she acquired a modest log building and set up a hurdy-gurdy house—or dance hall—the first in the territory to be run by a woman.

The descriptive term "hurdy-gurdy" was left over from California gold-rush days, when dance hall music was provided by a wheezy hand organ. Josephine—given the affectionate nickname "Chicago Joe" by her customers—actually featured somewhat more sophisticated musical fare, supplied by a three-piece orchestra that occupied a small platform off to one side of the premises. At the rear was a well-stocked bar where customers could buy 50-cent drinks for themselves and their dance partners. The girls, imported from Chicago, received a share of both the bar receipts and the two-bit charge that was levied for dances, and they could augment their income by making other arrangements on their own. A touch of class was lent to Josephine's establish-

The Duke

ment by the "Duke." a mysterious figure believed to be the black sheep of a titled British family, who helped to keep the patrons orderly and the dance hall staff disciplined.

Largely because her fresh-faced Chicago lasses (*overleaf*) outshone most frontier bawds, Josephine's place flourished. She moved into larger quarters in 1874, invested some of her growing capital in local real estate and formed alliances with influential figures in Helena's business and political worlds.

But in 1885, at the height of her reign as queen of the local underworld, Josephine's political friendships proved

unable to protect her from the prospect of ruination. That year, under pressure from farmers and other family men who had begun to pour into the territory, the Montana legislature ordered the prohibition of hurdy-gurdy houses, and shortly afterward Chicago Joe was arrested. Her trial became the first test of the new law.

Conviction seemed certain after the police testified that she employed "lewd women to dance with male visitors" and that her establishment was "a typical hurdy-gurdy place." Then Chicago Joe's attorney, a former territorial governor named I. D. McCutcheon, offered his defense. The statutes of Montana, he noted, provided that "all words be interpreted according to their common use." This meant, he said, that a hurdy-gurdy house literally must be a house utilizing a hurdy-gurdy—a definition that hardly fitted Chicago Joe's place, where the music was supplied by a piano, a violin and a cornet. Impressed by the counsel's pristine logic, the jury found her not guilty.

But Chicago Joe could read the handwriting on the wall. Within a year, she altered her premises to include a variety theater—complete with heavily curtained stalls on the second floor where her girls could entertain between the acts and sometimes in lieu of them. When the doors of her place closed at her death in 1899, a local paper pronounced a cool epitaph: "Her life in some respects was an eventful one." But Helenans accorded her a splendid funeral procession, and many of the city's leading citizens came to pay their last respects to this Montana pioneer.

CHICAGO JOE

BERTHA

LUCILLE

RUBY

ROXIE

LOUISE

BILLY

MONICA

LILLIE

ANNETTE

JACKIE

Fights between men were at least as popular. These bouts were usually held in saloons, and they were not so much exhibitions of skill as tests of endurance—for participants and spectators alike. An 1867 prize fight in Cheyenne between John Hardey and John Shannessy for a purse of $1,000 ran 126 rounds—each round lasting until one man or the other was knocked down, at which point the boxers rested for 30 seconds. The referee, no doubt exhausted himself, finally allowed that Hardey had won on a foul.

Judging from contemporary accounts, such contests rivaled the animal fights for gruesomeness. On the other hand, the accounts are so clearly exaggerated that it is often hard to discern where the fun leaves off and the facts begin. In 1877 the Dodge City *Times* covered a prize fight between Nelson Whitman and Red Hanley, who was billed as the "Red Bird from the South." The *Times* reporter took detailed notes on Hanley's demolition: "During the forty-second round Red Hanley implored Norton [the referee] to take Nelson off for a little while till he could have time to put his right eye back where it belonged, set his jawbone and have the ragged edge trimmed off his ears where they had been chewed the worst. This was against the rules of the ring so Norton declined, encouraging him to bear it as well as he could and squeal when he got enough. About the sixty-fifth round Red squealed unmistakably and Whitman was declared winner. Red retired from the ring in disgust."

Besides serving as an arena for boxing matches, the saloon was the setting for many other forms of Western entertainment—including, of course, the most basic of all: drinking. When it came to seeking solace at the end of a weary day, the first recourse of most men on the frontier was an alcoholic elixir—usually beer or bourbon, but often a homemade beverage bearing some such suggestive name as Tarantula Juice, Skull Bender or redeye. A few gulps of such a potent potable were sufficient, as experienced swiggers put it, to make a "hummingbird spit in a rattlesnake's eye" or to be "sure death at a thousand yards."

Testimony to the efficacy of these liniments for the soul runs through all of the Old West's history and legend. Of record, for example, was the peddler who, arriving in a tough Idaho gold camp in the 1860s and being fearful of thieves, fortified himself with two drinks of a local concoction called Sheepherder's Delight—made up of clear alcohol, plug tobacco and prune juice for color and taste, and strychnine to enhance the jolt. Thereafter he stole his own pack of wares and hid it so cunningly that he never found it again.

The Western saloon varied greatly with its place and time. In the agrarian communities of Kansas and Nebraska it was usually an unadorned and placid hangout where most customers drank moderately and only occasionally came to blows, and it didn't change much in the passing years. But in the tough, mostly male boomtowns, thriving on cattle or precious metals or an influx of railroad construction workers, the saloon was the core of the community. It rapidly developed solid creature comforts for drinking and gambling men, including one irresistible attraction—women, sometimes the only women in town.

Moved by the same spirit of adventure that had attracted men to the West, unattached females arrived in the boomtowns in a dead heat with the saloons. There, typically, they danced with the cowboys or the miners or railroad workers, sang a song or two if they were able, shilled drinks, enticed the men into small back rooms for amorous interludes, and split all fees with the proprietor.

More professional were the traveling taxi dancers: girls employed—often as a troupe—as dance partners for patrons who would pay a fee of 25 cents or so directly to the proprietor for each dance. Some dance hall girls—professionals and amateurs alike—were simply prostitutes, daring of dress and flexible of morals. But others could have passed muster at Sunday school, as was noted by entertainer Eddie Foy, a perceptive observer of the Western scene.

"Many of those girls," said Eddie in his autobiography, "were personally as straight as a deaconess. I knew some who were widows, some married ones with worthless or missing husbands, and not a few of them had children. The girls were merely hired entertainers. Their job was to dance with the men, talk to them, perhaps flirt with them a little bit and induce them to buy drinks—no more."

Many saloonkeepers, willing to try anything that would draw a crowd, added to their premises a stage for variety shows and short plays—a new entertainment twist that did not necessarily mean a discontinuation of dancing or prostitution. The early saloon-theaters tended to be modest. Denver's Apollo Hall, which opened in 1859 when the town was only a year old, occupied the drafty second floor of a white frame building; the saloon was on the street-level floor. The nearby gold camp of Georgia Gulch gave its first saloon-theater the grand name of Mountaineer Hall, and when it was completed in 1861, the *Miner's Record* described it as "elegantly fitted for the accommodation of all pleasure seekers and lovers of the drama." In fact, the new temple of the arts was less than a thing of beauty. It consisted mainly of two shelves—one large, one small —scooped out of the mountainside to serve as auditorium and stage. The most impressive appointment was a long bar with three bartenders who dispensed beer at 15 cents a glass and the hard stuff for two bits a shot. The performers' dressing rooms were screened off from the stage by bed sheets, and on opening night the box office was the crate in which the troupe's upright piano had arrived.

The players imported by the saloonkeepers were frequently as rough-hewn as the surroundings. Two favorites, for example, were a Mrs. De Granville, who did a strong-woman act and was billed as "the woman with the iron jaw," and Pearl Ardine, a jig dancer whose tour de force was to pick up money thrown to her and place it in her stocking without missing a beat.

In the late 1870s the manager of a saloon-theater in Silverton, Colorado, drew up a list of instructions for variety players—and in the process said a good deal about the performers as well as the atmosphere prevailing in his establishment. The document included these rules: "No kicking at the orchestra, especially from the stage; no fighting or quarreling will be allowed; drunkenness will subject the offender to a severe penalty or an immediate discharge; every lady will be required to dance on the floor after the show."

While these rude halls were played by many entertainers barely worthy of the name, they also attracted some professionals of very real talent. Mart Taylor, a durable stage celebrity in the Washoe silver-mining region of Nevada, was among them. Taylor, whose most impressive physical adornment was a nose of Cyrano de Bergerac proportions, was a man of many parts. He billed himself as the Taylor Family Troupe; but as his audiences discovered, he *was* the Taylor family, all of it —a solo artist whose boundless versatility filled an entire evening's bill of song, dance, rhyme and patter. In a typically "original, vastly comical, and highly poetical performance"—as his own program notes put it—he played all the turns: "*Opening Lines* by Mart Taylor, *Peep at the Mines (new poem)* by Taylor, *Taylor's Nose* by Mart Taylor, Esq., *My Sister* by Her Disconsolate Brother," and a half dozen others.

To this wholesale virtuosity—clearly a tough set of acts to follow—Taylor always appended his specialty, billed as "*A Local Song,* in which strictly complimentary mention will be made of the male citizens of this place." Taylor prepared for this particular act by briefing himself, as soon as he arrived in a new town, on the foibles, peccadilloes and follies of the community's leading citizens. Then, armed with a generous supply of foolscap, he would compose a lyric incorporating the gibes he had in mind and join the pages together to form an impressive scroll. As a finale to his show he would dramatically unroll his composition—often 20 feet or more in length—and sing it out while his victims writhed and their fellow townsmen roared.

Eddie Foy was another talented saloon performer who mined a lode of local material from his audiences, a practice which on at least one occasion backfired. Foy, a song-and-dance man who would become one of the greatest stage personalities of his time, made a road trip to Dodge City in 1878 as a brash youngster of 22. He was booked into the *Comique* ("Comikew," according to the cowpunchers)—a saloon, dance hall, gambling house and theater all in one. Having met such gunfighting citizens of Dodge as Wyatt Earp, Doc Holliday and Bat Masterson, and finding them unexpectedly mild-mannered and soft-spoken, Foy was emboldened to poke fun at his audience from the stage.

His mischievous sallies proved to be a tactical error. As Bob Wright recalled: "He dressed pretty loud and had a kind of Fifth Avenue swaggering strut, and made some distasteful jokes about the cowboys. This led to their capturing Foy by roping him, ducking him, in a friendly way, in a horse trough, riding him around on horseback, and taking other playful familiarities with him, just to show their friendship."

Foy, blessed with youthful resilience, took the hazing in good part. "I was determined to be nonchalant,"

Available to waltz, polka or mazurka for a fee, pinafored girls down 25-cent drinks with the patrons of a dance hall in Cripple Creek, Colorado, during the 1890s. As in other mostly male mining towns across the West, the dance hall business was so good that the girls worked all night long.

he later wrote, "and not let them see that they were worrying me, even if they broke my neck." His tormentors liked his spunkiness. As Wright remembered, "They played several pranks on him, which Foy took with such good grace that he thereby captured the cowboys completely. Nothing he could say or do offended them. They made a little god of him." He played Dodge that entire summer and went on to tour the vast Western circuit of boomtowns.

Sooner or later all but the most straitlaced Western communities got some form of saloon entertainment, but its nature was far from predictable. In Cheyenne, "Professor" James McDaniel—perhaps the most inventive of all barroom impresarios—installed a stereoscopic device in his Eddy Street saloon, opened just two months after the town was born. Patrons could look through the eyepieces of the stereoscope at three-dimensional images that McDaniel described as "choice pictures of art." A county judge, however, described them as "obscene and lascivious pictures" and fined McDaniel $25. The saloonkeeper happily paid up and continued to reap a bonanza from his visual edifications.

In the early days of his enterprise, McDaniel achieved another bizarre first in Cheyenne's entertainment history by hiring one A. C. Clark to walk back and forth on a platform above the bar for 60 hours without sleep, food or drink. Clark did his best and made it to the 50-hour mark, at which point a doctor ordered the pedestrian marathon halted.

Lest anyone in Cheyenne fail to realize that McDaniel's saloon was something special, the proprietor ran overwrought advertisements in the local papers to call attention to the place. "Ye Gods!" one ad exclaimed. "What nectar the professor concocts in those little china mugs. Better than the dew on a damsel's lips." A mixed drink more commonly known as a Tom and Jerry was described as containing whiskey plus "hen fruit, saccharine substance and lacteal fluid"—i.e., egg, sugar and milk.

McDaniel labeled his place a "museum-saloon," justifying this unique title not just with the so-called art of his stereoscope but with all manner of strange and wondrous exhibits that he added within a year of going into business. They included some stuffed animals, some live ones such as snakes and bears, a dwarf billed as the "Lilliputian Wonder," and "Miss Charlotte Temple, the great English giantess."

In 1869, still testing the outer limits of saloon showmanship, McDaniel made a trip back East and returned with a new stock of marvels. The Cheyenne *Leader* noted with awe that among them were the "world renowned Circassian [albino] girl who is but nineteen years of age and a beauty of the rarest description," as well as "American and Egyptian porcupines, wonderful white parrots, anacondas and monkeys and apes. No other town in the West can boast of an exhibition equal to the McDaniel's Museum."

Two months later McDaniel added a stage for the presentation of variety shows and legitimate productions. They were so enthusiastically attended that he went further; by the mid-1870s he was the proprietor of two playhouses in Cheyenne, in which he presented such attractions as *Richard III, Our American Cousin* and *Cinderella*.

Consummate showman that he was, McDaniel had not failed to recognize—and fulfill—the craving of his fellow townsmen for real drama. Legitimate theater was high on the list of entertainment priorities everywhere beyond the Missouri, no matter what the nature of the community. Nowhere was it more enthusiastically supported than in Salt Lake City, capital of the Mormon sect, where it got off to an early and auspicious start.

The Mormons, whose dictum was moderation in all things, were a special kind of audience. They did not permit the hard liquor, plug tobacco and rough humor of the boomtown saloon-theaters, but they did want entertainment; indeed they were led in this appetite by Brigham Young, President of the Mormon Church, who attached such importance to wholesome amusement that he decreed a state-sponsored program of theatrical fare. To those who questioned his stand, Young pointed out that Joseph Smith, founder of Mormonism, had said: "Men are that they might have joy."

Accordingly, in 1861 Young ordered the construction of an elaborate playhouse, its interior to be reminiscent of London's famous Drury Lane Theatre. By spring of the following year a local stock company was treading its boards with short plays and other light entertainments; and before another two years had passed, it was not uncommon for traveling actors from the East

to present full-length dramas at the Salt Lake City Theatre with supporting players drawn from the local company. Young himself had a private box in the theater, but he often preferred to sit in his rocking chair in the pit —under a chandelier he had made with his own hands —with two or three of his smallest children on his lap, rocking them while he enjoyed the action on the stage.

All fine theater was appreciated in the Mormon capital, but heavy drama was usually leavened with a comic afterpiece. *Othello* was followed by *Two Bonnycastles,* described in the playbill as a "laughable farce"; the gloom and violence of *Macbeth* was counteracted by a subsequent performance of a "screaming comedy" called *The Bridegroom, or Love in All Corners.* "If I had my way," said Brigham Young, "I would never have a

tragedy played on these boards. There is enough of tragedy in every-day life, and we ought to have amusement when we come here."

Few towns in the West had the resources and inspired leadership of Salt Lake City, and professional theater did not always come easily. In small farming communities, the theater had to battle its way up from lowly beginnings—usually amateur productions in town halls, court houses and even living rooms.

When the professionals arrived, they quickly discovered—as Eddie Foy did—that they might get into trouble if they failed to take local tastes and sensitivities into account. In the 1870s, residents of Grand Forks, Dakota Territory, were angered by a production of *Only a Farmer's Daughter* because it poked fun at a rural community; the local newspaper announced grimly that no more such offerings would be tolerated.

Contrariwise, those who heeded local custom fared well. In the winter of 1869-1870 the husband-and-wife team of James and Louisa (Louie) Lord left Chicago with a troupe of players and followed the railroads to the West. Kansas took an immediate liking to them. "Their plays," said the Paola *Western Spirit*, "have been well selected and have characters that contained much useful moral instruction, while contributing to the infinite amusement of those present." The Hays *Star-Sentinel* later hailed them for never letting "a low epithet or immoral idea" creep into their performances. Their standing in the state was further strengthened by a policy of recruiting new members of their company from the towns in which they played.

Journalist Frank Montgomery, who greatly admired the golden-tressed Louie but had seen more polished theater back East, followed the Lords' career with considerable interest while he was working on a number of small-town Kansas newspapers. The actors of the troupe, he commented in a column, "were brave beyond conception. They would storm the heights of a Shakespeare play with the same intrepidity with which they skirmished in the fields of simple melodrama. Desdemona, Portia, Topsy, Lady of Lyons were to Louie Lord such a small tax on her versatility that she passed from one to the other with no effort at all. To be sure, certain superelegant people might complain that her Lady Macbeth was attended with too much of the gay abandonment of Topsy, but to the great common people this was only an additional source of pleasure, for they could be sure always that they were seeing the star." As for Mr. Lord, Montgomery made it clear that the actor's most memorable dramatic achievement was the sleeping scene in *Rip Van Winkle*. But Montgomery's sweet-and-sour comments notwithstanding, the Lords became a Kansas institution, welcomed in all the cities and hamlets of the state.

Traveling players such as the Lords were the backbone of theater in the West, and they went everywhere. One of the best and most far-ranging companies was led by an actor-manager named Jack Langrishe. During the 1860s and 1870s, he took his polished professional troupe from Denver into the most remote gold camps of Colorado and Montana, playing wher-

ever there was anything remotely resembling a theater. Langrishe in his way, as the Lords in theirs, knew his audience, and he early became accustomed to having enthusiastic spectators or even local stagehands get into the act. One night his company put on Bulwer-Lytton's tearful drama *Alice, or The Mysteries* in a theater in Central City, Colorado. At a crucial point in the tangled web of plot, the leading man—playing to the hilt a bereaved and distraught character—gazed beseechingly toward heaven and cried, "Alice! Why don't you speak to me?" Down from the rafters came the gruff voice of a stage carpenter: "Damn it, Alice ain't up here!" The troupe was not disturbed by this unrehearsed piece of business; the audience loved it, and that was all that counted.

In 1882 another traveling troupe had a more discomfiting encounter with audience participation when they played *Uncle Tom's Cabin* at the Bird Cage Theatre in the rowdy silver-mining town of Tombstone, Arizona. Just as the drama's heroine, Eliza, was crossing an imaginary frozen river—with a real, carefully trained bloodhound baying at her heels—a drunken cowboy rose to her rescue and shot the dog down. Audience sympathies abruptly veered from Eliza to the dead dog, and the offender was beaten mercilessly until he himself was rescued and thrown in jail. The next day the remorseful cowboy offered not only money but his own horse in recompense for his canine victim.

Despite its peculiar hazards, the Western stage was host to many of the illustrious names of the 19th Century American theater, as well as some performers prominent on the British stage. Among the most distinguished of the entertainers to tread the Western boards were two of the formidable Booths; both Junius Brutus Booth Jr. and his equally renowned younger brother Edwin got in on the very ground floor of Western theater, performing for the forty-niners. Harry Chapman—member of a famous British acting family—was so versatile that, enacting a death scene on frontier stages, he could keel over and land with head and shoulders hidden in the orchestra pit, and there play his own funeral dirge on a violin while the rest of the "corpse" lay stiffly in view. Sarah Bernhardt, playing Camille in 1881, incurred the disapproval of critic Ed Howe of the Atchison, Kansas, *Globe*. She appeared onstage, he wrote, "walking as though she had but one joint in

THE PLAY.

"All the World's a Stage, and Men and Women Merely Players."

VOL. I.   TOPEKA, SATURDAY, MAR. 10, 1883.   NO. 48.

Crawford's Opera House,

Lester M. Crawford,

Proprietor .... and .... Manager

PROGRAME

THE

Fay Templeton

OPERA CO.,

In Gilbert and Sullivan's Æsthetic Comic Opera

PIRATES OF PENZANCE

Seth M. Crane	The Pirate King
Marie Celine	Mable
J. C. Armand	Frederick
Alice Vane	Ruth
Burton Adams	General Stanley
Mlle. Girard	Edith
Ed. Morris	The Sergent
Alice Baldwin	Kate
W. P. Guiberson	The Lieutenant
Cora Crane	Maude
Warren Ashley	Samuel
Irene Avenal	Mary
Joseph Le Brasse	The head of the police
Isabel Fuller	Jenny
A. J. Hennessey	Rudolph
Herminie Palaccia	Susette
Alex J. McKirdy	Boldwood
Carrie Wing	Eliza
Mr. Jamison	Wilberforce
Leon Du Ville	Jane
Clara Douglas	Selina

To-night "Olivette," by the same company.

her body, and no knees. Her first action was to shake hands with the stage company with arms as long and wiry as the tentacles of a devil fish. Her dress was of white and costly stuff, and cut so low in front that we expected every moment that she would step one of her legs through it."

No comet ever blazed a more coruscant pathway across the skies of the Old West than did Adah Isaacs Menken, who toured the region in the early 1860s, with particular success in the mining towns of Nevada. Adah was variously billed as a dramatic actress, a poetess, a danseuse, a male impersonator and an equestrienne. She was all these things and more; what made her so provocative was that she did what she did in a state of comparative undress. Moreover, she did it on a horse—"a wild, untamed stallion of Tartary," the show bills called him—which somehow made the act even more titillating.

"She is the most undressed actress now tolerated on the American stage," sniffed one reviewer, not saying how he had come into possession of this fact. Nothing but a "shape artist," scoffed Mark Twain, who happened to be working as a reporter on the *Territorial Enterprise* when Adah arrived in Virginia City, Nevada, in 1864. Neither comment seems to have dampened the enthusiasm of the silver miners, who turned up to see her in vast numbers.

Although she did appear in other melodramas, such as the racy *French Spy,* which was described as a "leg show," Adah's principal vehicle was an extravaganza called *Mazeppa,* in which she was required to impersonate Ivan Mazeppa, a Tartar prince. It was common for actresses to play men, a tradition that even permitted Sarah Bernhardt to take on the role of Hamlet; however this particular case of male impersonation called for a high degree of adaptability. To begin with, there were *"them limbs* and *that bust,"* as one drama critic described Adah's major talents (the italics are his). The difficulty was compounded by the role's frequent demand for scanty costuming. There was no way Adah could look like Ivan but, trouper that she was, she did not let this deter her.

The plot gave much scope for action. Ivan Mazeppa, with the poor judgment typical of 19th Century dramatic heroes, falls in love with the already-betrothed daughter of a Polish nobleman. As punishment for his effrontery, he is stripped naked and "condemned to be bound by hempen lashings to a fiery, untamed steed," which, given the quirt, gallops away to the hills. In the second act the horse reaches home in Tartary, where the king, indignant at the humiliation of his son, raises a punitive expedition and sets off for Poland. Equally indignant and eager to reclaim his Polish girl friend, Prince Ivan rides along in such haste for vengeance as to neglect a change of costume. Thus, at the finale, he reappears onstage still without—as the Virginia City *Union* explained with amazement—"even a shirt collar or a pair of spurs."

Adah met the challenge of a costume appropriate to the nude scene by wearing a single garment described by local fashion experts as either a maillot (tights) or a chiton (tunic); this was considered a cheat by some viewers and very risqué by others. One reviewer who definitely did not feel cheated was Mark Twain. Rising above his previous antipathy, he gave her an unqualified rave. She may have been a shape artist, but so far as

Adah Isaacs Menken strikes a pose of seductive languor in a melodrama entitled *Mazeppa*. Her sparsely clad figure packed boomtown theaters, prompting an overeager critic to state: "Prudery is obsolete now."

Twain was concerned she was a *great* shape artist, and he went to call on Adah in her room at the International Hotel to tell her so in person. There, according to his account, he read and appraised her poetry and she charmingly criticized his prose.

As the plot of Menken's chief dramatic vehicle indicates, most plays presented on Western stages were melodrama—gut-gripping, emotionally charged material with evocative titles like *The Widow's Victim, A Husband's Vengeance, Ten Nights in a Bar Room* and *The Romance of a Poor Young Man*. Surprisingly, however, the same audiences who feasted on these overdrawn and often bombastic plays also loved Shakespeare. There was scarcely a theatergoer west of the Missouri River, it seemed, who did not have some acquaintance with a good half dozen of the Bard's works, and the ranks of the townsmen held some true Shakespeare buffs—knowledgeable and demanding aficionados who came to know the lines as well as or better than the actors themselves. These frustrated hams

loved nothing so much as to attach themselves to visiting Shakespearean troupes and perform bit parts for the length of the engagement. Failing that, they could always roar out lines of dialogue or address pointed suggestions to the actors from the pit.

At least a part of the widespread interest in Shakespeare doubtless resulted from the great desire for cultural improvement that characterized Victorian America. In 1882 this vogue resulted in the arrival of one of the most unlikely visitors ever to grace the Old West: the British playwright-poet Oscar Wilde. He came on a lecture tour, a popular mode of entertainment during that period. Nineteenth Century Americans wanted to be informed on everything from Arctic exploration to the mysteries of zoology. They heard lectures from the likes of feminist Amelia Bloomer on practical attire for women, preacher Henry Ward Beecher on abolition, P. T. Barnum on temperance, and Victoria Woodhull on free love. Wilde's subject was Aestheticism—sim-

A circus parade wends its way down the muddy main street of Abilene, Kansas, before a crowd of gawkers in 1895. Townspeople eagerly awaited the visits of such Eastern-based extravaganzas, which crisscrossed the West each year in special trains that might contain as many as 65 cars.

ply, the science of the beautiful, or art for art's sake.

Wilde was known throughout the country as the inspiration for the languid leading character in Gilbert and Sullivan's comic opera *Patience,* which mercilessly satirized the cult of Aestheticism. Lecture audiences soon discovered that the real Oscar almost outshone his caricature in elegance and refinement. His knee breeches were hailed as the most ridiculous attire ever seen in America. His manner of speech—liberally sprinkled with such outlandish expressions as "too too" and "too utterly utter"—became a national laugh, as did his fondness for sunflowers, lilies and other blooms.

After he spoke in San Francisco a newspaper reported on the effect he had produced: "Sunflower buttonhole bouquets are worn; sunflower fans are fashionable in the theaters. The rage is too-too. If one asks another early in the afternoon what time it is, the reply is, 'two to two.' Young ladies when asked their age say they are not quite two-two; employers when vexed by their employees tell them to go to to. Articles of dress are labeled 'too exquisitely too too, too utterly utter, too sweetly sweet.' Even the locomotives have caught the fever and 'too-too.'"

Oscar did not mind being laughed at. For one thing, he found the tour highly satisfying from a financial viewpoint: all of his travel expenses were paid, and his income at times exceeded $1,000 a month. But the Western swing of the trip was not a notably aesthetic experience. The prairies, "so somber and lovely" at first sight, quickly lost their charm and he announced that they "reminded me of a piece of blotting paper." In Salt Lake City he lectured to a sellout crowd in a theater that had changed but little since Brigham Young had built it two decades before, except that the kerosene lighting had by now given way to gaslight. He later gave his decidedly unfavorable opinion of the city's chief attraction: "The Tabernacle has the shape of a soup-kettle and decorations suitable for a jail. It was the most purely dreadful building I ever saw."

As this apostle of wit and manners, beauty and taste, simplicity and grace made his way through the West, "aesthete" became a fighting epithet. In Denver, in anticipation of his arrival, one scarlet lady wore an enormous sunflower for a bonnet and was arrested for it. The charge lodged against her was not that of making sport of the effeminate Oscar but of creating a ribald dis-

turbance among her customers. Residents of Denver and the nearby mining town of Leadville—also on his itinerary—waited gleefully for the acid comments they were sure were about to drip from the pen of Eugene Field, the dramatic critic and managing editor of the Denver *Tribune.* He was known for his ability to strip away pretensions and cut people down to size (it was Field who once said of a Shakespearean actor: "He played the king as though he expected somebody else to play the ace").

To the astonishment of his readers, Field sternly admonished them to behave. "Oscar Wilde will be here next week, and there is no reason why he should not be well received. Any development of the rudeness which is called smartness will be a disgrace to Denver."

When Wilde stepped off the train he was observed to be somewhat bigger and shaggier than expected—more like the Irishman he had been born than the Londoner he had become. There was talk that, in spite of his predilection for too-utterly-utters and sunflowers, he had a crafty hand at cards and knew how to hold his liquor. Something about his Custer-style long hair, his impressive build and his good-natured acceptance of the raillery directed at him made his reception committee think he might not be such a fop after all.

But when he appeared on the Denver stage to speak on the niceties of interior decoration, he seemed every bit as ridiculous as had been rumored. The *Times* reporter described the Aesthete as making his way onstage with "a languid, dreamy sort of walk such as one would think a lovesick girl would have in wandering through a moonlit garden. A merry decorous laughter went up." However, Eugene Field did not laugh; reviewing the lecture afterward, he commented that Wilde had made "an excellently good impression."

In Leadville, site of the Matchless Silver Mine, Wilde "stumbled onto the stage with a stride more becoming a giant backwoodsman than an aesthete"—or so the Leadville *Herald* reporter claimed. Oscar opened his talk with an injunction to Leadville's miners to study the Gothic school of Pisan art; having thus won their somewhat baffled attention, he then launched into a discourse on gold. He urged his listeners to follow the example of Benvenuto Cellini in valuing gold not as wealth but as the raw material of fine art. Recounting events in this town later, he said that he read the min-

ers "passages from the autobiography of Benvenuto Cellini and they seemed much delighted. I was reproved by my hearers for not having brought him with me. I explained to them that he had been dead for some little time, which elicited the enquiry, 'Who shot him?'"

After this performance, Wilde was invited to do the town with a party of miners. Well-wishers in Denver had reminded him that Leadville was "the toughest as well as the richest city in the world and that every man carried a revolver"; and he had been warned that Leadville's hardboiled citizens were likely to shoot him or his traveling manager or both. Oscar—according to Oscar—had replied that "Nothing they could do to my traveling manager would intimidate me." Still, Wilde was a little nervous in Leadville, having heard reports that some sort of "reception" was awaiting him.

Touring Leadville's palaces of pleasure with his miner hosts after the lecture, Wilde watched dance hall girls and variety performers, listened politely to brass bands and piano players, gambled and consumed great quantities of liquor. Finally, at one or two o'clock in the morning, it was time for supper—which his companions casually suggested they have down in the Matchless Mine, as a suitable climax to the sight-seeing tour. Wilde found the idea charming, and soon he was climbing into an ore bucket in the No. 3 shaft to be lowered into the bowels of the mountain.

Down in the pit a reception committee of some dozen miners—co-conspirators with Oscar's hosts—awaited their victim, each armed with a bottle of whiskey. At the bottom of the shaft, Wilde chatted cheerfully with the miners and partook of each bottle as it made the rounds. By the end of the first round some of the miners were a trifle dizzy, but Wilde seemed merely refreshed. It was nearly dawn before Oscar was hauled back to the surface in the ore bucket, showing neither fatigue nor the effects of drink. He was later asked what had transpired below. "Having got into the heart of the mountain, I had supper," the Aesthete replied in tones of complete satisfaction, "the first course being whisky, the second whisky, and the third whisky."

When the miners recovered from Oscar's visit, they voted him an honorary life membership as one of them. And the Leadville *Herald,* heartily approving the way he played the gaming tables and held his liquor, paid the ultimate tribute: "There is no piousness in him."

A quick-change artiste gets top billing in this female-filled Cheyenne variety program.

A mixed bag of energetic troupers

For the amusement-starved townsman, the epitome of entertainment was to be found in the rollicking variety theater, which usually served as a saloon and gambling parlor as well. There, he could sit back and whoop it up while a procession of assorted crowd-pleasers—singers, dancers, musicians, comedians, acrobats, specialty performers—paraded across the tiny stage. A typical program, like the one reproduced at left, offered more than 20 acts calculated to satisfy every taste—from the maudlin to the bawdy—of a predominantly male patronage. After the show, the female performers were expected to join the audience for drinking and dancing.

The appetite for variety theater in the West was almost insatiable. Cheyenne supported at least 17 such halls in the late 1870s, when the population of the town was less than 4,000. Dodge City's Comique Theater, featuring such attractions as a one-legged tightrope walker and a high-kicking cancan line, repeated its shows all night long. Tombstone's Bird Cage Theatre also operated around the clock for the benefit of local miners, with the help of a resident troupe of dancing girls who doubled as barmaids between stage turns and were available for other favors in private cubicles on the perimeter of the main room.

The variety theater spawned scores of performers who traveled constantly from town to town. Occasionally they tarried long enough to pose for publicity photographs in local studios. The surviving portraits provide a rare look at the troupers—including some now nameless—who wowed them out West.

FLY'S GALLERY.   Tombstone, Ariz

The great Eddie Foy, a variety-circuit hit as a wisecracking song-and-dance man, had this portrait made in 1882 at a Tombstone studio near the O.K. Corral, scene of the West's most famous gunfight the year before.

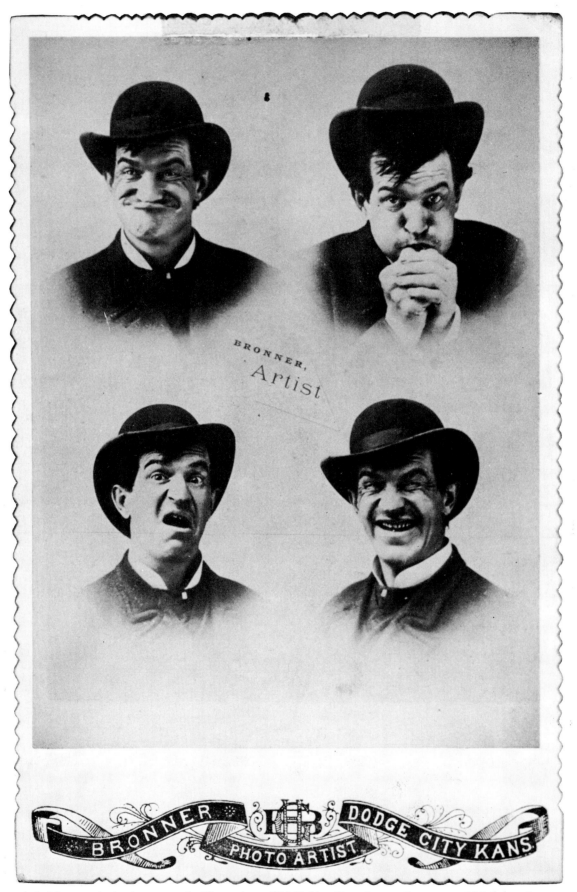

A facial contortionist, known to the West only as Old Rubber Face, immortalizes some of his impressions — probably used in a comedy routine involving the rube and the city slicker, stock characters of variety-theater humor.

A. E. RINEHART,

DENVER, COLO.

Annie Weigel, costumed for her role as Bronco Kate in the 1882 musical melodrama *Brittle Silver, or How a Mine and Maiden Were Lost and Won,* was a perky songstress who married co-star David Kelley, later a Denver millionaire.

A pair of unknown snake charmers exhibit their slippery charges for the benefit of a Wichita photographer. Like most such acts, they used fierce-looking but harmless bull snakes, which were frequently billed as deadly pythons or cobras.

R. G. Gardner, 1042 MAIN ST., KANSAS CITY.

Master Willie Sidney, headlined as the "Champion Light-Weight Roller Skater of the World" during his Dodge City engagement in 1885, stands tall on his wheels while proudly showing off an assortment of his medals and trophies.

Nast
1624 Curtis Street,
Denver, Colo.

A team of child acrobats, their names unrecorded, demonstrate their balancing prowess in a Denver studio. Youthful troupers were a common sight on the variety circuit; usually they traveled with parents who also were performers.

Fly's Gallery; Nola Forrest Tombstone, A. T.

Comedienne Nola Forrest, dolled up for an engagement at Tombstone's Bird Cage Theatre, was billed as "the people's choice" and so dazzled a local bookkeeper that he embezzled $800 to buy jewelry for her.

6 | A tenacious town that made it big

"A fine sketch of Denver," said the *Rocky Mountain News* of this 1874 watercolor, a collaborative effort by two French artists who were touring the West. Other local papers concurred. "Denver," glowed the *Times,* "is given the air of a metropolis."

And rightly so. At the time, Denver was well on its way to attaining the urban greatness that was every Western town's dream. Founded 16 years earlier, when gold was discovered along the South Platte River, the town had survived fire, flood and home-grown vi-olence to become a territorial capital boasting more than 14,197 citizens. Soon it would rank as the richest, raciest community between St. Louis and San Francisco.

Denver owed its enviable stature largely to the wealth of nearby mines. Yet any one of the other towns in the Pikes Peak region might well have waxed more prosperous on the proceeds of Rocky Mountain minerals but for Denver's outsized share of visionary businessmen, many of whom arrived with the first waves of gold seekers.

They built banks, railroads and smelt-ers; then, turning to the finer things in life, they outdid each other in erecting opulent mansions, opera houses and other tokens of culture. Most of them lived to hear no less a cosmopolite than world-ranging journalist Richard Harding Davis hail their city in 1892 as "a smaller New York in an encircling range of white-capped mountains." The mountains, in fact, were on just one side of the city—but Denverites forgave Davis his error, attributing it to a dazzlement that was only natural.

Denver sprawls beside Cherry Creek and the South Platte River *(foreground)*, with Pikes Peak *(center)* looming in the distance.

ROCKY MOUNTAIN NEWS.

THE MINES AND MINERS OF KANSAS AND NEBRASKA.

VOL. 1.   CHERRY CREEK, K. T., SATURDAY, APRIL 23 1859.   NO. 1.

THE OPENING OF JAPAN.

The present age is signalized by the
rapid succession of striking events in the
history of divine providence. Nations and
continents which had maintained a rigid
exclusiveness, or had been enveloped in
unbroken obscurity, are now brought into
friendly communication with the rest of
the world, and doors are opening for the
introduction of the gospel where before it has not been allowed a fo

Scarcely had the news of
of China to the commerce
ty of the Western worl
tidings came that a t
States, granting th
been ratified by
This empire
dred mile
being li
a pop
con
ar

CAPE HORN TO BE AVOIDED.—A company has been formed at New York to establish a line of powerful tug steamers to
tow vessels through the Straits of Magel-
lan, from ocean to ocean, thus obviating
the delay, dangers and difficulties of the
stormy passage around Cape Horn. It is
calculated that fully twenty days would be
saved to vessels passing through the straits,
compared with doubling the Cape.

ALPHABETICAL CONUNDRUMS.

Why is the letter A, like a meridian?
Because it is in the middle of day.
Why is the letter B, like
Because it makes
Why is th
Because

not
shoe
the U
not far
12,000,000
a value of 4,
men, and 32,5
these are made
largest shoe shop i
is Philadelphia. Ev
Massachusetts is a shoe
has 21¾ shoe houses, doing
$62,000,000 annually. New
55 houses in the trade, doing a bus
$16,000,000.

are ne
in use by goo
writer employed mo
proportion of the whole. Few seamen
use as many as 10,000 English words,
and ordinary people not more than 3,000.
In all Shakespeare there are not more
than 15,000 words, and in all Milton but
8,000. There were but 800 of the Egyptian hieroglyphics

THE WORLD WITHOUT A SAB-BATH.

What would it be? Labor without
   solace; probation with-
      without day.
         of the

d is similar to the prai-
haps a little more

v; in fact this
counties of
onsists of
lar, and
tes.
ving
he

COMMUNICATIONS RECEIVED BY THE NEBRASKA IMMIGRA-TION SOCIETY.

MONROE, N. T. Nov. 30, 1858.
DEAR SIR: The Circular of the Nebraska Immigration Society of which you
are Secretary has been received, and I
will cheerfully give any information that
at any and all times. In regard to

or is worth from $1 to 2

not banished. it will overthrow one hundred thousand men in England; for now it
is so common that he hath seen plough-
men take it at the plough."

according to the annu-
Commissioner of Indian
ented to Congress, there are
e limits of the United States
450,000 Indians, comprised in 175
oes, with 44 of which we have treaties.
There have been 393 treaties ratified
with them since the adoption of the Constitution, by which 581,163,188 acres of
land are acquired, and the entire cost of
fulfilling them will be about $19,816,311.
From the lands that have been sold, the
government has received a surplus of at
least $100,000,000 above the expense in-
curred for their acquisition, survey and
sale. The whole amount of trust funds
held on Indian account is $19,670,619.

YANKEE VISIT TO CARLYLE.

The Rev. Theodore Clapp, of New Or-
leans, in an autobiography, gives the following account of his introduction to the
"Great Censor of the Age," Thomas
Carlyle. Having received letters from
Mr. Bancroft, the American Ambassador
at the English Court, he called at the door
of his residence. A lady, with a very intelligent appearance, received the visitor.
"I have called this morning, he said, "to
see Mr. Carlyle; is he at home?" She
replied, "Mr. Carlyle has just entered
his study, and no gentleman can see him
this morning. If the Queen of England
should now call and request an interview,
it would not be granted." The Doctor
asked if she could oblige him by taking a written message to his study. An
affirmative answer was given, when he
wrote with a pencil the following words:
" Dear Sir: No gentleman, but a man
is at your door—a Unitarian, a Yankee,
a Democrat, and a radical, all the way
from the banks of the Mississippi; a care-
reader, and a great admirer of Mr.
yle, and begs the favor of a short in-
w, which must be granted now, or
this side of the grave."
etter of introduction was sent with
ne note. Directly the invitation
alk up sir; I shall be happy to

Dr. Clapp's account of this in-

ived in the most kind and
manner. The topics on
rsed were so numerous
room even to mention
quial style is plain, easy
d bears no resemblance
writings; has none of
monly called transcen-
rsation was protracted
ough I rose several
nsisted on my staying
at I acceeded to his
time was spent in
ries concerning the
States, the peculi-
ent, laws, manners,
ature, &c. He pro-
fied with the infor-
him in regard to

GROWERS.—The'
Guardian gives an
ion of seven head
I. G. Freeman,
of Chinese Sugar
compressed in the
g of the stalks are
racter; when thus
ito the stomach, it
lass, cutting, and in
g through the coats
ng violent inflama-
examination in this
the cause of death.
should be known to
nay be the means of
s destruction of their
danger, there is no-
y feeding the bagasse.
opical cane is consider-
for everything but fuel.
ribune.

emembar M'Donald Clark,
ll known in New York a
the "Mad Poet." During
of his life Clarke was made
Astor House table, and often-
rrant man of genius could be
ating its hospitalities when other
re closed on his fallen fortunes.
ne knew Clarke by sight; and one
ile quietly taking his dinner, two
erners, seating themselves,
ed a conversation intended for the
s of Clarke. One said:
"Well! I have now been in New York
two months, and have seen all I wish to
see with one exception."
"Ah" said the other, "what is that?"
"M'Donald Clarke, the great poet,"
responded No. 1, with strong emphasis.
Clarke raised his eyes slowly from his
plate, and seeing the attention of the table
was on him, stood up, placing his hand on
his heart, and bowing with great gravity
to the Southerners, said:
"I am M'Donald Clarke, the great
poet."
The Southerner started in mock surprise, gazed at him in silence for a few
moments, and then, amidst an audible titter of the company, drew from his pocket,
a quarter-dollar, and laying it before
Clarke, still looking at him without a smile.
Clarke raised the quarter in silence and
dignity, bestowed it in his pocket, drew
thence a shilling, which he deposited before the Southerner with these words:
"Children half price."
The titter changed to a roar, and the
Southerners were missing instanter.

What key is that that opens the gate of
misery? Whis-key.

Mile-high hopes for mile-high Denver

For the first dozen years after the town's shaky beginning in 1858, Denver's citizens swung between expectations of unlimited expansion and panic fear that everything would vanish overnight. In between, they carried on with the stubbornly optimistic faith that hard times only meant things had to get a lot better sooner or later. In the end, although an anomaly and an apparent violation of reason, Denver became a glowing jewel of the West, splendidly justifying its founders' highflying hopes.

Like many another Rocky Mountain burg, Denver grew from a dream of gold. But the first strike in the immediate vicinity, while not exactly an illusion, proved so thin that within a few months the hordes who had headed west in answer to the tocsin were plodding eastward again—threadbare, hungry and bitter. In 1859 another discovery, 30 miles from the infant town, made a few early and lucky comers rich, but likewise turned out to be a hardscrabble way for most of them to retrieve a few grains of gold with shovel, pan or sluice box. With almost nothing on which to pin their belief, a few obstinate holdouts clung to the view that one day Denver would strike it rich. They were right—not only gold but silver, and by the ton measure.

Meanwhile Denver had to do everything the hardest possible way. Even its location—alongside skinny Cherry Creek, where it flowed into the South Platte River in the foothills of the Front Range of the Rockies —seemed the unlikeliest of places for a town. Neither the creek nor the river held enough water to bear boats of any appreciable size—except in moments of devastating flood. The close-looming Rockies presented an awesome 14,000-foot barrier to travel farther west. Ferocious Indians in the area were ready to defend the land they owned under an 1851 treaty. Local weather was capricious—capable of blizzards as late as May, yet not to be trusted for enough moisture to grow a crop without irrigation. The most impressive natural vegetation around the town's mile-high location consisted of scraggly cottonwood trees and chokecherry shrubs, whose mouth-puckering fruit gave the creek its name.

Still, Denver might easily have burst into bloom in this inhospitable terrain much earlier than it did. Rumors of gold in the area—known as the Pikes Peak region, after its most conspicuous landmark—had long been circulating. Ever since the early years of the 19th Century, mountain men working in the beaver streams of the Rockies had known that the glittering stuff was there, but they were not interested in back-breaking labor with pick and shovel. The Indians, too, may have been aware that gold was present; white traders and trappers had heard a legend that the Arapahos, a powerful local tribe, once fired gold bullets during a battle against the Pawnees.

Ironically, the first responsible report of a strike in the Pikes Peak region came from a group of Indians who originated in Georgia and had taken up the white man's life. In 1850 a band of Cherokees panned a little dust from Cherry Creek while on their way to goldrush California. Eight years later, when California's promise of easy wealth had faded and the Indian argonauts had returned to the East, their tales of gold in the foothills of the Rockies began to find interested listeners, among them a Georgian named William Green Russell, who had a Cherokee wife. Russell led a party of gold hunters to Cherry Creek in June 1858. They

The first issue of the *Rocky Mountain News* makes a backdrop for this photograph of publisher William Byers and his wife, Elizabeth. At the time, Denver was made up of two antagonistic settlements on either side of Cherry Creek, whose name Byers chose for a compromise dateline.

Boisterous citizens of two-year-old Denver—not quite past its log-cabin days—paid Mademoiselle Carolista, the star of a variety troupe, $170 to dance along a tightrope above Larimer Street. As the *Rocky Mountain News* reported, the spectators roundly applauded "the brave little woman."

found little gold on the creek itself but made a more encouraging strike a few miles away on the Platte.

Meanwhile a party from Lawrence, Kansas Territory, having spent the summer unsuccessfully prospecting about 65 miles to the south, along the flanks of Pikes Peak, got word of Russell's success and came to pitch camp beside the Platte in September. Having no luck there, they moved to a grove of cottonwoods on the east bank of Cherry Creek and named their campsite St. Charles. Shortly afterward, a few members of the Russell party pitched winter camp on the west bank of the creek and named the spot Auraria, after a town back in Georgia. In happy anticipation of a future rush of miners and settlers, each outfit organized itself into a town company and marked off boundaries, streets and building lots. That the Indians rightfully owned the land bothered them not a whit. They assumed that the federal government would rectify the situation and, indeed, the Indians' title was summarily extinguished by Congress five years later.

As the winter of 1858 approached, a few hardy souls dug in to protect their newly platted communities. The rest started home, talking up the advantages of the towns to everybody they met and showing off their smidgens of gold—which rumor quickly exaggerated into sackfuls. A rush to Cherry Creek began. James W. Denver, governor of Kansas Territory, recalling that Cherry Creek lay within the boundaries of the territory's Arapahoe County, sent out a set of county administrators. On the trail, this group encountered yet another band of town boomers, led by William Larimer. A teetotaling major general of the Pennsylvania militia, Larimer had been an engineer, banker, merchant, freighter and a member of the Nebraska legislature. He had recently added to these career credits the founding of La Platte City, Nebraska, and he considered town promotion to be his real calling.

After barely surviving a blizzard, Larimer reached Cherry Creek in the waning days of November, too late to stake a claim to a desirable townsite—but not too late to jump someone else's claim. A few Georgians were holding the fort in Auraria, and Larimer wisely acknowledged their precedence. However, St. Charles possessed just one half-finished cabin and one resident, Charles Nichols. Judiciously combining persuasion with threats of violence, Larimer got Nichols to throw in his lot with him and they named their new creation "Denver City." This attempt to win the goodwill of Governor Denver misfired, since the Governor had been replaced in office by the time Larimer arrived.

From the first, the matching pair of hamlets bestriding Cherry Creek were hotly competitive, and at least one murder grew out of the endless disputes over their relative merits. But a shared plight—a shortage of supplies as winter halted traffic from the East—drew them together for a time. Relief came appropriately on Christmas Eve, 1858, when trader Richens Wootton arrived from Taos, New Mexico Territory, with his Mexican wife and a wagonload of goods. He had intended to trade with the Indians for furs, but he could not resist the pleas, cash and gold of Cherry Creek's 300 residents. "Uncle Dick," as he came to be known before the dawn of Christmas Day, had brought along two barrels of Taos Lightning, a devastating potion distilled from wheat in New Mexican pueblos. In the spirit of the season, Uncle Dick broached his barrels and invited all comers without charge.

The party went on well into Christmas Day, mostly outdoors—since, up to that time, there were hardly any indoors available—before a roaring bonfire. A dance got started and was stoically witnessed by a band of Arapahos. Larimer and others made speeches, and everybody drank to the future or to any other pretext for raising the tin cup. "Although there are good things come up from Old Taos," went one rather ungratefully phrased toast, "its whiskey ain't worth three skips of a louse." The toasts naturally included wistful testaments to absent feminine beauty, which was a little unfair to Wootton's wife and the other females who were in attendance. A. O. McGrew, who had pushed his belongings west in a wheelbarrow, recited a bit of doggerel that was to become the community's credo:

Speculation is the fashion even at this early stage,
And corner lots and big hotels appear to be the rage.
The emigration's bound to come, and to greet them
  we will try
Big pig, little pig, root, hog, or die.

McGrew was right on target. While Denverites and Aurarians whiled away the winter drinking and gambling—to the distress of General Larimer, a fastidious man in such matters—stories of fabulous gold strikes spread and grew throughout the East. In 1859 alone an estimated 100,000 people left home for the Pikes Peak region, and enough of them settled around Cherry Creek to send the hopes of boosters soaring. Not all of the newcomers were the sort of citizens that Larimer had hoped to attract. At about this time a pioneer brothel keeper who called himself Pink S. wrote a letter to a girl back in Ohio, saying, "The Emigration is comeing in continually and our town is building almost like a 2d sanfrancisco. It allready contains any amt. of Liquor and gambling saloons, and *one or two H Hs or assignation houses* are to be supplied from Mexico and St. Louis & Cincin. . . ."

The first Cherry Creek business not primarily concerned with entertainment was a general store, opened under the sign of Blake & Williams. The next—a visionary project, considering the local shortage of basics —was the watchmaking shop and jewelry store of J. D. Ramage. Kinna & Nye opened a hardware store.

The early businessmen included a remarkable number of dynamic entrepreneurs who would leave an indelible imprint on Denver. John Edward Good, a farm boy from French Alsace, arrived in an ox wagon loaded with merchandise to stock another general store; his enterprise got off to a ragged start, however, when his clerk decamped with the entire inventory, while Good was back East buying more wares. Luther Kountze, one of five brothers of an Omaha banking family, opened a modest gold assay office in a rear room of a new drugstore operated by Walter Cheesman. Henry Brown, a contractor from St. Joseph, Missouri, opened a carpentry business and took up a 160-acre homestead on high ground southeast of the confluence of Cherry Creek and the South Platte. Two decades later, the land would be the royal roost of the silver kings.

Early on, the townspeople of Cherry Creek acquired a properly extraordinary voice—a bragging, scolding, counseling, jealous, defensive, aggressive and thoroughly irrepressible newspaper: the *Rocky Mountain News,* edited and published by William Newton Byers. Like Denver itself, William Byers was an anomaly, a man seemingly shaped by his background for anything but journalism. As an Iowa farm boy he had received little formal education, and most of that was in the rudiments of surveying. In his early 20s he took the Oregon Trail west and helped to survey the Oregon-Washington boundary before joining the California gold rush. Returning home via Panama, he served with Larimer in the Nebraska legislature, got admitted to the bar, dabbled in real estate and was busy dealing in lots in Omaha when he heard of the Pikes Peak gold strike.

New towns needed newspapers, and Byers saw no compelling reason why he should not seize the opportunity. He promptly rounded up a used hand press and a couple of helpers, but his start for Pikes Peak was slightly delayed when he got mixed up in a street corner scuffle one night in Omaha. Spotting some Irish toughs beating up a German immigrant, Byers rushed to the rescue — and had his right collarbone shattered by a shotgun blast. While recuperating, he showed his somewhat cavalier regard for previous experience in any field of endeavor by writing one of the 15 guidebooks to the Pikes Peak region that were published in and around Kansas Territory in 1859.

Byers and his helpers finally embarked for Pikes Peak on March 8, 1859, traveling in two wagons. One vehicle carried the press, a supply of paper, the type and the ponderous smooth-surfaced stone slabs on which type was laid out in the perfectly flat arrays required for printing. The heavy-laden wagon bogged down in Omaha mud before the expedition had proceeded a quarter of a mile. It had to be unloaded before the oxen could work it free — a useful trial for what proved to be a frequent occurrence.

Byers was not quite sure where he was going, hence he decided to name his publication for the Rocky Mountains rather than some specific town. However he did have some idea of what he was going to say when he got there. Aboard the press wagon was type already set into two timeless pages of his presumptive paper. Along with features about such newly historic events as the opening of Japan by Commodore Perry in 1854, the preset pages included a number of advertisements. The forethoughted publisher had sold space to Omaha merchants and wholesalers who hoped to receive orders for supplies from men in the new diggings. Even with this advance revenue in hand, however, the *News* threatened to begin as a shoestring venture. Thus, Byers was only too happy to accept a financial windfall of $300 in cash invested by Dr. A.F. Peck, an Omaha surgeon who had found the money in the pockets of

a hanged horsethief whose cadaver he had dissected.

Arriving at Denver-Auraria on April 17, 1859, Byers was plunged at once into a scene seething with life and purpose. Along both banks of Cherry Creek stood neat rows of log cabins and rough clapboard buildings. Bullwhackers, Indians, miners and mountain men mingled in the wide, straight dirt streets. Prospectors eager to file their mining claims packed the office of the town recorder. Merchants priced their wares in pinches of gold dust, the customary medium of exchange, and after business hours swept up tidy sums in spilled dust from their dirt floors.

Byers immediately rented an attic above a saloon and installed his printing plant. Then he scoured the town for local copy to be added to the two pages he had brought from Omaha. Speed was essential; a man named Jack Merrick was at that very moment setting type for the maiden issue of another paper, the *Cherry Creek Pioneer,* in a cabin on the other bank. Denverites and Aurarians bet heavily on which sheet would hit the street first. Fascinated townsfolk jammed the cramped loft where Byers and his men labored. The weather did not help Byers either. A wet snow had been falling for two days, and the attic's unshingled roof leaked such gouts of water that a tarpaulin had to be rigged over the press.

Around dawn of April 23, Byers emerged from under the wet tarpaulin and began handing out smudgy copies of the first issue of the first volume. Jack Merrick had lost the race by 20 minutes. Whether depressed by his defeat or impressed by the quality of the *News,* he soon sold his press and type to Byers for $25 worth of flour and bacon, then went off prospecting.

Since there had been so little time for legwork, the first six-page issue of the *News* displayed certain weaknesses. A report of a murder and a subsequent hanging, for instance, omitted the names of both the murderer and the victim. But Byers really spread himself in his editorials. "With our hat in our hand and our best bow," he wrote with fleeting humility, "we make our first appearance upon the stage in the capacity of Editor." He lauded the region's gold-mining prospects and predicted that "a new State will be organized west of Kansas and Nebraska ere this year is out with a hundred thousand inhabitants." His estimate was 17 years off but was exactly in tune with his audience. From then on the *News*

Awed Denverites view a grim morning-after scene wrought by floodwaters of Cherry Creek on May 19, 1864. Gone without a trace was the *Rocky Mountain News* building, but one month later the paper's publisher, William Byers, purchased the premises — complete with a flagpole *(center left)* — of an unscathed rival sheet, the *Commonwealth*.

plugged unceasingly for the creation of a Colorado Territory as a first step toward statehood.

Byers and the *News* had arrived just in time to bear witness to one of Denver's bitterest disappointments. The editor would quickly show himself to be his town's staunchest defender in adversity.

During that spring of 1859, gold seekers and their families had poured into the area in ox wagons, buggies or on foot. Few of them were properly equipped to hunt gold, either by training or by the provisions they carried, and many were destitute and ill. As one woman wrote home to a sister: "I was taken with the ague before we left Columbus—had to be carried on a bed six days—sleeping on the ground—rained in on us—cold —snowed—besides almost starved to death—oh the suffering I have seen—men starving—one man that went out—went eight days without eating anything but a snake he killed and cooked. . . ." Daniel Blue of Illinois watched his two brothers die of starvation after their pack horse ran off with their supplies. Blue himself was found by a wandering Arapaho hunter half-crazed, eating the body of one of his brothers.

Little but disillusionment awaited the sorry pilgrims; the diggings along Cherry Creek and the South Platte proved sparse even for veteran miners and downright barren for the neophytes. Before the summer was out, the rush became a two-way traffic as embittered argonauts headed back East with cries of "hoax" and "humbug" on their lips. An outward-bound traveler wrote, "We met one thousand people in one day coming back and hundreds of beggars—hundreds starved to death—22 in one spot laid by the road side dead."

Citizens of Auraria and Denver City, still positive that limitless mineral wealth lay somewhere in the area, looked upon the retreating throngs as little better than traitors. When Eastern and Midwestern newspapers reported the disenchantment of the returning argonauts, an angry *News* thundered back: "We are informed that the returning emigration are giving currency to many absurd and false stories . . . such for instance as that 'Denver and Auraria were burned—that all the old citizens were hung or fled the country—that a vigilance committee guarded the road, and whenever an emigrant wagon approached it was surrounded and plundered, the cattle or horses killed and the owners compelled to flee for their lives'—all of which are so monstrously and outrageously false we wonder that people can be found who will believe them."

As the reverse tide continued and outside press reports grew more negative, the *News* coined a scornful new word for the emigrants—Gobacks: "We hope that this class are all again safely at home with their Pa's and Ma's, their sweethearts, or 'Nancy and the babies. . . .' Farewell to these 'gobacks.' They have had their day and soon will be forgotten." With sublime confidence, Byers predicted: "Before six months have passed away hundreds who are wending their way toward the states will be again as anxious as ever before to visit the Gold mines of the South Platte."

Byers was uncannily correct. As Denver-Auraria reached its nadir of adversity, its golden dream condemned as a cruel sham by half the nation, dramatic reprieve was at hand. During that same spring of 1859, an impoverished prospector named John H. Gregory had been panning a bare living out of a rocky declivity above Clear Creek about 30 miles west of Denver. Suddenly in May, his claim began to yield pans worth $4 each, and within a week he had taken out $972. "By God," he cried, "now my wife can be a lady!" A miner named George Jackson made a similar strike nearby. Within two weeks Gregory Gulch had 30,000 miners. Gobacks turned west again in droves.

Despite the very real riches in Gregory Gulch, Denver might have been forced to endure further slurs from the nation's press but for the testimony of that great friend of the West, Horace Greeley, editor of the vastly influential *New York Tribune*. Greeley arrived in June. "As to gold," he wrote in a dispatch sent off to the *Tribune* by stagecoach, "Denver is crazy. She has been low in the valley of humiliation and is suddenly exalted to the summit of glory. The stories of days' works, and rich leads that have been told to me today—by grave, intelligent men—are absolutely bewildering. I do not discredit them but I shall state nothing at second hand. I have come to lay my hands on the naked indisputable facts."

The miners, enchanted to receive so famous a visitor, gave Greeley an exhaustive tour of Gregory Gulch and even let him pan $4 worth of gold from a crevice. (To ensure that every moment of his trip was pleasurable, the crevice had been carefully salted.) Greeley sent to the *Tribune* an enthusiastic report of "gold vis-

Horses that pulled a tram uphill and then freeloaded on the way down were familiar sights after Denver got its first streetcar system in 1871. For effect, this photographer improved the incline by tilting his camera.

HENRY BROWN

DAVID MOFFAT

NATHANIEL HILL

WALTER CHEESMAN

JOHN EVANS

DENNIS SHEEDY

Six kings of the West's queen city

HENRY BROWN, an Ohio orphan bound out to a farmer at seven, made himself a master carpenter, ran sawmills on the Pacific Coast and became one of Denver's big rich by turning a 160-acre homestead into a posh suburb. Then he sank his fortune into building a luxury hotel—and sank back to poverty in the 1893 depression.

DAVID MOFFAT, an Omaha real-estate millionaire at 20 and bankrupt at 21, rebounded to forge a financial empire whose loans kept Denver banks afloat during the 1893 panic. He went broke building a Denver-to-Salt Lake City rail line, with a seven-mile-long tunnel through the Rockies that was finished after his death.

NATHANIEL HILL, a chemist, took 72 tons of Colorado ore to Europe, studied smelters there and returned in 1868 with an efficient process for refining gold, silver and copper. To consolidate his and Colorado's gains, he won election to the U.S. Senate and helped persuade the Treasury of the wisdom of heavy silver purchases.

WALTER CHEESMAN, a druggist whose canny land purchases turned him into Colorado's biggest taxpayer, organized a firm in 1869 to pipe potable water to Denver when wells began to run dry. He was reviled for enriching himself by his water monopoly but admired for pumping some of the profits into philanthropy.

JOHN EVANS, a physician with entrepreneurial flair, made medical history back in Illinois by proving that cholera is infectious—and also made a fortune in real estate. Appointed the second territorial governor of Colorado in 1862, he went on to help create Denver's electrical streetcar system, a university and three railroads.

DENNIS SHEEDY made a false start in Denver as a store clerk in 1864, left for Montana and returned 17 years later with fabulous riches from a cattle empire covering eight states. He poured his wealth into stores, smelters and railroads, built a mansion, then added a stable for his cow ponies that was almost as large.

ible to the naked eye." He showed a copy of this testament to Byers. Realizing that such a verdict was as valuable to Denver as gold itself, Byers repeated it in the first extra edition of the *News* he ever put out. As often happened in those days of uncertain transportation, the *News* was short of newsprint, but Byers printed his extra on brown wrapping paper, adding editorially that it "will give satisfaction to the public mind and at once set to rest the cry of 'humbug.' Let us then rejoice that a brighter day is dawning."

There would still be Gobacks, the luckless, the improvident, the unskilled and fainthearted. And the placer deposits of free gold soon petered out. But hard-rock miners then moved in to hack more fortunes out of gold-bearing quartz. In September 1859, oxen slowly hauled up to Gregory Gulch the components of the region's first stamp mill. This steam-powered device, freighted across the plains in pieces over a period of about a month, consisted of four 400-pound iron hammers that fell like pile-drivers onto chunks of quartz, pulverizing the ore so that the gold could be extracted by chemical treatment. Two more stamp mills arrived by December and many more followed, greatly increasing the production of gold.

Denver-Auraria shared in the wealth from the outlying gold camps. A roving *New York Tribune* reporter, Henry Villard, noted early in 1860 that, between them, the two towns embraced 29 wholesale and retail houses, 15 hotels and boardinghouses, 23 bars, 11 restaurants, 2 schools, 2 theaters and 1 newspaper—the *News.* The towns had lawyers, doctors, shoemakers, tailors and barbers. Town lots had jumped in price from tens to hundreds of dollars. Everybody was making money. One busy merchant hung on the door of his establishment a sign saying, "Gone to bury my wife—back in half an hour."

To men like Byers it seemed increasingly absurd to split the dividends of the boom between two towns. On April 3, 1860, largely at the editorial urging of the *News,* Denver City and Auraria voted to merge and took the combined name of Denver. Social groups began to form. A Masonic Lodge and a Ladies Union Aid Society were organized. Celebrations took on a more decorous tone—in some quarters at least. Noting that 22 women attended a gala in July 1860, the *News* was moved to say: "Social parties are getting

very frequent and in fashionable dress, sumptuous fare and unexceptionable character, they cannot be excelled away down East."

A strong financial community began to coalesce. It gained one of its brightest stars when David Moffat arrived from Omaha on St. Patrick's Day in 1860 and opened a book and stationery store. He would stay, he announced, long enough to make $75,000, then he intended to retire to New York. But the book business did so well that Moffat went on to found the First National Bank of Denver and forgot all about New York. Meanwhile Luther Kountze expanded his little backroom gold office into a bank and later joined his brother Charles in founding the Colorado National Bank. On another financial front, the risk and the high cost of freighting gold dust (5 per cent of the shipment's value) persuaded E. H. Gruber and two brothers named Clark to put up a solid two-story brick structure beside Cherry Creek and fill it with minting machinery (coining money was not yet a federal monopoly). Their first $10 gold eagle, struck on July 20, 1860, was presented to Editor Byers.

For his part, Byers was already showing vision as an empire-builder. Denver, he foresaw, would need to outlast the precious minerals of the mountains. Throughout his 19 years on the *News* he was to advocate irrigation and other enlightened agricultural techniques for the area. In 1860 he homesteaded 160 acres of land near Denver and later established an experimental farm, testing irrigation and crop rotation, and trying out strains of fruit, nut trees and grape vines. Not many people took his advice in the early days, but those who did found it good. One, Rufus Clark, though unrelated to the gold-minting Clarks, became a millionaire anyway by producing an always-scanty commodity—food. In 1860, when Denver's population had reached 4,126, he sold his potato crop to Denverites and outlying miners for $30,000.

But as always in Denver's history, prosperity was a prologue to peril. Passions that would soon erupt into civil war farther east were astir in Denver, too—and they took a particularly violent form in the youthful town. The Southern cause, in addition to enjoying support among respectable Denverites, attracted a stratum of no-good hellions, locally known as "bummers." They hung out at gambler Charley Harrison's Criterion Sa-

210

loon. Harrison was a bald but luxuriantly bearded Southerner, affable and deadly. He made himself the crime-boss of Denver, using strong-arm tactics to acquire control of saloons, brothels and—some said—even the municipal government. By mid-1860, Editor Byers had concluded that Harrison and his renegades posed a grave threat to the future of the town.

Denver was accustomed to violence. In the first two years of the *News's* existence, the paper reported 15 murders, two duels and several differences of opinion in which a man had an ear or nose bitten off. Byers felt strongly about crime, horrendous or minor, and he was not at all reluctant to wield the *News* as the weapon of his displeasure, no matter how trifling might be the infraction. "Some unprincipled scamp, not having the fear of the devil," he wrote on one occasion, "has got into the habit of milking our cow. That same fellow or his brother has been stealing our wood from the door after it was cut and prepared for the stove."

The editor's readiness to denounce sin precipitated himself, and ultimately Denver, into a dangerous confrontation. On July 12, 1860, Harrison casually killed a blacksmith who attempted to join him in a poker game. "We are led to think that the act was wanton and unprovoked, in short a cold blooded murder if called by its right name," wrote an outraged Byers in the *News.* He went on to warn that "the terrors that swept over the fields of California at various times, and first purified its society, will be reenacted here with terrible results to outlaws and villains."

Sure enough, within three days a secret 100-man Denver Committee of Safety was organized; the vigilante group certainly included some of Denver's leading citizens, and Byers himself was probably among them. The bummers, rightly interpreting Byers' editorial as a threat, struck first. Four well-liquored rogues invaded the *News* office, seized Byers at the make-up stones and marched him off to the Criterion, where he was offered to Harrison as a blood sacrifice. Harrison was known to boast that in his lifetime he intended to kill 12 white men in order "to have a jury of my peers in hell," but he was not yet ready for a direct confrontation with the vigilantes. He led the editor to a back door, advising him to prepare the *News* for siege.

When the same four bummers showed up to destroy the *News* office that afternoon, Byers had his shotgun handy. He wounded one bummer, and the town marshal —running to join the fray—finished the man off. The other three surrendered and were run out of town by the vigilantes, but the conflict continued. The bummers tried to burn down the *News* office. Byers, fearing an attack in the streets, took to wearing disguises on his way to and from work.

Soon the Committee of Safety retaliated. Masked men broke into the houses of suspected malefactors, wrung testimony from reluctant witnesses and hanged or shot a number of suspected murderers and thieves. "We never hanged on circumstantial evidence," Byers said in later years. "I have known a great many such executions but I don't believe one was ever unjust. But when proved guilty they were always hanged. There was no getting out of it."

Although crime declined, sectional tensions continued. After Fort Sumter fell and the government in Washington began pulling out some of the West's already scanty troops, Denver seethed with rumors that Harrison's hoodlums were buying up all available firearms at fancy prices and planning to loot the town.

Fueling their secessionist sentiments at the Criterion bar one night, the bummers issued from the saloon in a body and ran up a Confederate flag on the roof of a store next door. A crowd of furious Unionists soon gathered and faced off against the gang of bellicose bummers. Pistols were cocked and knives drawn, but when a man named Sam Logan scaled the roof and tore down the banner, the bummers sullenly retreated indoors.

Into this explosive atmosphere on the afternoon of May 27, 1861, rolled a stagecoach bearing the first governor of the newly formed Colorado Territory—organized by Congress just three months earlier. President Lincoln had sent out Governor William Gilpin with orders to hold Colorado for the Union at all costs. The Pennsylvania aristocrat seemed a thoroughly impressive choice. Then 47, he had been educated abroad, spent a year at West Point, edited a newspaper, became an attorney, crossed the continent in an 1843 expedition led by the explorer John Charles Frémont, fought in the war against Mexico and battled Indians along the Santa Fe Trail.

Gilpin was warmly greeted by a Denver that had yet to mark its third birthday, but along its treeless, dusty streets crowded nearly $700,000 worth of construction: saloons, stores, hotels, theaters and the offices of doctors, lawyers and claim agents. To protect this eminently vigorous town and the gold-rich mountains behind it, Gilpin had persuaded the federal government to let him issue a proclamation calling for the organization of a regiment: the First Colorado Volunteers.

Since Colorado had neither treasury nor taxes, Gilpin confidently issued—and Denver merchants confidently accepted—$375,000 worth of drafts on the U.S. Treasury to buy uniforms, arms and supplies for the regiment. As for payments to his troops, the Governor made do with repeated and extravagant promises of future emolument.

"Gilpin's Pet Lambs," as the Volunteers were called by the bummers and anyone else anxious to start a fight, took to their mission with enthusiasm, but no major engagements were fought in the city. However, a brief skirmish in a pleasure house operated by one of Harrison's lady friends considerably disheveled the place and its inmates. A few nights later, gunfire erupted from the Criterion, wounding two soldiers of the Volunteers —one in an ankle and the other through the lobe of an ear. Thereupon the Volunteers sounded a bugle, wheeled a cannon up to the Criterion and aimed it at the front door. The men inside wisely surrendered, and Harrison himself was chained up for the night. The next day he was fined $5,000 and run out of town—an event that signaled the conclusion of the Civil War within Denver's city limits.

The bearded saloonkeeper came to a macabre end. In May 1874, while serving as a Confederate guerrilla in southeast Kansas, he was bushwhacked by a party of pro-Union Osage Indians, who considered his bald pate a poor trophy and scalped his chin instead.

Meanwhile serious work for the Volunteers lay ahead. In February 1862, Confederate General Henry H. Sibley marched northwest out of San Antonio with a force of 3,700 Texans. In the grand strategy of the Confederacy, Sibley's campaign had the ultimate goal of separating all of the West from the Union and the immediate objective of capturing Denver and all of Colorado's mines—which, the year before, had produced $7 million in gold.

The Volunteers, at this point, had 1,342 men under arms. Being unpaid, these hard-rock miners customarily lived off the country and were as undisciplined

a military unit as has ever been assembled. But they were willing—even eager—to fight. Sibley moved up the Rio Grande, easily scattering such forces as opposed him. He took one Union fort after another, with only token resistance from the garrisons, until he reached the town of Las Vegas in northeastern New Mexico, only 330 miles from Denver. Governor Gilpin then sent the Volunteers under Denver's Colonel John Slough to intercept the Confederates.

Approaching the enemy position, Slough issued orders to Major John Chivington, a six-foot five-inch black-bearded Methodist evangelist. Slough gave Chivington 400 mounted men and sent him out to raid and reconnoiter but—by all means—to avoid a general engagement. However, Chivington, a bloodthirsty swashbuckler out to make a name for himself, unexpectedly met some Texan scouts in a narrow defile called Glorieta Pass and scattered them in a savage charge. The next day, while Slough engaged Sibley's main body, Chivington led a flank attack, burned the Confederate supply train and bayoneted 500 horses and mules. Sibley withdrew to Texas.

Byers proudly printed in the *News* a letter from a captured Texan to his wife. "They were regular demons," the Southerner wrote of the Colorado Volunteers. "Had it not been for the devils from Pikes Peak, this country would have been ours." Denver later referred to Chivington's disobedient charge as the "Gettysburg of the West."

If the rout of the Texans had indeed saved the West, the Union government turned out to be strangely ungrateful, refusing to make good Gilpin's drafts. Denver merchants, facing heavy losses, demanded the recall of the Governor. Byers led the attack; he had favored William Larimer for the post, and besides, Gilpin had given the *News* only a portion of the territorial government's printing contracts. Bowing to Denver's sentiments, President Lincoln replaced Gilpin with John Evans, a wealthy and renowned physician who had founded Northwestern University, and, more to the point, helped form the Republican party in Illinois. His first words on alighting from the stagecoach in Denver on May 16, 1862, were appropriate: "Let us pray." Denver was indeed in dire straits. Now that Gilpin's scrip had been declared worthless, the town sank into a business de-

Grandiose schemes of the dashing Baron von Richthofen

One of the most flamboyant, and least successful, of Denver's movers and shakers was a Prussian aristocrat with a penchant for business schemes as unlikely as his name: Baron Walter von Richthofen. The freewheeling nobleman arrived in Denver in the late 1870s and soon began throwing his funds and charm into bizarre ventures. The first of these far-fetched schemes involved the promotion of a new suburb south of Denver, in an area so remote that even the lure of an elegant beer garden and a special railroad link failed to produce customers.

Undaunted, the baron tried again east of Denver with a suburb called Montclair. His new gimmick was to sell huge lots to newly rich Denverites as sites for posh country estates. The baron trundled his prospects to

The visionary von Richthofen

Montclair in horse-drawn carriages, and he galloped alongside with a pack of wolfhounds to provide a taste of country living. The sales clincher was often a peek at the baron's own im-

posing castle *(below)*, whose grounds were stocked with bears and wild canaries. This edifice took two years to build, but the busy baron and his English wife lived there only three years before departing for London and a stylish Regent Street residence.

Von Richthofen hastened back to Denver during the financial panic of 1893 and attempted to recoup his large losses by promoting the most ambitious of his projects—a luxurious health spa with mineral water piped in from a well 20 miles away. But when he died in 1898, his vision of a "Colorado Carlsbad" died with him. It remained for his nephew Manfred, the Red Baron of World War I, to immortalize the von Richthofen name with the deadly aerial flourishes of his "Flying Circus" in the French skies.

Rising in crenelated splendor, the baron's stone castle — centerpiece of his Montclair suburb — displayed his family coat of arms on the central tower.

The Windsor Hotel, opened in 1880 by silver baron H. A. W. Tabor, reflected Denver's affluence. It boasted 176 marble mantelpieces and a taproom whose floor was studded with 3,000 silver dollars.

pression that lasted all through the winter of 1862-63.

Even worse was to come with the spring of 1863. Denver in that unseasonably dry and windy spring was a firetrap. Most homes and many business structures were built of logs or pitch-laden sawed pine, with roofs of tinder-like split shakes. The fire department that the city fathers had organized the previous summer was, for all practical purposes, still a piece of paper, and therefore as vulnerable to flame as the town itself. And burn Denver did. At 3 a.m. on April 19 a drunk kicked over the stove in the Cherokee Hotel. That night, the

wind was boxing the compass in unpredictable gusts, and for three hours the flames leaped about in capricious fury. By dawn the center of town was a black ruin. The *News* escaped, but half its advertisers were gone. Total damage was reckoned at $350,000.

Denver set about rebuilding with entirely characteristic enterprise. Small boys scratched through the ruins, salvaging and straightening nails; doing so, a kid with pluck and luck could make a princely $10 a day. The ashes were still smoldering when Luther Kountze reopened the Colorado National behind a pine-board

214

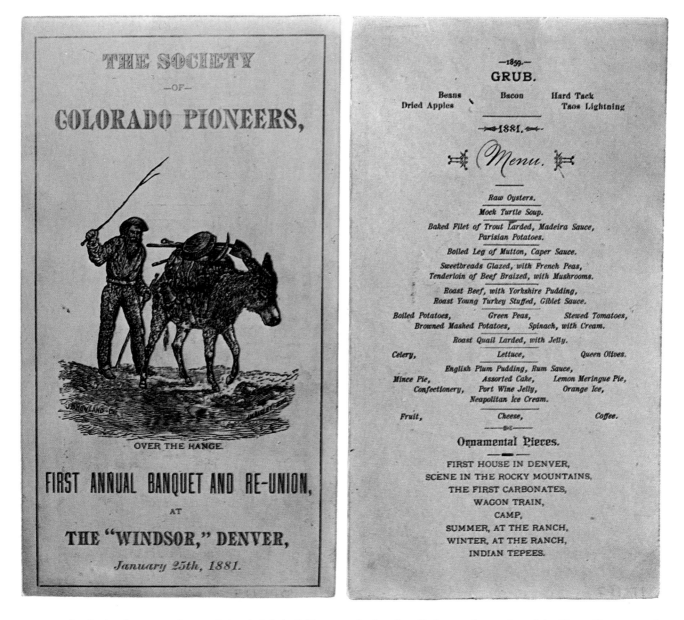

counter in the back room of a surviving brick building. Within months, the town was back on its feet.

But the hard luck was not yet ended. Having been tested by fire, the town would next undergo trial by water. Most of the major business buildings were located either on the banks of Cherry Creek or—as in the case of the *News*—actually in its bed, raised up on pilings. Byers had picked the spot as diplomatically neutral ground between the antipathetic villages of Auraria and Denver City. The spring of 1864 was as wet as 1863's had been dry. Week after week black thun-

derheads roiled over the peaks of the Front Range, and repetitious downpours saturated the hills around Cherry Creek's headwaters. Denver got only a few showers and was not alarmed, but just after midnight on May 20 a wall of water came thundering down the creek.

The star reporter for the *News,* a longiloquent Irishman known as "Professor" Goldrick, later described the event in a few thousand colorfully chosen words. "Precipitately and in paroxysms," he wrote in part, "the tempestuous torrent swept along, now twenty feet in the channel's bed, and bridging bank to bank with billows high as hills piled upon hills—with broken buildings, tables, bed-steads, baggage, boulders, mammoth trees, leviathan logs and human beings buffeting with the billowcrests." As for the *News* building, "down it sank, with its union flag staff, into the maelstrom." Gone forever was the 3,000-pound steam-powered press Byers had imported from the East. Byers himself was at home, but he escaped only narrowly. His friend Chivington came by in a rowboat and rescued the entire Byers family from the roof of their house.

When it was all over, Denver counted up a million dollars in damages and estimated the death toll at 20. Any other town might have concluded that the gods were out to wipe it off the map for good. But Denver, starting with the Gobacks, had never been able to think of hardship as anything worse than a temporary inconvenience on the road to destiny.

Among the first enterprises to recover was the *News*. By now Byers was no shoestring operator but a prosperous publisher busy investing in mining claims in partnership with Governor Evans. He bought out a rival paper, the *Commonwealth*—founded in Denver two years before—and took over its plant, which had escaped the flood. The first issue of the revivified *News* noted that the "spasmodic stream called Cherry Creek is now entirely dry, and its broad channel's sands are once more glistening in the sunshine."

The flood had knocked almost as big a hole through Denver as had the fire. It swept away a sawmill, a church, stores and their stocks and account books. The city hall and all its records vanished—a loss which subsequently led to endless confusion over land titles. The owners of some valuable real estate, however, were beyond worrying about titles. "Lost on the night of the 19th," read an ad in one of Denver's surviving newspapers, "four first class building lots. Anyone who will overtake and return them will be liberally rewarded."

Within months Denver had largely repaired the ravages of the deluge. But by then the town had other concerns. A spate of Indian raids in the vicinity impaired travel to the town and dampened commerce almost as effectively as the flood. To deal with this fresh problem, Governor Evans pleaded with the government in Washington to send troops or let him raise volunteers to fight the warriors. By the time he got permission and had put Chivington in command of 750 volunteers, the

Indians had calmed down and abandoned the warpath in return for government handouts of beef.

Chivington and other warhawks claimed the Indians were merely settling down for the winter and would return to the attack in the spring. Furthermore, Chivington, backed by Byers, was seeking election as a Territorial delegate to Congress, and he yearned for glory. At dawn on November 29, 1864, his 750 troops attacked a band of some 700 Cheyennes under Chief Black Kettle, encamped at Sand Creek, 130 miles southeast of Denver. During the morning, the volunteers slaughtered 163 Cheyennes, mostly women and children, scalped most of their victims and even sliced off the breasts of slain squaws.

The massacre split Denver. Byers hailed it as "among the brilliant feats of arms in Indian warfare." But Sand Creek roused such horror among other Denverites and throughout the U.S. that Evans was forced to resign, and Chivington was finished politically. The bloody deed also enraged surviving Cheyennes and other Indians in the Territory, and several tribes united in a final effort to drive out the treacherous white men. Sand Creek brought on three more years of raids and reprisals before the Indians were finally subdued.

Denver soon had to endure another grievous injury to her pride as well as her prosperity. When the rails of the Union Pacific and Kansas Pacific railroads first began tracing their iron paths outward from the Missouri River, Denverites assumed that, almost as a matter of divine right, a main line would come through town. As early as 1862, Evans, backed by a public subscription and the support of such community leaders as Byers and banker David Moffat, had sent Territorial Surveyor General F. A. Case to check the feasibility of a rail route across the great wall of the Rockies. Case traced a course up toward the summit of the continental massif, more or less following an existing stage road through Berthoud Pass—named for the Army explorer who had discovered it. But the surveyor reported discouragingly that even with a three-mile tunnel at the 11,316-foot summit of the pass, the grade would be pretty steep. Undismayed, Evans and Byers continued to maintain that the route, though admittedly a little precipitous in some segments, was clearly the only practicable passage through the Rockies—if one began with the assumption that the main line had to go through Denver.

General Grenville Dodge, the U.P.'s master engineer, agreed that it would be a good thing to bring the rails through Denver. But the Berthoud route looked a lot steeper to him than it did to Byers. Dodge opted for Bridger's Pass in Wyoming, a longer but flatter passage. Denver was plunged into angry despair. Some fainthearts, agreeing with U.P. Vice-President Thomas C. Durant that Denver was "too dead to bury," moved their businesses to the new town of Cheyenne, 100 miles north of Denver on the U.P. main line.

Such a thought never entered the minds of leaders like Byers, Evans and Moffat. Soon they were busily organizing the Denver Pacific Railroad Company (most such ventures almost automatically included "Pacific" in their titles) to build a branch line between Denver and Cheyenne. The *News* waxed ecstatic over the flatness of the proposed branch. "It is said to be better than the road from St. Petersburg to Moscow, so famous for its natural grade line," the editor wrote.

In a series of intricate financial and political deals, the new company won a grant of federal lands along its right of way, raised some $500,000 by floating a bond issue in Denver and environs, and acquired additional capital from the U.P. by agreeing to let the U.P. use the Denver Pacific tracks. With the funds from these various sources, Evans and his friends got the road built, profiting handsomely in the process. Evans was to have driven in a final spike of solid silver to symbolize the road's completion, but the workman entrusted with the spike pawned it to buy whiskey. An iron spike wrapped in silver paper was hastily substituted.

On June 22, 1870, the first Denver Pacific train rolled into town drawn by a U.P. locomotive rechristened the "D. H. Moffat" for the occasion. The Kansas Pacific, meanwhile, had been persuaded that Denver was worthy of inclusion in its rail empire, and the K.P. tracks arrived just 52 days later.

But having two railroads in hand merely whetted the appetites of Denver's businessmen, who now launched on their own into an orgy of railroad-building. Evans, who had become something of a one-man conglomerate in business while still governor, began construction of the narrow-gauge Denver, South Park & Pacific. A network of rail lines pushed west and south from Denver, squeezing through narrow canyons and switchbacking dizzily up nearly vertical slopes.

These new roads were pursuing a glittering new prize: silver. By the late 1860s the shine had gone off the gold-mining bonanza, leaving only the prospect of tremendous labor for moderate rewards. But just as Denver began to worry about this latest cloud on the horizon, its luck turned again. In 1869, Colorado miners had discovered that a lot of the heavy rock they had been impatiently thrusting aside in their search for gold was high-grade silver ore that could be economically reduced by new smelting processes developed in Europe. It was Pikes Peak all over again—swarms of prospectors, instant mining towns, a voracious demand for supplies. Railroads made fortunes hauling ore out of the mining camps and hauling in everything from blasting powder to pianos. And more was to come.

In 1875 prospector Will Stevens and his partner, a Michigan metallurgist named Alvinus B. Wood, were running a fairly profitable gold placer operation near the semiabandoned mining town of Oro City, about 75 miles southwest of Denver. Wood became curious about the heavy black sand that regularly clogged their sluices. He assayed it and found it to be carbonate of lead carrying 40 ounces of silver to the ton. The discovery set off the biggest bonanza yet. Leadville, as Oro City was renamed, became the center of a stupendously rich mining area.

The richest single silver strike was made three years later when Horace Austin Warner Tabor, a struggling storekeeper in Oro City, staked a pair of German prospectors to $17 worth of tools, grub and whiskey for a one-third share in whatever they found. While seeking a continuation of an already high-yielding vein owned by somebody else, the Germans discovered what became the lucrative Little Pittsburgh mine. After buying out his original partners, Tabor developed the mine in combine with David Moffat. The Little Pittsburgh brought Tabor $1.5 million—the start of a fortune that eventually amounted to almost $9 million.

In the centennial year of 1876—to the immense, if long deferred satisfaction of its boosters—Colorado finally achieved statehood. Nevertheless, 1876 had its personal drawbacks for Byers. One spring afternoon a gray-eyed, demurely pretty milliner and divorcée named

As a final touch to a spectacular gift, H. A. W. Tabor presented programs in embroidered silk covers to the 1,500 opening-night patrons at the $750,000 opera house that he gave to Denver in 1881.

INAUGURAL ENTERTAINMENT.

TABOR GRAND OPERA HOUSE.

DENVER, - COLORADO.

Wm. H. Bush, - - - Manager.
N. Mc Tabor, - - - Treasurer.

MONDAY EVENING, SEPT. 5, 1881.

Hattie E. Sancomb waylaid him in the street within a block of his home and began popping away at him with a pearl-handled revolver. The noise attracted, among others, the editor's wife, Elizabeth. She scrambled into the family buggy, which was standing hitched in the driveway, and scooped up Byers before Mrs. Sancomb had scored a single hit. Soon all Denver knew that Byers had tried to break off an affair with Mrs. Sancomb, and thereby aroused her fit of pique.

Prior to this contretemps, Byers had within his grasp the Republican nomination for governor—which was then tantamount to election. But Denver had by now become too proper to tolerate sex scandals. The Republicans dropped Byers for John Routt, a Civil War hero whom President Ulysses S. Grant had named as Colorado's last territorial governor and who was duly elected as the state's first governor.

As the capital of the Union's newest and by all odds most glamorous state, Denver simply exploded. The city's population—a mere 4,759 in 1870—ballooned to 35,629 in 1880. In the next decade, it tripled to 106,713, a third of the state's total head count. All of the state's new prosperity from mines, railroads, farms and ranches funneled through Denver. Discoveries of coal and iron launched a steel industry, and new foundries and machine shops turned Denver overnight into an industrial giant, the world's manufacturing center of mining machinery.

Denver's magnates did their best to live up to their huge incomes. By the score they moved to the high ground southeast of town, where contractor Henry Brown had subdivided his old homestead in the serene confidence that Denver would grow out to meet him. He had even set aside land to be donated for a state capitol. In a pun on Henry's high hopes for his high land, Denverites had named the area Brown's Bluff.

The joke wore thin as the mansions of the new big rich proliferated. These monuments to wealth featured a dozen different modes of architecture and certain stylistic mixtures that had never been seen anywhere else on earth. John Edward Good, who had begun as the proprietor of a general store and became a beer baron, built a $250,000 stone castle fashioned to remind him, pleasantly, of his impoverished youth in Alsace. David Moffat's four-story house, with huge white marble columns reaching to the roof line, had a $25,000 stained-glass window sent from Tiffany's of London.

Nor did the magnates let down their standards within their edifices. Gold-plated doorknobs were common, but the fittings in Roger Woodbury's bathrooms were of solid silver from his own mines. Steel king Lawrence Phipps had a pipe organ built into his house. Real-estate mogul Charles Kitteredge could seat 100 people at his dining table. Silver miner Sam Hallett's wife, Julia, could write letters at a desk once owned by Marie Antoinette. In the reception room of financier Crawford Hill's mansion hung what had been Thomas Jefferson's chandelier, and cement potentate Charles Boettcher had one that had been in the White House.

By this time, Denver had already managed to take care of the fundamental amenities. A city gasworks went into operation in January 1871, supplying fuel for Denver's first street lights, which were tended by a corps of lamplighters who thriftily turned them all off on moonlit nights. In the following year came the first water mains, supplied from deep artesian wells. The year 1879 saw the first telephones, dubbed "galvanic muttering machines" by subscribers trying to make head or tail of the sounds that came over the wires.

Electric lights began to succeed gas in 1880. Byers, who had sold the *News* two years earlier but remained a force in Denver life, became postmaster and inaugurated free home-delivery of mail. In 1885, Byers and Evans, inspired by the invention of a professor at the five-year-old University of Denver, set out to replace the city's horsecars with electric streetcars which would draw power from charged cables buried in the streets. The system was an instant popular success — until the first rainy day. Water seeping down to the cables carried current to the hoofs of the harnessed horses and mules. The shocks were nonfatal but nevertheless set off some lively stampedes.

Denver's first real place of public recreation, Riverfront Park, grew out of the persistent delusion — stridently abetted by Byers and the *News* — that the South Platte River was navigable. A few adventurers like the roving reporter Henry M. Stanley — later famous for his discovery of Dr. Livingstone — had successfully traversed the stream, but most attempts to float anything down it to the Missouri River and the Gulf came to grief. Nevertheless, in the ebullient 1880s, a syndicate of promoters built a sidewheel steamer to carry ex-

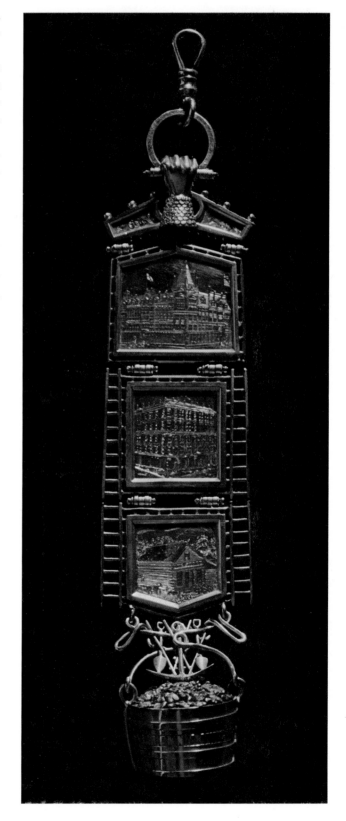

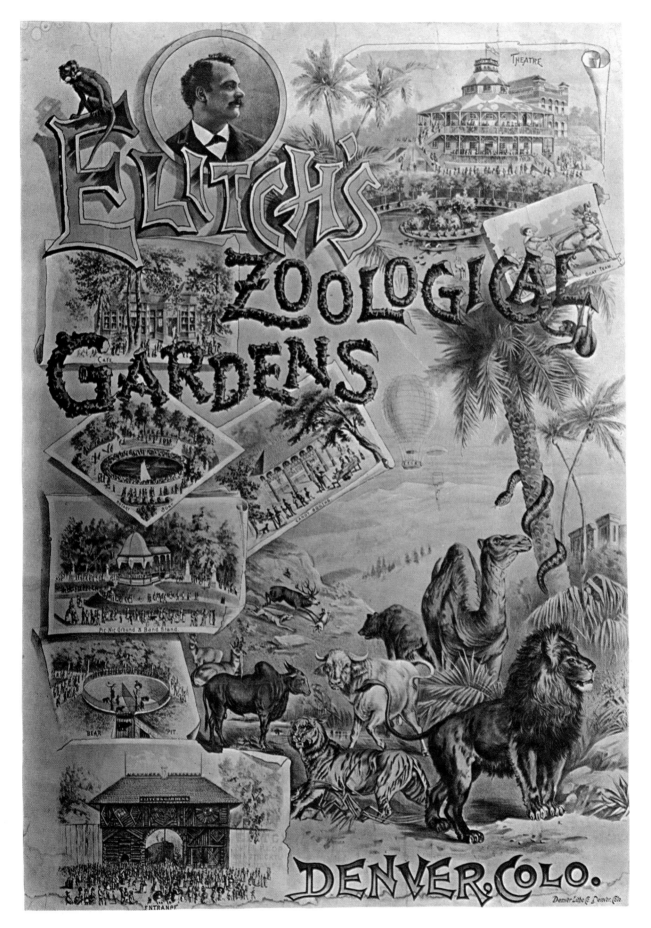

cursionists along the Platte. When the vessel predictably ran aground, the syndicate dammed the river, creating a lake about the length of four city blocks, and relaunched the sidewheeler as a showboat christened *H.M.S. Pinafore.*

To the accompaniment of band music the boat continued to take families on picnic excursions around its little basin. Riverfront Park grew up on the banks of this inland sea, and there Denver staged fairs, rodeos, horse races, fireworks displays and baseball games. When the Denver nine played at home, sometimes against teams as prestigious as the Chicago White Stockings, its supporters encouraged the players by stationing kegs of beer at each base and offering $20 gold pieces for stolen bases and home runs.

More parks followed. The famous Elitch's Gardens was too decorous to permit public dancing but delighted Denver's young with roller coasters, carousels and a zoo, while diverting their elders with concerts, light opera and classical plays.

The increasingly luxurious tastes of Denver's increasingly well-heeled citizens were reflected in the five-story, 300-room Windsor Hotel. By the time it was completed in 1880, it had cost its builders $350,000. Its operating company, headed by silver millionaire H. A. W. Tabor, spent another $200,000 installing three elevators and a ballroom floor slung on cables to provide built-in bounce. All rooms had gaslights and most had fireplaces. For cleanliness addicts there were 60 bathtubs, a swimming pool and steam baths with areas denoted as "sudsatorium, frigidorium and lavatorium." In its main dining room, gourmets could order frogs legs, guava jelly, prairie chicken, trout, venison and bear meat, then top it all off with ice cream from the Windsor's steam-powered freezer.

None of the silver barons who came down from the hills to pitch camp on Brown's Bluff made more of a splash than Tabor. Having lavished on Leadville a fire department, a street railway, an opera house and a telephone company, he sought a larger stage. He moved to Denver, got elected lieutenant governor, and in 1881 presented Denver with a splendiferous opera house full of carved Japanese cherrywood, mammoth French mirrors, embroidered silk draperies that cost $50 a yard, tapestries copied from the palace at Fontainebleau, a crystal chandelier aglow with a hundred gas jets, one

wall that was mostly stained glass and a prominently displayed picture of Shakespeare. The picture lasted only until someone told Tabor who the subject was. "Hell!" said Tabor, "what did Shakespeare ever do for Denver? Put a picture of me up there." They did.

On opening night Tabor's box was empty. He was estranged from the wife who had sustained him through 26 hardscrabble years and he had taken up—but not publicly—with a cute blue-eyed blonde divorcée, Mrs. Elizabeth McCourt Doe, known as "Baby Doe." Eventually Tabor induced his wife to divorce him and in 1883 went off to Washington with Baby Doe to fill out the last 30 days of the term of Senator Henry Teller, who had resigned to become Secretary of the Interior in President Chester A. Arthur's cabinet. Tabor disrupted the business of the Senate by constantly inviting fellow solons out for a drink. After a sumptuous wedding ceremony in Washington, he and Baby Doe returned to Denver and settled into a suite at the Windsor, where Tabor had one room permanently reserved for his poker games. He occasionally amused his bride by flinging handfuls of silver dollars from the balcony to scrambling crowds below.

Baby Doe longed for respectable domesticity, so Tabor bought a mansion and filled its lawns with cast-iron animals and a few alabaster nudes that shocked the ultra-proper. Silver kings, politicians, sporting men of all sorts, actors and concert artists attended Baby Doe's parties, but she never quite made the grade with Denver high society. In one generation, Denver had reached the stage of putting on airs, and to the high-nosed, whist-playing matrons of Brown's Bluff, later known as "The Sacred 36," Baby Doe was beyond the pale.

And so, at first, was Margaret "Molly" Tobin Brown, who had come to Leadville from Hannibal, Missouri. At 19, short on literacy but long on Irish charm, she married James Joseph "Leadville Johnny" Brown—no relation to Henry, creator of the elite suburb. Brown discovered gold in the previously silver-rich Little Jonny mine and set her up in a stately Brown's Bluff palace that was guarded by imported Egyptian sphinxes and stone lions. But it took more than a big house and trips to Paris, from which she returned hautely coutured and speaking French, to break into Denver society. It took the *Titanic.* On that ship when it began to sink after striking an iceberg on its

221

maiden voyage, she grabbed command of a lifeboat, pistol in hand to enforce the women-and-children-first tradition, and kept up the spirits of her fellow castaways by singing hymns. After that, even Brown's Bluff noticed the Unsinkable Molly Brown.

Within 30 years after the city's founding, everything about Denver had grown astonishingly—including its adversities. For two decades, U.S. government purchases of silver had kept the mines of Colorado profitable. As long as times were prosperous, the Treasury could afford to spend nearly $50 million a year on silver. But all that was changed by the depression of 1893, an unfavorable balance of trade and run on U.S. gold reserves by European holders of American bonds. Congress in 1893 halted further buying of silver by the Treasury. Silver prices plummeted, then fell still farther when India, a great consumer of the metal, stopped making silver coins.

Times grew terribly hard. In Denver suicides and holdups were daily occurrences. Silver kings like Tabor, whose life styles depended entirely on yearly incomes of millions from the mines, crashed down in ruin. Unemployed miners flooded into Denver. With more charity than good sense, the city gave them lumber for building boats in which to float down the South Platte to a fresh start elsewhere. Most were shipwrecked.

But Denver did not go broke. Without the additional resources developed by far-sighted men, the panic of 1893 might well have wrought permanent harm. But the good years had fattened Denver beyond starving, and permanent roots in agriculture and industry had been put down. Before the century was out, some who had hazarded their fortunes on Denver's development would see still one more fantastic boom: the Cripple Creek gold rush which would surpass even the tremendous bonanza of Leadville.

And thus to Denver, the unlikeliest candidate, came all the good things dreamed of, schemed for, struggled for by all the men and women who had crossed the great rivers to found a new urban civilization. The community had many chances to vanish in the sorrowful way of more than two thousand other towns in the Old West. But Denver was obstinate. It was also superbly lucky. And so it became, beyond any man's license to dispute the title, truly the Queen City of the Plains.

222

The broad, paved artery of 16th Street cuts through the Queen City of the Plains in an 1895 view from Capitol Hill, formerly Brown's Bluff. Hidden by buildings behind the domed county courthouse is the confluence of Cherry Creek and the South Platte River, where Denver began.

An unshakable sense of solidarity

Midway through a 15-week tour of frontier towns in 1865, roving journalist Albert Richardson of the *New York Tribune* observed, "Western emigration makes men larger, riper and more fraternal." Their camaraderie was everywhere visible — in chance encounters on the streets, in a constant round of festive gatherings and in a wealth of organizations: debating societies, sewing clubs, church auxiliaries and all-male groups like the Masons or the Grand Army of the Republic *(below)*, composed of Union veterans.

Nor did Richardson have to look far for reasons to account for the powerful sense of community that he discerned. Western townsmen were drawn together by remoteness and shared hardships on the one hand, and by a vision of an unlimited future on the other. Summing up his impressions at journey's end, he compared these amiable settlers to his own friends back East and concluded, a bit harshly, that the latter "have never thawed out from the freezing their fathers got on Plymouth Rock."

The West Union, Nebraska, G.A.R. Post — plus families — celebrates at an 1886 picnic, complete with a band and a thatch sunshade.

Lanterns hanging over an 1890s lawn party in Orofino, Idaho, augur a feast lasting to late hours.

Masquerades like this 1890s dance in Englewood, Kansas, were regular festive fare in wintertime.

229

Townsfolk of Guthrie, Oklahoma, showing off one of the bounties of their newly settled region, surround 100 pounds of catfish.

Content to watch the world go by, a solitary townsman relaxes outside a barber shop on the main—and only—street of Murray, Idaho.

TEXT CREDITS

For full reference on specific page credits see bibliography.

Chapter 1: Particularly useful sources for information and quotes in this chapter were: Lewis E. Atherton, *Main Street on the Middle Border,* Indiana University Press, 194; Everett Dick, *The Sod House Frontier 1854-1890,* Johnsen Publishing Company, 1954; Albert D. Richardson, *Beyond the Mississippi,* American Publishing Company, 1867. 17 —Jackson quotes, Griswold, pp. 146-9; 19—young emigrant quote, Barnard, p. 311; 23—Taylor quote, Griswold, p. 89; 40—Cordley quote on Lawrence, Cordley, pp. 59-61. Chapter 2: Particularly useful sources for information and quotes: Everett Dick, *The Sod House Frontier 1854-1890,* Johnsen Publishing Company, 1954; Paul W. Gates (with a chapter by Robert W. Swenson), *History of Public Land Law Development,* Public Land Law Review Commission, 1968; Kansas State Historical Society, *Kansas Historical Collections,* Vol. VIII, 1903-4, Vol. XII, 1911-12, Vol. XIV, 1915-18; M. M. Marberry, *The Golden Voice,* Farrar, Straus & Co., 1947; Glenn Chesney Quiett, *They Built the West,* D. Appleton-Century Co., 1934; John W. Reps, *The Making of Urban America,* Princeton University Press, 1965; Albert D. Richardson, *Beyond the Mississippi,* American Publishing Company, 1867. 57—Mark Twain quote, Atherton, *Main Street on the Middle Border,* pp. 10-11; 60—Pastor Metz quote, Shambaugh, p. 72; 61—Burlington & Missouri quote, Overton, p. 103; 65—Bryce quote, Atherton, *Main Street,* p. 13. Chapter 3: Particularly useful sources for information and quotes: Robert R. Dykstra, *The Cattle Towns,* Alfred A. Knopf, Inc., 1968; Robert M. Wright, *Dodge City, the Cowboy Capital,* Wichita Eagle Press, 1913; W. F. Thompson, "Peter Robidoux: A Real Kansas Pioneer," *Kansas Historical Collections,* Vol. XVII, 1926-1928. 98 —merchant quoted on farm women, Atherton, *The Frontier Merchant in Mid-America,* p. 25; 98—exasperated merchant quoted, Atherton, *Frontier Merchant,* p. 22. Chapter 4: Particularly useful sources for information and quotes: Howard R. Lamar, *Dakota Territory 1861-1889,* Yale University Press, 1956; selections reprinted from *History of Wyoming* by T. A. Larson by permission of University of Nebraska Press; Henry F. Mason, "County Seat Controversies in Southwestern Kansas," *Kansas Historical Quarterly,* Vol. II, No. 1, Feb. 1963; Richard Reinhardt, "Tapeworm Tickets and Shoulder Strikers," *The American West,* Vol. III, No. 4, Fall 1966; Gilbert Stetler, "The Birth of a Boom Town," *Annals of Wyoming,* Vol. 39, No. 1, April 1967. 130—brilliant speeches quote, Saltiel and Barnett, p. 9. Chapter 5: Particularly useful sources for information and quotes: Margaret G. Watson, *Silver Theatre,* The Arthur H. Clark Company, 1964; Lloyd Lewis and Henry Justin Smith, *Oscar Wilde Discovers America (1882),* Harcourt Brace Jovanovich, Inc., 1936; Melvin Schoberlin, *From Candles to Footlights,* The Old West Publishing Company, 1941; Campton Bell, "The Early Theatres, Cheyenne, Wyoming, 1867-1882," *Annals of Wyoming,* Vol. XXV, 1953. 167—Wright on brass band, Wright, pp. 204-5; 167—*Times* quote, Wright, p. 238; 172—dance hall girls quote, Foy, pp. 105-6; 173—Foy description, Wright, p. 298; 177—Brigham Young quote, Pyper, p. 168; 178—Montgomery quote, Malin, p. 243; 178-80—Bernhardt quote, Brown, p. 184. Chapter 6: Particularly useful sources for information and quotes: Phyllis F. Dorset, *The New Eldorado,* Macmillan, 1970; Edith Kohl, *Denver's Historic Mansions,* Sage Books, 1957; Louisa Arps, *Denver in Slices,* Sage Books, 1959; selections from *The First Hundred Years—An Informal History of Denver and the Rocky Mountain News* by Robert L. Perkins. © 1959 by the Denver Publishing Company. Reprinted by permission of Doubleday & Company, Inc. 206—Denver quote, Greeley, p. 97.

PICTURE CREDITS

The sources for the illustrations in this book are shown below. Credits from left to right are separated by semicolons, from top to bottom by dashes.

Cover—Benschneider, courtesy Nebraska State Historical Society. 2 —From the Collection of David R. Phillips. 6 through 9—Courtesy Kansas State Historical Society, Topeka. 10,11—Joseph E. Smith from the Collection of David R. Phillips. 12,13—Courtesy of The Oakland Museum, Andrew J. Russell Collection. 14,15—Joe Clark, HBSS, from the Collections of Greenfield Village and the Henry Ford Museum. 16 —Courtesy Western History Collections, University of Oklahoma Library. 18,19—Courtesy Museum of New Mexico. 20—Courtesy Wyoming State Archives and Historical Department. 21—Courtesy Utah State Historical Society. 22—Courtesy Kansas State Historical Society; Sharlot Hall Museum, Prescott, Arizona. 23—Center, courtesy Idaho State Historical Society; others, Kansas State Historical Society. 24,25—Courtesy Solomon D. Butcher Collection/Nebraska State Historical Society. 26—Nicholas Fasciano. 28,29—Courtesy Chicago Historical Society Library. 30,31—Courtesy Kansas State Historical Society. 34,35—Courtesy Library, State Historical Society of Colorado. 37—Courtesy Church Archives, The Church of Jesus Christ of Latter-day Saints. 38—Courtesy Nebraska State Historical Society. 40 through 43—Courtesy Kansas State Historical Society. 44,45—Joseph E. Smith from the Collection of David R. Phillips. 46,47—Courtesy Kansas State Historical Society. 48,49—Courtesy Brigham Young University Library. 50,51—Courtesy Museum of New Mexico. 52—Courtesy Nebraska State Historical Society. 54 through 59—Courtesy Kansas State Historical Society. 62,63—Geneva, San Francisco, and Douglass certificates, courtesy Nebraska State Historial Society; Cherokee City certificate courtesy Denver Public Library, Western History Department; others, courtesy Kansas State Historical Society. 64,65—Courtesy Kansas State Historical Society. 66 through 69—Kansas State Historical Society, courtesy Mrs. Thornton Hooper. 72,73—Courtesy Solomon D. Butcher Collection/Nebraska State Historical Society. 75 through 77 —Courtesy Kansas State Historical Society. 78 through 87—Courtesy Western History Collections, University of Oklahoma Library. 88,89 —Courtesy Kansas State Historical Society. 90—Courtesy Solomon D. Butcher Collections/Nebraska State Historical Society. 91—Courtesy Kansas State Historical Society. 92,93—Courtesy Western History Collections, University of Oklahoma Library. 94—Courtesy Denver Public Library, Western History Department. 95—Courtesy Frances Seely Webb Collection. 96 through 101—Courtesy Kansas State Historical Society. 103—Courtesy Lexington Library and Historical Association. 104—Courtesy Denver Public Library, Western History Department—Henry Groskinsky, courtesy Boot Hill Museum, Inc., 500 W. Wyatt Earp, Dodge City, Kansas. 105—Henry Groskinsky, courtesy Boot Hill Museum, Inc. 107—Courtesy Arizona Historical Foundation and Historical files of Herb and Dorothy McLaughlin. 108,109—Courtesy Kansas State Historical Society. 110,111— Henry Groskinsky, courtesy Boot Hill Museum, Inc. 112,113—

Courtesy Kansas State Historical Society. 114,115 — Courtesy Boot Hill Museum, Inc. 116,117 — Courtesy Denver Public Library, Western History Department. 118 — Courtesy Montgomery Ward. 120 — Courtesy Boot Hill Museum, Inc. — courtesy Kansas State Historical Society. 121 through 125 — Henry Groskinsky, courtesy Boot Hill Museum, Inc. 126,127 — Courtesy Wyoming State Archives and Historical Department. 128 — Courtesy Yankton County Historical Society, Yankton, South Dakota. 129 — Henry Groskinsky, courtesy Boot Hill Museum, Inc. 130,131 — Courtesy Nebraska State Historical Society. 132,133 — Courtesy Sharlot Hall Museum, photo #X73-867P. 134 — Henry Groskinsky, courtesy Boot Hill Museum, Inc. 135 — Courtesy Solomon D. Butcher Collection/Nebraska State Historical Society. 136 — Courtesy The Beinecke Rare Book and Manuscript Library, Yale University. 138,139 — Courtesy Barker Texas History Center. 140,141 — Courtesy Pioneers' Museum, Colorado Springs, Colorado. 144,145 — Copied from the Collections of the Arizona Historical Society. 146 — Courtesy Dorothy Jencks Collection, Yankton, South Dakota. 148 — Courtesy Kansas State Historical Society — courtesy Nebraska State Historical Society. 149 — City Bank currency courtesy Kansas State Historical Society; others, courtesy Nebraska State Historical Society. 150,151 — Courtesy Kansas State Historical Society. 152 — Courtesy Montana Historical Society, Helena. 153 — Courtesy Robinson Museum, Pierre, South Dakota. 154 — Courtesy Denver Public Library, Western History Department — Henry Beville, courtesy Library of Congress. 155 — Courtesy Wyoming State Archives and Historical Department. 156 — Courtesy Wyoming State Archives and Historical Department; Western History Research Center, University of Wyoming; Denver Public Library, Western History Department — Kansas State Historical Society. 157 — Courtesy Kansas State Historical Society; Wyoming State Archives and Historical Department; Denver Public Library, Western History Department — Kansas State Historical Society. 158-159 — Courtesy Wyoming State Archives and Historical Department. 160,161 — Courtesy Kansas State Historical Society. 162 through 165 — Cour-

tesy Montana Historical Society. 166 — Courtesy Kansas State Historical Society. 167 — Courtesy Western Historical Research Center, University of Wyoming. 168 through 171 — Courtesy Montana Historical Society. 174,175 — Courtesy Denver Public Library, Western History Department. 177 — Courtesy Longmont Pioneer Museum Collection, Longmont, Colorado. 179 — Courtesy Performing Arts Research Center, The New York Public Library, Astor, Lenox and Tilden Foundations. 180 — Courtesy Hoblitzelle Theatre Arts Library, Humanities Research Center, University of Texas at Austin. 181 — Courtesy Museum of the City of New York, Theatre and Music Collection. 182,183 — Courtesy Kansas State Historical Society. 185 — *Harpers Bazaar,* June 10, 1882, copied by Henry Beville, courtesy Library of Congress. 186,187 — Courtesy Denver Public Library, Western History Department. 188 — Courtesy Wyoming State Archives and Historical Department. 189 — Courtesy Burton Devere Collection. 190 — Courtesy Boot Hill Museum, Inc. 191 — Courtesy Denver Public Library, Western History Department. 192,193 — Courtesy Boot Hill Museum, Inc. 194 — Courtesy Nebraska State Historical Society. 195 — Courtesy Bird Cage Theatre, Tombstone, Arizona. 196,197 — Arthur Shay, courtesy Denver Public Library, Western History Department. 198 — Newspaper courtesy Library, State Historical Society of Colorado; photograph courtesy Denver Public Library, Western History Department. 200,201 — Courtesy Library, State Historical Society of Colorado. 204 through 215 — Courtesy Denver Public Library, Western History Department. 215 — Copied by Arthur Shay. 218,219 — Arthur Shay, courtesy Library, State Historical Society of Colorado. 220 — Arthur Shay, courtesy Elitch's Gardens, Denver, Colorado. 222,223 — Courtesy Denver Public Library, Western History Department. 224,225 — Courtesy Solomon D. Butcher Collection/Nebraska State Historical Society. 226,227 — Courtesy Idaho State Historical Society. 228,229 — Courtesy Kansas State Historical Society. 230,231 — Courtesy Western History Collections, University of Oklahoma Library. 232,233 — Courtesy Idaho State Historical Society.

ACKNOWLEDGMENTS

The editors give special thanks to the following persons who read and commented on portions of the book: Dr. Paul W. Gates, Dept. of History, Cornell Univ.; Dr. Robert Athearn, Dept. of History, Univ. of Colorado; Dr. T. A. Larson, Dept. of History, Univ. of Wyoming; Dr. Howard R. Lamar, Dept. of History, Yale Univ.

The editors also wish to thank: Lee Bennet, Marfa, Texas; Prof. B. Bowen Carlsen, Univ. of Colorado; Greeley Municipal Museum, Greeley, Colo.; David Crossen, Research Historian, Western History Research Center, Univ. of Wyoming; Peggy Cullen, Public Relations, Montgomery Ward, Chicago; Jean C. Dallas, Director and Curator, The Riley County Historical Society and Museum, Manhattan, Kans.; James H. Davis, Photo Archivist, Idaho Historical Society, Boise; Eugene D. Decker, Archivist, Joseph W. Snell, Asst. State Archivist, Kansas State Historical Society, Topeka; Prof. John N. De Haas, Architecture Dept., Montana State Univ.; Mr. and Mrs. Burton Devere, Tombstone; Michael Fargo, Fine Arts Dept., Topeka Public Library; Bert M. Fireman, Curator, Arizona Collection, Arizona State Univ.; Prof. Emil Fischer, Kansas State Univ. School of Architecture, Manhattan, Kans.; Gail Gardner, Prescott; James I. Garner, Prescott Courier, Prescott; Eleanor Gehres, Dir., A. D. Mastrogiuseppe, Picture Librarian, Opal Harber, Hazel Lundberg, Kay Kane, Sandra Turner, Archivists, Western History Dept., Denver Public Library; Hazel Gribble, Librarian, Columbus Public Library, Columbus, Kans.; Jack Haley, Asst. Curator, Western History Collections, Univ. of Oklahoma Library; David Hartley, Dir., Robinson Museum, Pierre, S.D.; Katherine A. Halverson, Chief, Laura Hayes, Curator, John Cornelison, Archivist, Historical Research and Publ. Div., Wyoming State Archives and Historical Dept., Cheyenne; George R. Henrichs, Exec. Dir., Boot Hill Museum, Inc., Dodge City; Pauline Henson, Prescott; William Hunley Jr., Bird Cage Theatre, Tombstone; James Potter, State Archivist, Mrs. Opal Jacobsen, Photo Librarian, Robert Pettit, Museum Curator, Donald Snoddy, Archivist, Nebraska State Historical Society; Dorothy Jencks, Yankton; Ken Kimsey, Sharlot Hall Museum, Prescott; Charlotte LaRue, Photo Curator, Museum of the City of New York; Terry Mangan, Chief Photo Archivist, Michael Sievers, Research Historian, Colorado State Historical Society; John Meek, Curator, Longmont Pioneer Museum, Longmont, Colo.; Harriett C. Meloy, Librarian, Lory Morrow, Photo Archivist, Montana Historical Society; Rita Napier, Dept. of History, Univ. of Kansas; Arthur Olivas, Museum of New Mexico; Henrietta Perry, Curator, Rosemary Hetzler, Asst. Curator, Pioneers' Museum, Colorado Springs; David R. Phillips, Chicago; Lester Ward Ruffner, Prescott; Cassandra Tiberio, Asst. Librarian, Western Historical Collections, Univ. of Colorado Libraries; Larry Viskochil, Ref. Librarian, Chicago Historical Society; Nelson Wadsworth, Salt Lake City; John Wallace, Dir., Lexington Historical Soc., Lexington, Mo.; George Warren, State Archivist, Terry Ketelsen, Lynda Snyder, Staff Archivists, Colorado State Archives and Public Records; Capt. Stephen Whitfield, Army Corps of Engineers, Lafayette, La.; Muriel Wolle, Boulder; Dr. Florence B. Yount, Prescott.

BIBLIOGRAPHY

Andreas, A. T., *History of the State of Kansas.* A. T. Andreas, 1883.

Arps, Louisa A. W., *Denver in Slices.* Sage Books, 1959.

Atherton, Lewis E.:
The Frontier Merchant in Mid-America. Univ. of Missouri Press, 1971.
Main Street on the Middle Border. Indiana University Press, 1954.
"James and Robert Aull — A Frontier Missouri Mercantile Firm," *Missouri Historical Review.* Vol. 30, 1935.
"The Services of the Frontier Merchant," *Mississippi Valley Historical Review.* Vol. 24, 1937.

Baker, J., and L. Hofer, *History of Colorado.* Linderman Co., 1927.

Barnard, Hon. E. H., "Early Fremont," *Nebraska State Historical Society Publications 1887.* Vol. 11, No. 7.

Beach, Mrs. Alfred, *Women of Wyoming.* S. E. Boyer & Co., 1927.

Bell, Campton, "The Early Theatres, Cheyenne, Wyoming, 1867-1882," *Annals of Wyoming.* Vol. XXV, 1953.

Billington, Monroe, "Susanna Medora Salter — First Woman Mayor," *Kansas Historical Quarterly.* Vol. XXI, No. 3, Autumn 1954.

Boner, Harold, *The Giant's Ladder.* Kalmbach Publ. Co., 1962.

Brown, Dee, *The Gentle Tamers: Women of the Old Wild West.* G. P. Putnam's Sons, 1958.

Buchanan, John and Doris, *A Story of the Fabulous Windsor Hotel.* The A. B. Hirschfeld Press, 1956.

Catt, Carrie, and Nellie Shuller, *Woman Suffrage and Politics.* Charles Scribner's Sons, 1923.

Chaplin, B. B., "The Legal Sooners of 1889 in Oklahoma," *Chronicles of Oklahoma.* Winter 1957.

Clanton, O. Gene, "Intolerant Populist? The Disaffection of Mary Elizabeth Lease," *Kansas Historical Quarterly.* Vol. XXXIV, No. 2, Summer 1968.

Clark, Archie L., "John Maguire: Butte's 'Belasco'," *The Montana Magazine of History.* Jan. 1952.

Cordley, Richard, *Pioneer Days in Kansas.* The Pilgrim Press, 1903.

Crowley, Elmer, "The History of the Tabor Grand Opera House," M.A. thesis. University of Denver, 1940.

Dallas, S., *Cherry Creek Gothic.* University of Oklahoma Press, 1971.

Danker, Donald F., "Columbus, a Territorial Town in the Platte Valley," *Nebraska History.* Vol. XXXIV, 1953.

Dempsey, David, with Raymond P. Baldwin, *The Triumphs and Trials of Lotta Crabtree.* William Morrow, 1968.

Dick, Everett:
The Lure of the Land. University of Nebraska Press, 1970.
The Sod-House Frontier 1854-1890. Johnsen Publishing Co., 1954.

Donaldson, Thomas, *The Public Domain.* Johnson Reprint Corp., 1970.

Dorset, Phyllis Flanders, *The New Eldorado.* Macmillan, 1970.

Dunn, Esther Cloudman, *Shakespeare in America.* First published 1939. Reissued 1968 by Benjamin Blom, Inc.

Dykstra, Robert R., *The Cattle Towns.* Alfred A. Knopf, Inc., 1968.

Ellis, David M., ed., *The Frontier in American Development.* Cornell University Press, 1969.

Faulk, Odie B., *Tombstone: Myth and Reality.* Oxford U. Press, 1972.

Fite, Gilbert C., *The Farmers' Frontier 1865-1900.* Holt, Rinehart and Winston, Inc., 1966.

Foy, Eddie, and A. F. Harlow, *Clowning through Life.* Dutton, 1928.

Gates, Paul W.:
Fifty Million Acres: Conflicts over Kansas Land Policy, 1854-1890. Cornell University Press, 1954.

(With a chapter by Robert W. Swenson), *History of Public Land Law Development.* Public Land Law Review Commission, 1968. *Landlords and Tenants on the Prairie Frontier.* Cornell University Press, 1973.

Gibson, Arrell M., "Medicine Show," *American West.* Vol. IV, No. 1, Feb. 1967.

Gower, Calvin, "Lectures, Lyceums, and Libraries in Early Kansas, 1854-1864," *Kansas Historical Quarterly.* Vol. XXXVI, Summer 1970.

Greeley, Horace, *An Overland Journey.* Saxton, Barker & Co., 1860.

Griswold, Don and Jean, *Colorado's Century of "Cities."* 1958.

Gruberg, Martin, *Women in American Politics.* Academia Press, 1962.

Heaton, Rev. I. E., "Sketch of the First Congregational Church in Fremont, Nebraska," *Nebraska State Historical Society Publications 1887.* Vol. II, No. 7.

Henderson, Myrtle E., *A History of the Theatre in Salt Lake City from 1850 to 1870.* Evanston, Illinois, July 1934.

Hollon, W. Eugene, "Rushing for Land: Oklahoma, 1889," *The American West.* Vol. 3, No. 4, Fall 1966.

Idaho Yesterdays, Idaho Historical Society. Winter 1968-9, Dec. 4, pp. 13-22.

Ingalls Union, Ingalls, Kansas, Jan. 17 and Feb. 7, 1889.

Jacksonian, Cimarron, Kansas, Jan. 18, 1889.

Johnson, A. R., compiler, *Residence and Business Directory of Cheyenne.* The Leader Printing Co., 1884-85.

Jones, W., and K. Forrest, *Denver, A Pictorial History.* Pruett, 1973.

Kansas Historical Collections, Vol. VIII (1903-4), Vol. XII (1911-12), Vol. XIII (1913-14), Vol. XIV (1915-18), Kansas State Historical Society.

Karolevitz, Robert F.:
Doctors of the Old West. Superior Publishing Company, 1967.
Newspapering in the Old West. Superior Publishing Company, 1965.
Yankton: A Pioneer Past. North Plains Press, 1972.

Kelsey, Harry E., *Frontier Capitalist, Life of John Evans.* Pruett, 1969.

Kingsbury, George Washington, *History of Dakota Territory,* Vol. I. The S. J. Clarke Co., 1915.

Kohl, Edith, *Denver's Historic Mansions.* Sage Books, 1957.

Lamar, H. R., *Dakota Territory 1861-1889.* Yale Univ. Press, 1956.

Lambert, William, and Keith Wheeler, "The Easygoing Man behind the Image." LIFE, Oct. 23, 1964.

Larson, T. A., *History of Wyoming.* Univ. of Nebraska Press, 1965.

Lewis, L., and H. J. Smith, *Oscar Wilde Discovers America.* Harcourt Brace Jovanovich, 1936.

Lyman, George D., *The Saga of the Comstock Lode.* Scribners, 1934.

MacLane, John F., *A Sagebrush Lawyer.* Pandick Press, Inc., 1953.

Malin, James C.:
"Dodge City Varieties—a Summer Interlude of Entertainment, 1878," *Kansas Historical Quarterly.* Vol. XXII, 1956.
"James A. and Louie Lord: Theatrical Team—Their Personal Story, 1869-1889," *Kansas Historical Quarterly.* Vol. XXII, 1956.

Marberry, M. M., *The Golden Voice.* Farrar, Straus and Co., 1947.

Mason, Henry F., "County Seat Controversies in Southwestern Kansas," *Kansas Historical Quarterly.* Vol. II, No. 1, February, 1933.

McNeal, T. A., *When Kansas Was Young.* Macmillan, 1922.

Minutes of the Cheyenne City Council. August 7, 8, 15, 16, 17, 19 and 20, 1867. Wyoming State Archives and Historical Department.

Mullen, Robert R., *The Latter-day Saints: The Mormons Yesterday and Today.* Doubleday, 1966.

Olson, James C., *History of Nebraska.* Univ. of Nebraska Press, 1955.

Overton, Richard C., *Burlington Route.* Alfred A. Knopf, Inc., 1965.

Pearson, Hesketh, *Oscar Wilde.* Harper and Brothers, 1946.

Penniman, Howard R., *Sait's American Parties and Elections.* Appleton-Century-Crofts, Inc., 1952.

Perkins, Robert L., *The First Hundred Years: An Informal History of Denver and the Rocky Mountain News.* Doubleday, 1959.

Pomeroy, Earl S., *The Territories and the United States 1861-1890.* University of Pennsylvania Press, 1947.

Pyper, G. D., *The Romance of an Old Playhouse.* Seagull Press, 1928.

Quiett, G. C., *They Built the West.* D. Appleton-Century, 1934.

Reinhardt, Richard, "Tapeworm Tickets and Shoulder Strikers," *American West.* Vol. III, No. 4, Fall, 1966.

Reps, John W., *The Making of Urban America.* Princeton University Press, 1965.

Reynolds, C., *Pioneer Circuses of the West.* Westernlore Press, 1966.

Richards, O. H., "Memories of an 89'er," *Chronicles of Oklahoma.* Spring, 1948.

Richardson, Albert D., *Beyond The Mississippi.* American Publishing Company, 1867.

Robbins, Roy M., *Our Landed Heritage: The Public Domain 1776-1936.* University of Nebraska Press, 1962.

Ruggles, Eleanor, *Prince of Players.* W. W. Norton, 1953.

Saltiel, E. H., and George Barnett, compilers, *History and Business Directory of Cheyenne.* L. B. Joseph, Feb. 1868.

Schell, H. S., *History of South Dakota.* Univ. of Nebraska Press, 1961.

Schoberlin, Melvin, *From Candles to Footlights.* The Old West Publishing Company, 1941.

Shambaugh, Bertha M. H., *Amana, the Community of True Inspiration.* State Historical Society of Iowa, 1908.

Smiley, Jerome C., ed., *History of Denver, With Outlines of the Earlier History of the Rocky Mountain Country.* Times-Sun Publ. Co., 1901.

Stetler, Gilbert A., "The Birth of a Frontier Boom Town: Cheyenne in 1867," *Annals of Wyoming.* Vol. 39, No. 1, April 1967.

Streeter, B. F., *Prairie Trails & Cow Towns.* Devin Adair, 1963.

Taft, R., *Artists and Illustrators of the Old West.* Scribners, 1953.

Thompson, W. F., "Peter Robidoux: A Real Kansas Pioneer," *Kansas Historical Collections.* Vol. XVII, 1926-28.

Van Orman, Richard A.:
"Hotels of the Old West," *American History Illustrated.* Oct. 1968.
"The Bard in the West," *Western Historical Quarterly.* Vol. V, No. 1.

Wagoner, Jay J., *Arizona Territory 1863-1912.* University of Arizona Press, 1970.

Watson, Margaret G., *Silver Theatre.* The Arthur H. Clark Co., 1964.

Williams, B. J., *Senator John James Ingalls.* Univ. Press of Kansas, 1972.

Willson, Clair Eugene, "Mimes and Miners—A Historical Study of the Theater in Tombstone," *University of Arizona Bulletin, Fine Arts Bulletin.* No. 1, Oct. 1, 1935.

Wright, Robert M., *Dodge City, the Cowboy Capital.* Wichita Eagle Press, 1913.

Young, Fredric R., *Dodge City.* Boot Hill Museum, Inc., 1972.

Young, J. H., *The Toadstool Millionaires.* Princeton Univ. Press, 1941.

Zornow, William Frank, *Kansas: A History of the Jayhawk State.* University of Oklahoma Press, 1957.